The Official SAT Subject Tests in U.S. History and World History Study Guide™

The College Board
New York, NY

About the College Board

The College Board is a mission-driven not-for-profit organization that connects students to college success and opportunity. Founded in 1900, the College Board was created to expand access to higher education. Today, the membership association is made up of over 6,000 of the world's leading educational institutions and is dedicated to promoting excellence and equity in education. Each year, the College Board helps more than seven million students prepare for a successful transition to college through programs and services in college readiness and college success — including the SAT® and the Advanced Placement Program®. The organization also serves the education community through research and advocacy on behalf of students, educators and schools.

For further information, visit www.collegeboard.org.

Copies of this book are available from your bookseller or may be ordered from College Board Publications, P.O. Box 86900, Plano, TX 86901. 800 323-7155. The price is $18.99.

Editorial inquiries concerning this book should be addressed to the College Board, SAT Program, 45 Columbus Avenue, New York, New York 10023-6992.

ISBN 13: 978-0-87447-769-6

ISBN 10: 087447-769-7

Library of Congress Card Catalog Number: 2006016432

Printed in the United States of America

12

Distributed by Macmillan

CONTENTS

World History 123

The SAT Subject Test Answer Sheets 223

The SAT Subject Tests™

About SAT Subject Tests

SAT Subject Tests™ are a valuable way to help you show colleges a more complete picture of your academic background and interests. Each year, nearly one million Subject Tests are taken by students throughout the country and around the world to gain admission to the leading colleges and universities in the U.S.

SAT Subject Tests are one-hour exams that give you the opportunity to demonstrate knowledge and showcase achievement in specific subjects. They provide a fair and reliable measure of your achievement in high school — information that can help enhance your college admission portfolio. The U.S. History and World History Subject Tests are a great way to highlight your understanding, skills and strengths in history.

This book provides information and guidance to help you study for and familiarize yourself with the U.S. History and World History Subject Tests. It contains actual, previously administered tests and official answer sheets that will help you get comfortable with the tests' format, so you feel better prepared on test day.

The Benefits of SAT Subject Tests

SAT Subject Tests let you put your best foot forward, allowing you to focus on subjects that you know well and enjoy. They can help you differentiate yourself in a competitive admission environment by providing additional information about your skills and knowledge of particular subjects. Many colleges also use Subject Tests for course placement and selection; some schools allow you to place out of introductory courses by taking certain Subject Tests.

Subject Tests are flexible and can be tailored to your strengths and areas of interest. These are the **only** national admission tests where **you** choose the tests that best showcase your achievements and interests. You select the Subject Test(s) and can take up to three tests in one sitting. With the exception of listening tests, you can even decide to change the subject or number of tests you want to take on the day of the test. This flexibility can help you be more relaxed on test day.

Who Should Consider Subject Tests?

Anyone can take an SAT Subject Test to highlight his or her knowledge of a specific subject. SAT Subject Tests may be especially beneficial for certain students:

REMEMBER

Subject Tests are a valuable way to help you show colleges a more complete picture of your academic achievements.

- Students applying to colleges that require or recommend Subject Tests — be aware that some schools have additional Subject Test requirements for certain students, majors or programs of study
- Students who wish to demonstrate strength in specific subject areas
- Students who wish to demonstrate knowledge obtained outside a traditional classroom environment (e.g., summer enrichment, distance learning, weekend study, etc.)
- Students looking to place out of certain classes in college
- Students enrolled in dual-enrollment programs
- Home-schooled students or students taking courses online
- Students who feel that their course grade may not be a true reflection of their knowledge of the subject matter

Who Requires the SAT Subject Tests?

Most college websites and catalogs include information about admission requirements, including which Subject Tests are needed or recommended for admission. Schools have varying policies regarding Subject Tests, but they generally fall into one or more of the following categories:

- Required for admission
- Recommended for admission
- Required or recommended for certain majors or programs of study (e.g., engineering, honors, etc.)
- Required or recommended for certain groups of students (e.g., home-schooled students)
- Required, recommended or accepted for course placement
- Accepted for course credit
- Accepted as an alternative to fulfill certain college admission requirements
- Accepted as an alternative to fulfill certain high school subject competencies
- Accepted and considered, especially if Subject Tests improve or enhance a student's application

In addition, the College Board provides a number of resources where you can search for information about Subject Test requirements at specific colleges.

- Visit the websites of the colleges and universities that interest you.
- Visit College Search at www.collegeboard.org.
- Purchase a copy of *The College Board College Handbook*.

Some colleges require specific tests, such as mathematics or science, so it's important to make sure you understand the policies prior to choosing which Subject Test(s) to take. If you have questions or concerns about admission policies, contact college admission officers at individual schools. They are usually pleased to meet with students interested in their schools.

Subject Tests Offered

SAT Subject Tests measure how well you know a particular subject area and your ability to apply that knowledge. SAT Subject Tests aren't connected to specific textbooks or teaching methods. The content of each test evolves to reflect the latest trends in what is taught in typical high school courses in the corresponding subject.

The tests fall into five general subject areas:

English	**Languages**	
Literature	Reading Only	Languages with Listening
History	French	Chinese
United States History	German	French
World History	Italian	German
Mathematics	Latin	Japanese
Mathematics Level 1	Modern Hebrew	Korean
Mathematics Level 2	Spanish	Spanish
Science		
Biology E/M		
Chemistry		
Physics		

Who Develops the Tests

The SAT Subject Tests are part of the SAT Program of the College Board, a not-for-profit membership association of over 6,000 schools, colleges, universities and other educational associations. Every year, the College Board serves seven million students and their parents, 23,000 high schools, and 3,800 colleges through major programs and services in college readiness, college admission, guidance, assessment, financial aid and enrollment.

Each subject has its own test development committee, typically composed of teachers and college professors appointed for the different Subject Tests. The test questions are written and reviewed by each Subject Test Committee, under the guidance of professional test developers. The tests are rigorously developed, highly reliable assessments of knowledge and skills taught in high school classrooms.

Deciding to Take an SAT Subject Test

Which Tests Should You Take?

The SAT Subject Tests that you take should be based on your interests and academic strengths. The tests are a great way to indicate interest in specific majors or programs of study (e.g., engineering, pre-med, cultural studies).

You should also consider whether the colleges that you're interested in require or recommend Subject Tests. Some colleges will grant an exemption from or credit for a freshman course requirement if a student does well on a particular SAT Subject Test. Below are some things for you to consider as you decide which test(s) to take.

Think through your strengths and interests

- List the subjects in which you do well and that truly interest you.
- Think through what you might like to study in college.
- Consider whether your current admission credentials (high school grades, SAT® scores, etc.) highlight your strengths.

Consider the colleges that you're interested in

- Make a list of the colleges you're considering.
- Take some time to look into what these colleges require or what may help you stand out in the admission process.
- Use College Search to look up colleges' test requirements.
- If the colleges you're interested in require or recommend SAT Subject Tests, find out how many tests are required or recommended and in which subjects.

Take a look at your current and recent course load

- Have you completed the required course work? The best time to take SAT Subject Tests is at the end of the course, when the material is still fresh in your mind.

- Check the recommended preparation guidelines for the Subject Tests that interest you to see if you've completed the recommended course work.
- Try your hand at some SAT Subject Test practice questions on collegeboard.org or in this book.

Don't forget, regardless of admission requirements, you can enhance your college portfolio by taking Subject Tests in subject areas that you know very well.

If you're still unsure about which SAT Subject Tests to take, talk to your teacher or counselor about your specific situation. You can also find more information about SAT Subject Tests on collegeboard.org.

When to Take the Tests

We generally recommend that you take Subject Tests after you complete the relevant course work, prior to your senior year of high school, if possible. This way, you will already have your Subject Test credentials complete, allowing you to focus on your college applications in the fall of your senior year. If you are able to, take the United States History Subject Test or the World History Subject Test right after your courses end, when the content is still fresh in your mind.

Since not all Subject Tests are offered on every test date, be sure to check when the Subject Tests that you're interested in are offered and plan accordingly.

You should also balance this with college application deadlines. If you're interested in applying Early Decision or Early Action to any college, many colleges advise that you take the SAT Subject Tests by October or November of your senior year. For regular decision applications, some colleges will accept SAT Subject Test scores through the December or January administration. Use College Search to look up policies for specific colleges.

This book suggests ways you can prepare for the SAT Subject Tests in U.S. History and World History. Before taking a test in a subject you haven't studied recently, ask your teacher for advice about the best time to take the test. Then review the course material thoroughly over several weeks.

How to Register for the Tests

There are several ways to register for the SAT Subject Tests.

- Visit the College Board's website at www.collegeboard.org. Most students choose to register for Subject Tests on the College Board website.
- Register by telephone (for a fee) if you have registered previously for the SAT or an SAT Subject Test. Call, toll free from anywhere in the United States, 866-756-7346. From outside the United States, call 212-713-7789.

- If you do not have access to the Internet, find registration forms in *The Paper Registration Guide for the SAT and SAT Subject Tests.* You can find the booklet in a guidance office at any high school or by writing to:

  The College Board
  SAT Program
  P.O. Box 025505
  Miami, FL 33102

When you register for the SAT Subject Tests, you will have to indicate the specific Subject Tests you plan to take on the test date you select. You may take one, two or three tests on any given test date; your testing fee will vary accordingly. Except for the Language Tests with Listening, you may change your mind on the day of the test and instead select from any of the other Subject Tests offered that day.

Student Search Service®

The Student Search Service® helps colleges find prospective students. If you take the PSAT/NMSQT, the SAT, an SAT Subject Test, or any AP Exam, you can be included in this free service.

Here's how it works: During SAT or SAT Subject Test registration, indicate that you want to be part of the Student Search. Your name is put in a database along with other information such as your address, high school grade point average, date of birth, grade level, high school, e-mail address, intended college major and extracurricular activities.

Colleges and scholarship programs then use the Student Search to help them locate and recruit students with characteristics that might be a good match with their schools.

Here are some points to keep in mind about the Student Search Service:

- Being part of Student Search is voluntary. You may take the test even if you don't join Student Search.
- Colleges participating in the Search do not receive your exam scores. Colleges can ask for the names of students within certain score ranges, but your exact score is not reported.
- Being contacted by a college doesn't mean you have been admitted. You can be admitted only after you apply. The Student Search Service is simply a way for colleges to reach prospective students.
- Student Search Service will share your contact information only with approved colleges and scholarship programs that are recruiting students like you. Your name will never be sold to a private company or mailing list.

Keep the Tests in Perspective

Colleges that require Subject Test scores do so because the scores are useful in making admission or placement decisions. Schools that don't have specific Subject Test policies generally review Subject Test scores during the application process because the scores can give a fuller picture of your academic achievement. The Subject Tests are a particularly helpful tool for admission and placement programs because the tests aren't tied to specific textbooks, grading procedures or instruction methods but are still tied to curricula. The tests provide level ground on which colleges can compare your scores with those of students who come from schools and backgrounds that may be far different from yours.

It's important to remember that test scores are just one of several factors that colleges consider in the admission process. Admission officers also look at your high school grades, letters of recommendation, extracurricular activities, essays and other criteria. Try to keep this in mind when you are preparing for and taking Subject Tests.

Score Choice™

In March 2009, the College Board introduced Score Choice™, a feature that gives you the option to choose the scores you send to colleges by test date for the SAT and by individual test for the SAT Subject Tests — at no additional cost. Designed to reduce your test day stress, Score Choice gives you an opportunity to show colleges the scores you feel best represent your abilities. Score Choice is optional, so if you don't actively choose to use it, all of your scores will be sent automatically with your score report. Since most colleges only consider your best scores, you should still feel comfortable reporting scores from all of your tests.

REMEMBER

Score Choice gives you an opportunity to show colleges the scores you feel best represent your abilities.

More about collegeboard.org

collegeboard.org is a comprehensive tool that can help you be prepared, connected and informed throughout the college planning and admission process. In addition to registering for the SAT and SAT Subject Tests, you can find information about other tests and services, try The Official SAT Question of the Day™, browse the College Board Store (where you can order *The College Board College Handbook, The Official Study Guide for all SAT Subject Tests*™ or *The Official SAT Subject Tests in Mathematics Levels 1 & 2 Study Guide*™), and send e-mails with your questions and concerns. collegeboard.org also contains free practice questions for each of the 20 SAT Subject Tests. These are an excellent supplement to this Study Guide and can help you be even more prepared on test day.

Once you create a free online account, you can print your SAT admission ticket, see your scores and send them to schools.

Which colleges are right for you? College Search at www.collegeboard.org has two ways to help you. The College MatchMaker lists colleges that meet all of your needs. If you are already familiar with a school, use College QuickFinder for updates of essential information. Both methods help you find the latest information on more than 3,800 colleges, as well as easy access to related tools.

How will you pay for college? While you're at the College Board website, look at the Financial Aid EasyPlanner, to help you organize your finances. It can help you find answers to such questions as: What does the school of your choice cost? How much can you save? How much can you and your family afford to pay? How much can your family afford to borrow for your education? What scholarships are available to you?

SAT Subject Tests Schedule

Subject	Date					
	October	November	December	January	May	June
Literature	*	*	*	*	*	*
United States History	*	*	*	*	*	*
World History			*			*
Mathematics Level 1	*	*	*	*	*	*
Mathematics Level 2	*	*	*	*	*	*
Biology E/M	*	*	*	*	*	*
Chemistry	*	*	*	*	*	*
Physics	*	*	*	*	*	*
Languages: Reading Only						
French	*		*	*	*	*
German						*
Modern Hebrew						*
Italian			*			
Latin			*			*
Spanish	*		*	*	*	*
Languages with Listening						
Chinese		*				
French		*				
German		*				
Japanese		*				
Korean		*				
Spanish		*				

NOTES:

1. You can take up to three SAT Subject Tests on a single test day.
2. You must indicate which test or tests you plan to take when you register, but, except for the Language Tests with Listening, you can change which tests you actually take on the day of the test.
3. You may only use a calculator for Mathematics Level 1 and Mathematics Level 2 Subject Tests. You can take these tests without a calculator, but that will put you at a disadvantage.
4. You must bring an acceptable CD player if you are taking a Language with Listening test.
5. **The SAT Subject Tests offered on each test date are subject to change. Please visit collegeboard.org for the latest test schedule information.**

How to Do Your Best on the SAT Subject Tests

Get Ready

Give yourself several weeks before the tests to read the course materials and the suggestions in this book. The rules for the SAT Subject Tests may be different than the rules for most of the tests you've taken in high school. You're probably used to answering questions in order, spending more time answering the hard questions and, in the hopes of getting at least partial credit, showing all your work.

When you take the SAT Subject Tests, it's OK to move around within the test section and to answer questions in any order you wish. Keep in mind that the questions go from easier to harder. You receive one point for each question answered correctly. For each question that you try but answer incorrectly, a fraction of a point is subtracted from the total number of correct answers. No points are added or subtracted for unanswered questions. If your final raw score includes a fraction, the score is rounded to the nearest whole number.

Avoid Surprises

Know what to expect. Become familiar with the test and test-day procedures. You'll boost your confidence and feel a lot more relaxed.

- **Know how the tests are set up.** All SAT Subject Tests are one-hour multiple-choice tests. The first page of each Subject Test includes a background questionnaire. You will be asked to fill it out before taking the test. The information is for statistical purposes only. It will not influence your test score. Your answers to the questionnaire will assist us in developing future versions of the test. You can see a sample of the background questionnaire for the U.S. History and World History Subject Tests at the start of each test in the book.
- **Learn the test directions.** The directions for answering the questions in this book are the same as those on the actual test. If you become familiar with the directions now, you'll leave yourself more time to answer the questions when you take the test.
- **Study the sample questions.** The more familiar you are with the question formats, the more comfortable you'll feel when you see similar questions on the actual test.
- **Get to know the answer sheet.** At the back of this book, you'll find a set of sample answer sheets. The appearance of the answer sheets in this book may differ from the answer sheets you see on test day.

- **Understand how the tests are scored.** You get one point for each right answer and lose a fraction of a point for each wrong answer. You neither gain nor lose points for omitting an answer. Hard questions count the same amount as easier questions.

A Practice Test Can Help

Find out where your strengths lie and which areas you need to work on. Do a run-through of a Subject Test under conditions that are close to what they will be on test day.

- **Set aside an hour so you can take the test without interruption.** You will be given one hour to take each SAT Subject Test.
- **Prepare a desk or table that has no books or papers on it.** No books, including dictionaries, are allowed in the test room.
- **Read the instructions that precede the practice test.** On test day, you will be asked to do this before you answer the questions.
- **Remove and fill in an answer sheet from the back of this book.** You can use one answer sheet for up to three Subject Tests.
- **Use a clock or kitchen timer to time yourself.** This will help you to pace yourself and to get used to taking a test in 60 minutes.

The Day Before the Test

It's natural to be nervous. A bit of a nervous edge can keep you sharp and focused. Below are a few suggestions to help you be more relaxed as the test approaches.

Do a brief review on the day before the test. Look through the sample questions, answer explanations and test directions in this book or on the College Board website. Keep the review brief; cramming the night before the test is unlikely to help your performance and might even make you more anxious.

The night before test day, prepare everything you need to take with you. You will need:

- your admission ticket
- an acceptable photo ID (see page 12)
- two No. 2 pencils with soft erasers (Do not bring pens or mechanical pencils.)
- a watch without an audible alarm
- a snack

REMEMBER

You are in control.

Come prepared.

Pace yourself.

Guess wisely.

Know the route to the test center and any instructions for finding the entrance.

Check the time your admission ticket specifies for arrival. Arrive a little early to give yourself time to settle in.

Get a good night's sleep.

Acceptable Photo IDs

- Driver's license (with your photo)
- State-issued ID
- Valid passport
- School ID card
- Student ID form that has been prepared by your school on school stationery and includes a recognizable photo and the school seal, which overlaps the photo (go to www.collegeboard.org for more information)

The most up-to-date information about acceptable photo IDs can be found on collegeboard.org.

REMINDER **What I Need on Test Day**

Make a copy of this box and post it somewhere noticeable.

I Need	I Have
Appropriate photo ID	________
Admission ticket	________
Two No. 2 pencils with clean soft erasers	________
Watch (without an audible alarm)	________
Snack	________
Bottled water	________
Directions to the test center	________
Instructions for finding the entrance on weekends	________

I am leaving the house at ____________________ a.m.

****Be on time or you can't take the test.****

On Test Day

You have good reason to feel confident. You're thoroughly prepared. You're familiar with what this day will bring. You are in control.

Keep in Mind

You must be on time or you can't take the test. Leave yourself plenty of time for mishaps and emergencies.

Think positively. If you are worrying about not doing well, then your mind isn't on the test. Be as positive as possible.

Stay focused. Think only about the question in front of you. Letting your mind wander will cost you time.

Concentrate on your own test. The first thing some students do when they get stuck on a question is to look around to see how everyone else is doing. What they usually see is that others seem busy filling in their answer sheets. Instead of being concerned that you are not doing as well as everyone else, keep in mind that everyone works at a different pace. Your neighbors may not be working on the question that puzzled you. They may not even be taking the same test. Thinking about what others are doing distracts you from working on your own test.

Making an Educated Guess

Educated guesses are helpful when it comes to taking tests with multiple-choice questions; however, making guesses is not a good idea. To correct for random guessing, a fraction of a point is subtracted for each incorrect answer. That means random guessing — guessing with no idea of an answer that might be correct — could lower your score. The best approach is to eliminate all the choices that you know are wrong. Make an educated guess from the remaining choices. If you can't eliminate any choices, move on.

REMEMBER

All correct answers are worth one point, regardless of the question's difficulty level.

Cell phone use is prohibited in the test center or testing room. If your cell phone is on, your scores will be canceled.

10 Tips FOR TAKING THE TEST

1. **Read carefully.** Consider all the choices in each question. Avoid careless mistakes that will cause you to lose points.
2. **Answer the easy questions first.** Work on less time-consuming questions before moving on to the more difficult ones.
3. **Eliminate choices that you know are wrong.** Cross them out in your test book so that you can clearly see which choices are left.
4. **Make educated guesses or skip the question.** If you have eliminated the choices that you know are wrong, guessing is your best strategy. However, if you cannot eliminate any of the answer choices, it is best to skip the question.
5. **Keep your answer sheet neat.** The answer sheet is scored by a machine, which can't tell the difference between an answer and a doodle. If the machine mistakenly reads two answers for one question, it will consider the question unanswered.
6. **Use your test booklet as scrap paper.** Use it to make notes or write down ideas. No one else will look at what you write.
7. **Check off questions as you work on them.** This will save time and help you to know which questions you've skipped.
8. **Check your answer sheet regularly.** Make sure you are in the right place. Check the number of the question and the number on the answer sheet every few questions. This is especially important when you skip a question. Losing your place on the answer sheet will cost you time and even points.
9. **Work at an even, steady pace and keep moving.** Each question on the test takes a certain amount of time to read and answer. Good test-takers develop a sense of timing to help them complete the test. Your goal is to spend time on the questions that you are most likely to answer correctly.
10. **Keep track of time.** During the hour that each Subject Test takes, check your progress occasionally so that you know how much of the test you have completed and how much time is left. Leave a few minutes for review toward the end of the testing period.

If you erase all your answers to a Subject Test, that's the same as a request to cancel the test. All Subject Tests taken with the erased test will also be canceled.

7 Ways TO PACE YOURSELF

1. Set up a schedule. Know when you should be one-quarter of the way through and halfway through. Every now and then, check your progress against your schedule.

2. Begin to work as soon as the testing time begins. Reading the instructions and getting to know the test directions in this book ahead of time will allow you to do that.

3. Work at an even, steady pace. After you answer the questions you are sure of, move on to those for which you'll need more time.

4. Skip questions you can't answer. You might have time to return to them. Remember to mark them in your test booklet, so you'll be able to find them later.

5. As you work on a question, cross out the answers you can eliminate in your test book.

6. Go back to the questions you skipped. If you can, eliminate some of the answer choices, then make an educated guess.

7. Leave time in the last few minutes to check your answers to avoid mistakes.

REMEMBER

Check your answer sheet. Make sure your answers are dark and completely filled in. Erase completely.

After the Tests

Most, but not all, scores will be reported online several weeks after the test date. A few days later, a full score report will be available to you online. You can request a paper score report too, which arrives later. Your score report will also be mailed to your high school and to the colleges, universities and scholarship programs that you indicated when you registered or on the correction form attached to your admission ticket. The score report includes your scores, percentiles and interpretive information.

What's Your Score?

Scores are available for free at www.collegeboard.org several weeks after each SAT is given. You can also get your scores — for a fee — by telephone. Call customer service at 866-756-7346 in the United States. From outside the United States, call 212-713-7789.

Some scores may take longer to report. If your score report is not available online when expected, check back the following week. If you have requested a paper score report and you have not received it by eight weeks after the test date (by five weeks for online reports), contact customer service by phone at 866-756-7346 or by e-mail at sat@info.collegeboard.org.

Should You Take the Tests Again?

Before you decide whether or not to retest, you need to evaluate your scores. The best way to evaluate how you really did on a Subject Test is to compare your scores to the admission or placement requirements, or average scores, of the colleges to which you are applying. You may decide that with additional work you could do better taking the test again.

?

Contacting the College Board

If you have comments or questions about the tests, please write to us at The College Board SAT Program, P.O. Box 025505, Miami, FL 33102, or e-mail us at sat@info.collegeboard.org.

United States History

Purpose

The Subject Test in United States History emphasizes pre-Columbian times to the present as well as basic social science concepts, methods, and generalizations as they are found in the study of history. It is not tied to any textbook or instructional approach, but to your high school curriculum.

Format

This is a one-hour test with 90 to 95 multiple-choice questions. The questions cover political, economic, social, intellectual, and cultural history as well as foreign policy. The chart on the following page shows you what content the test covers and the approximate percentages of questions covering that content.

Content

The questions may require you to:

- recall basic information and require you to know facts, terms, concepts, and generalizations
- analyze and interpret materials such as graphs, charts, paintings, text, cartoons, photographs, and maps
- understand important aspects of U.S. history
- relate ideas to given data
- evaluate data for a given purpose, basing your judgment either on internal evidence, such as proof and logical consistency, or on external criteria, such as comparison with other works, established standards, and theories

Material Covered*	Approximate Percentage of Test
Political History	32–36
Economic History	18–20
Social History	18–22
Intellectual and Cultural History	10–12
Foreign Policy	13–17
Periods Covered	
Pre-Columbian history to 1789	20
1790 to 1898	40
1899 to the present	40
* Social science concepts, methods, and generalizations are incorporated in this material.	

How to Prepare

The only essential preparation is a sound, one-year course in U.S. history at the college-preparatory level. Most of the test questions are based on material commonly taught in U.S. history courses in secondary schools, although some of the material may be covered in other social studies courses. Knowledge gained from social studies courses and from outside reading could be helpful. No one textbook or method of instruction is considered better than another. Familiarize yourself with the directions in advance. The directions in this book are identical to those that appear on the test.

Score

The total score is reported on the 200-to-800 scale.

Sample Questions

All questions on the Subject Test in U.S. History are multiple choice, requiring you to choose the best response from five choices. The following sample questions illustrate the types of questions on the test, their range of difficulty, and the abilities they measure. Questions may be presented as separate items or in sets based on quotations, maps, pictures, graphs, or tables.

Directions: Each of the questions or incomplete statements below is followed by five suggested answers or completions. Select the one that is best in each case and then fill in the corresponding circle on the answer sheet.

1. Which leader of the national women's suffrage movement was responsible for the "winning plan" leading to the enactment of the Nineteenth Amendment?

   (A) Abigail Adams
   (B) Carrie Chapman Catt
   (C) Peggy Eaton
   (D) Emma Goldman
   (E) Carrie Nation

Choice (B) is the correct answer to question 1. Carrie Chapman Catt was influential in the 1920 ratification of the Nineteenth Amendment, which gave women the right to vote. In 1916, as president of the National American Woman Suffrage Association, Chapman Catt unveiled her "winning plan" for achieving women's suffrage (voting rights). Her plan was to lobby for suffrage at both the national and state levels. She thought that gaining key states would help persuade legislators at the national level. Her plan and her support of the war effort worked: the Nineteenth Amendment was ratified just four years later. None of the other women were leaders of the U.S. women's suffrage movement. Abigail Adams (A) was the wife of second U.S. President John Adams. Peggy Eaton (C) is known for her involvement in a scandal with John Henry Eaton, a member of President Andrew Jackson's cabinet, whom she eventually married. Emma Goldman (D) was a Lithuanian-born anarchist and radical activist who was deported in 1919. Carrie Nation (E) was a leader of the temperance movement in the United States.

2. The greatest source of federal revenue between 1865 and 1900 was

   (A) land sales
   (B) tariffs
   (C) property and corporate taxes
   (D) income taxes
   (E) bond sales

Choice (B) is the correct answer to question 2. The greatest source of federal revenue between 1865 and 1900 was tariffs. Tariffs are duties governments collect on goods that are imported into their country. To raise much-needed funds during the American Civil War, the United States established high tariffs on incoming goods from Europe. After the war, the high tariffs remained to raise federal revenue and to protect American manufacturers from competition with cheaper imported goods. Many opposed high tariffs because they restricted international trade and tended to make consumer goods more expensive, and these tariffs were eventually lowered. The other answers are incorrect. Land sales (A) and bond sales (E) did not generate as much federal revenue as tariffs did during this time period. Federal taxation of property and corporations (C) and of income (D) occurred primarily after the passage of the Sixteenth Amendment was ratified in 1913, ending a long battle about the constitutionality of federal taxation of income.

3. During the Progressive Era, Congress passed legislation to create the
   (A) Federal Reserve System
   (B) Interstate Commerce Commission
   (C) Agricultural Adjustment Act
   (D) Tennessee Valley Authority
   (E) Works Progress Administration

Choice (A) is the correct answer to question 3. During the Progressive Era of the early twentieth century, Congress did much to reform the country, including passing legislation to create the Federal Reserve System. President Woodrow Wilson signed this important legislation in 1913, helping to stabilize the nation's economy by setting up a system to control the money supply. The Federal Reserve System is a central U.S. banking system responsible for monetary policy. The Federal Reserve System regulates the creation of currency and sets interest rates. The other answers are incorrect, as none of the other acts or agencies was established during this time period. The Interstate Commerce Commission (B) was created earlier, in 1887. The Agricultural Adjustment Act (C), the Tennessee Valley Authority (D), and the Works Progress Administration (E) were all created later, during the New Deal of the 1930s.

4. Under Chief Justice Earl Warren, the Supreme Court did which of the following?
   (A) Restricted the rights of dissidents to receive passports
   (B) Developed a clear definition of obscenity still in use
   (C) Protected the rights of persons charged with criminal activity
   (D) Upheld state laws segregating public schools
   (E) Endorsed prayer in public schools

Choice (C) is the correct answer to question 4. Under Earl Warren, Chief Justice from 1953 to 1969, the Supreme Court ruled in favor of the plaintiff in *Miranda v. Arizona*, thereby protecting the rights of persons charged with criminal activity. With the 1966 Miranda case, the Court ruled that before persons accused of a crime are interrogated by the police, they must be informed of their right to remain silent and to have an attorney present. The decision established what has come to be known as the Miranda warning to arrested persons, famously beginning, "You have the right to remain silent. Anything you say can and will be used against you in a court of law. You have the right to an attorney..." The other answers are incorrect. In the 1958 *Kent v. Dulles* decision, the Supreme Court upheld the rights of dissidents to receive passports (A). Although the Supreme Court did rule on a definition of obscenity in *Roth v. United States* in 1957, Warren argued that the definition was still unclear (B). Clearer criteria for obscenity were established by the Supreme Court in 1973 with *Miller v. California*, after Warren had left the court. Under Warren, the Supreme Court also made the historic *Brown v. Board of Education of Topeka* decision in 1954, overthrowing legal segregation of public schools (D). In *Engel v. Vitale* (1962), the Supreme Court under Warren ruled that prayer in public schools was unconstitutional (E).

5. Louis Sullivan and Frank Lloyd Wright are best known for their work in

   (A) painting
   (B) poetry
   (C) science
   (D) architecture
   (E) philosophy

Choice (D) is the correct answer to question 5. Louis Sullivan and Frank Lloyd Wright are best known for their work in architecture. Louis Sullivan (1856–1924) was an American architect known for designing steel-framed buildings. Sullivan is considered to be the originator of the skyscraper. A member of the Chicago School of Architecture, Sullivan's influential buildings include the Wainwright Building in St. Louis and the Carson Pirie Scott department store in Chicago. Also associated with the Chicago School, Frank Lloyd Wright (1867–1959) was an American architect known for his "prairie houses," clean geometric lines, and style of integrating buildings into their natural surroundings. Among his most famous buildings are the Guggenheim Museum in New York City and the Fallingwater house in Bear Run, Pennsylvania. The other answers are incorrect.

6. "I believe that it must be the policy of the United States to support free peoples who are resisting attempted subjugation by armed minorities or by outside pressures.

   I believe that we must assist free peoples to work out their own destinies in their own way. . . .

   Should we fail to aid Greece and Turkey in this fateful hour, the effect will be far reaching to the west as well as to the east. We must take immediate and resolute action."

   The excerpt above states which of the following foreign policies?

   (A) The Gentlemen's Agreement
   (B) The Marshall Plan
   (C) The Good Neighbor policy
   (D) The Truman Doctrine
   (E) The Alliance for Progress

Choice (D) is the correct answer to question 6. The excerpt is taken from President Harry Truman's address to the U.S. Congress on March 12, 1947, in which he expressed what came to be known as the Truman Doctrine. Central to the Truman Doctrine is the idea that it is in the best interests of the United States to help governments resist and repress uprisings and invasions by organizations the United States deems undemocratic, with a focus on stopping the spread of communism. This doctrine was initially used, as the excerpt suggests, to help Greece and Turkey defeat a communist insurgency. Later, the Truman Doctrine was famously cited as an argument for U.S. involvement in Southeast Asia. The other answers are incorrect.

7. The decade following the War of 1812 has been characterized as the Era of Good Feelings for which of the following reasons?

   (A) All sections of the country supported the aims of the Hartford Convention.

   (B) Only one political party dominated national elections.

   (C) International cooperation produced a long period of peace.

   (D) Women gained political influence with the right to vote.

   (E) Abolitionists succeeded in restricting slavery in new territories.

Choice (B) is the correct answer to question 7. The decade following the War of 1812 has been characterized as the Era of Good Feelings largely because one political party dominated national elections. President James Monroe of the Democratic–Republican Party, elected with little opposition in 1816, ran unopposed in 1820 and was nearly unanimously reelected. The other main political party, the Federalists, was in the midst of collapse in 1816, and no other party or candidate gained national popularity for years to come. The other answers are incorrect. The Hartford Convention of 1814 (A) was only supported by delegates from New England, who met to discuss their disagreements with the South and the antitrade policies of President James Madison. Although some international peace occurred at the end of the Napoleonic Wars, it was during this decade that many South American nations revolted against Spain (C). Women did not gain the right to vote until 1920 (D). The Missouri Compromise of 1820 prohibited slavery in many territories, but permitted it in the territory of Missouri (E).

8. Puritans who remained within the Church of England founded the colony of

   (A) Massachusetts Bay

   (B) New Netherland

   (C) Plymouth Plantation

   (D) Rhode Island

   (E) Virginia

Choice (A) is the correct answer to question 8. Puritans who remained within the Church of England founded the colony of Massachusetts Bay. The term "Puritan" generally refers to a sect of English Christianity that originated in the 16th century. Puritans held beliefs about ethics, biblical interpretation, and church authority that differed from the core beliefs of the Church of England. Of those Puritans who remained within the official church, many, like the founders of the Massachusetts Bay Colony, found it easier to live and worship in the American colonies. The other answers are incorrect. The beliefs of some Puritans, such as the founders of the Plymouth Plantation (C) and Rhode Island (D), led them to separate from the Church of England. The settlers of New Netherland (B) were from the Netherlands and were not members of the Church of England. The founders of Virginia (E) were members of the Church of England who did not hold Puritan beliefs.

9. Michael Harrington's 1962 book, *The Other America*, primarily addresses the

   (A) growth of Communist Party membership
   (B) problems of migrant labor
   (C) failure of secondary education
   (D) increase in poverty
   (E) increase in gender inequality

Choice (D) is the correct answer to question 9. Michael Harrington's 1962 book, the full title of which is *The Other America: Poverty in the United States*, addresses the increase in poverty in the United States. A writer and activist, Harrington became an influential voice in U.S. society. *The Other America*, which reveals the impoverished conditions under which many U.S. citizens lived, attracted many readers, including Presidents John F. Kennedy and Lyndon B. Johnson, and is said to have led in part to President Johnson's declaration of a "war on poverty." The other answers are incorrect, as Harrington's book is not primarily focused on the Communist Party (A), migrant labor (B), secondary education (C), or gender inequality (E).

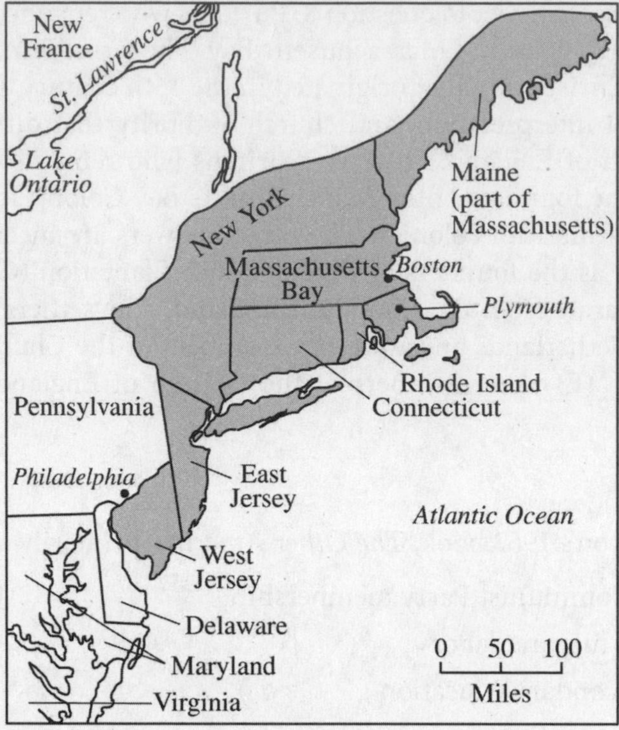

10. The shaded area in the map above represents the boundaries of

(A) King Philip's (Metacom's) domain in 1675
(B) the Powhatan Confederacy in 1680
(C) the Dominion of New England in 1688
(D) the Puritan colonies in 1710
(E) the Iroquois Confederacy in 1750

Choice (C) is the correct answer to question 10. The shaded area in the map above represents the boundaries of the Dominion of New England in 1688. The Dominion of New England was an administrative unit of the English colonies established by King James II in 1686. In 1688, New York and New Jersey were acquired by England from the Dutch and added to the Dominion. King James II established the Dominion to centralize military and political rule in order to enforce imperial policies such as the Navigation Acts, which restricted the colonies from trading with non-British companies. Highly unpopular with the colonists, the central administration by the Dominion and its enforcing British soldiers were met with severe resistance, collapsing with the overthrow of James II in the Glorious Revolution of 1688. The other answers are incorrect. In 1675 and 1676, King Philip (Metacom) was at war with colonists throughout the shaded region, but he never took full control of the territories (A). The Powhatan Confederacy was located south of the shaded area (B). Large portions of this area, including New York, were not Puritan colonies in 1710 (D). The Iroquois Confederacy was located west and north of the shaded area (E).

11. "In all things that are purely social we can be as separate as the fingers, yet one as the hand in all things essential to mutual progress."

    In the quotation above, Booker T. Washington seeks to

    (A) provide a formula for economic success for African Americans

    (B) demand integrated facilities for African Americans

    (C) promote religious harmony between whites and African Americans

    (D) promote labor unions in the United States South

    (E) gather support for abolishing slavery

Choice (A) is the correct answer to question 11. In the quotation above, Booker T. Washington seeks to provide a formula for economic success for African Americans. This quotation is taken from Washington's "Atlanta Compromise" speech, made to an audience of predominately white businessmen in 1895. Washington is arguing that white Southern businessmen would be wise to employ African Americans (instead of European immigrants) in the interests of "mutual progress." Washington believed that African Americans could achieve economic success by laboring for white-owned businesses, but he clearly felt the need to reassure white business owners that economic cooperation between the races did not mean social equality. The other answers are incorrect. In this address, Washington is mainly concerned with the economic cooperation between whites and African Americans, not integrated facilities (B) or religious harmony (C). Washington was seeking greater employment of African Americans, not modification of their working conditions through labor unions (D). Slavery had already been abolished by the time of this address (E).

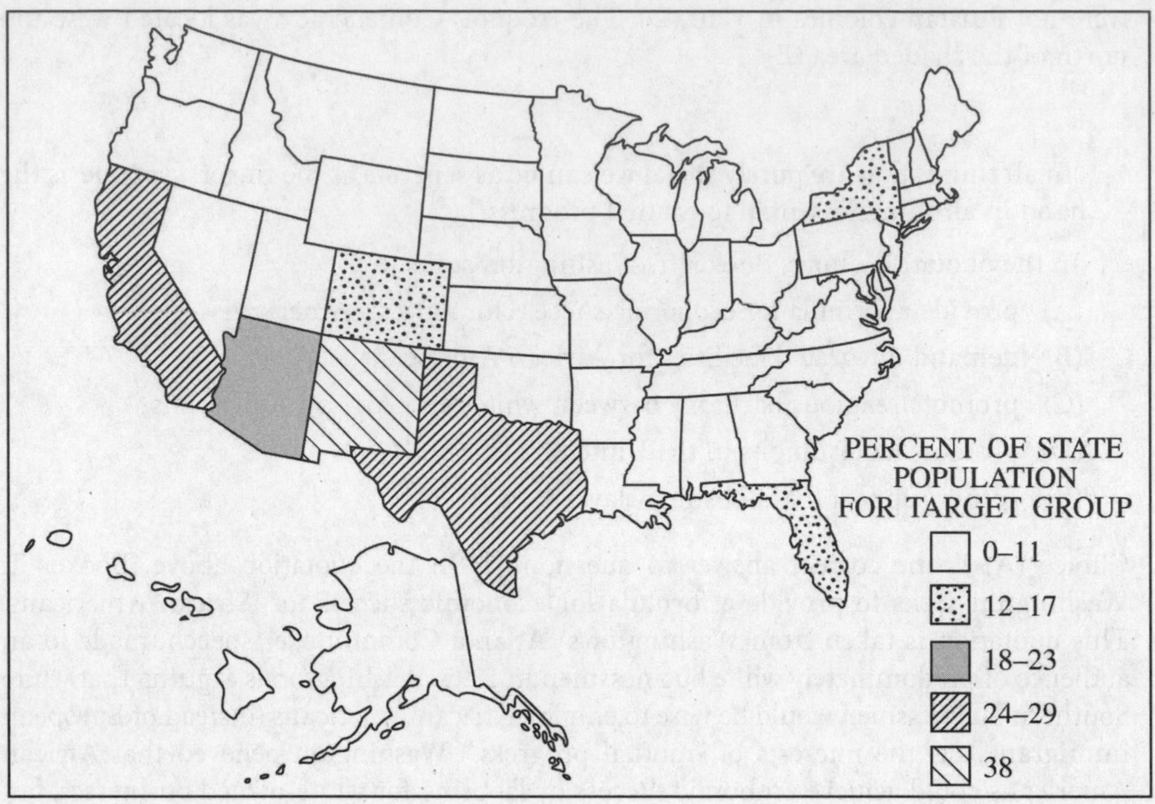

12. The late twentieth-century map above shows concentrations of which of the following groups?

(A) Conservative Republicans
(B) African Americans
(C) Liberal Democrats
(D) Christian fundamentalists
(E) Hispanics

Choice (E) is the correct answer to question 12. This map shows concentrations of Hispanics in the United States in the late twentieth century. The term Hispanic refers to people of Spanish or Latin American heritage. As shown by the map, the states with the highest percentage of Hispanics in the late twentieth century were located along or near the Mexican border, with the exception of Florida and New York, two states with historically large Hispanic populations. The other choices are incorrect. None of the other groups were represented demographically in the late twentieth century as shown on the map: there were higher proportions of Conservative Republicans (A), African Americans (B), and Christian fundamentalists (D) in Southern states such as South Carolina and Georgia, and higher proportions of Liberal Democrats (C) in such states as New Jersey, Massachusetts, and Illinois.

13. In the seventeenth century, women serving as indentured laborers had to
    - (A) remain unmarried until their indenture was over
    - (B) give their inheritance to their employers
    - (C) renounce all legal ties to their families
    - (D) pledge to produce specified amounts of spun wool and cotton thread
    - (E) live in separate buildings or dormitories supervised by matrons

Choice (A) is the correct answer to question 13. In the seventeenth century, women serving as indentured laborers had to remain unmarried until their terms of indenture were over. Indentured laborers were laborers who undertook contract work for an employer for a period of time without pay, in exchange for housing, food, training, and, in the case of many American indentured laborers, the cost of coming to a new country. Because the indentured servants were legally bound to their masters, they were prohibited from marrying while under contract. Women were also prohibited from becoming pregnant. The other answers are incorrect. Indentured servants were otherwise free persons and did not have to give up their inheritances (B), or renounce ties to their families (C). Most female indentured servants performed household duties and did not have to produce wool or cotton thread (D). Female indentured servants often lived in the main houses of their masters rather than in separate buildings or dormitories (E).

United States History – Practice Test 1

Practice Helps

The test that follows is an actual, previously administered SAT Subject Test in United States History. To get an idea of what it's like to take this test, practice under conditions that are much like those of an actual test administration.

- Set aside an hour when you can take the test uninterrupted.
- Sit at a desk or table with no other books or papers. Dictionaries, other books, or notes are not allowed in the test room.
- Tear out an answer sheet from the back of this book and fill it in just as you would on the day of the test. One answer sheet can be used for up to three Subject Tests.
- Read the instructions that precede the practice test. During the actual administration, you will be asked to read them before answering test questions.
- Use a clock or kitchen timer to time yourself.
- After you finish the practice test, read the sections "How to Score the SAT Subject Test in United States History" and "How Did You Do on the Subject Test in United States History?"
- The appearance of the answer sheet in this book may differ from the answer sheet you see on test day.

UNITED STATES HISTORY TEST

The top portion of the page of the answer sheet that you will use to take the United States History Test must be filled in exactly as illustrated below. When your supervisor tells you to fill in the circle next to the name of the test you are about to take, mark your answer sheet as shown.

○ Literature	○ Mathematics Level 1	○ German	○ Chinese Listening	○ Japanese Listening
○ Biology E	○ Mathematics Level 2	○ Italian	○ French Listening	○ Korean Listening
○ Biology M	● U.S. History	○ Latin	○ German Listening	○ Spanish Listening
○ Chemistry	○ World History	○ Modern Hebrew		
○ Physics	○ French	○ Spanish	**Background Questions:** ① ② ③ ④ ⑤ ⑥ ⑦ ⑧ ⑨	

After filling in the circle next to the name of the test you are taking, locate the Background Questions section, which also appears at the top of your answer sheet (as shown above). This is where you will answer the following Background Questions on your answer sheet.

BACKGROUND QUESTIONS

Please answer the two questions below by filling in the appropriate circle in the Background Questions box on your answer sheet. <u>The information you provide is for statistical purposes only and will not affect your test score.</u>

<u>Question I</u>

How many semesters of United States History have you taken from grade 9 to the present? (If you are taking United States History this semester, count it as a full semester.) Fill in only <u>one</u> circle of circles 1-4.

- One semester or less —Fill in circle 1.
- Two semesters —Fill in circle 2.
- Three semesters —Fill in circle 3.
- Four or more semesters —Fill in circle 4.

<u>Question II</u>

Which, if any, of the following social studies courses have you taken from grade 9 to the present? (Fill in ALL circles that apply.)

- One or more semesters of government —Fill in circle 5.
- One or more semesters of economics —Fill in circle 6.
- One or more semesters of geography —Fill in circle 7.
- One or more semesters of psychology —Fill in circle 8.
- One or more semesters of sociology or anthropology —Fill in circle 9.

If you have taken none of these social studies courses, leave the circles 5 through 9 blank.

When the supervisor gives the signal, turn the page and begin the United States History Test. There are 100 numbered circles on the answer sheet and 90 questions in the United States History Test. Therefore, use only circles 1 to 90 for recording your answers.

UNITED STATES HISTORY TEST

Directions: Each of the questions or incomplete statements below is followed by five suggested answers or completions. Select the one that is best in each case and then fill in the corresponding circle on the answer sheet.

1. During the seventeenth and eighteenth centuries, the English colonial system was based most explicitly on the economic and political principles of

(A) mercantilism
(B) free trade
(C) salutary neglect
(D) enlightened despotism
(E) physiocracy

2. The concept of the separation of powers, as articulated by the framers of the Constitution, refers to the

(A) right of free speech
(B) right of freedom of assembly
(C) organization of the national government in three branches
(D) separation of church and state
(E) political rights of confederated states

3. The Trail of Tears refers to the

(A) movement of slaves from eastern states into the West after the 1820's
(B) relocation of Cherokee Indians from the Southeast to settlements in what is now Oklahoma
(C) difficult movement of settlers over the Oregon Trail
(D) Lewis and Clark's expedition during the Jefferson presidency
(E) movement of thousands of people across the Great Plains during the California gold rush

4. All of the following reformers are correctly paired with the reform issue with which they were most involved EXCEPT

(A) Elizabeth Cady Stanton . . suffrage
(B) Sojourner Truth . . antislavery
(C) Harriet Beecher Stowe . . prohibition
(D) Emma Willard . . women's education
(E) Dorothea Dix . . treatment of people with mental and emotional disabilities

GO ON TO THE NEXT PAGE

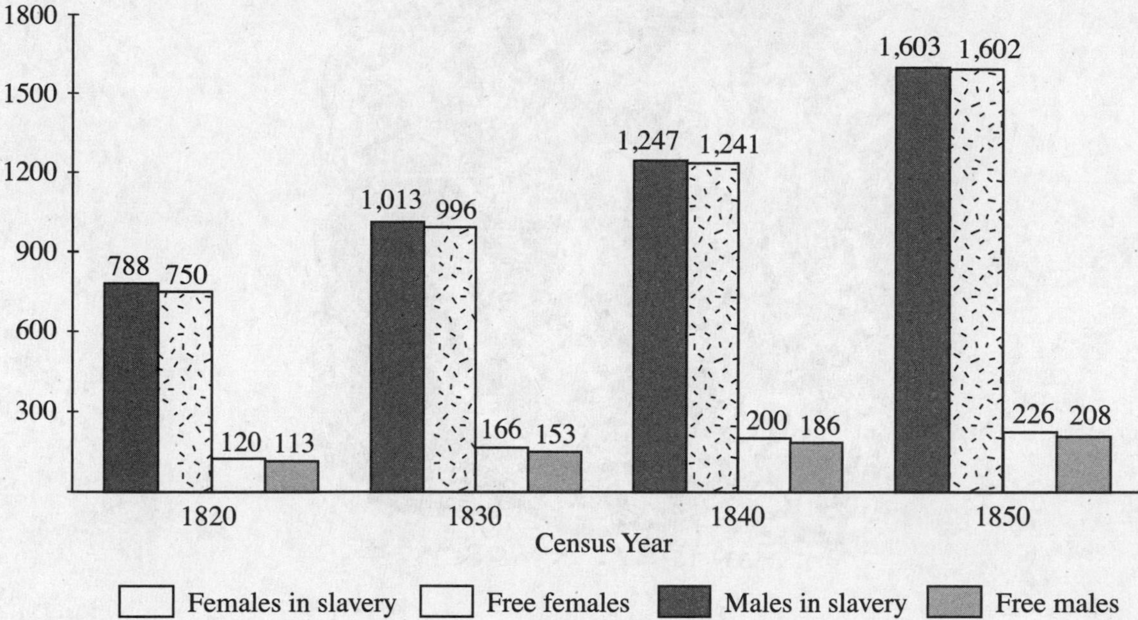

5. Which of the following statements about the period from 1820 to 1850 is supported by the diagram above?

(A) The percentage of the Black population held in slavery declined.
(B) The ratio of Black males to Black females remained fairly constant.
(C) Black males were more likely than Black females to be free.
(D) The number of Black females doubled every 20 years.
(E) The total Black population in each census exceeded two million.

GO ON TO THE NEXT PAGE

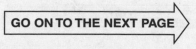

Punch Ltd.

6. The cartoon above illustrates popular reaction to publication of a theory by

   (A) Malthus
   (B) Darwin
   (C) Marx
   (D) Einstein
   (E) Freud

---

7. In the early years of the twentieth century, the majority of female workers employed outside of the home were

   (A) widowed
   (B) divorced
   (C) married with young children
   (D) married with grown children
   (E) young and unmarried

8. President Franklin D. Roosevelt attempted to "pack" the Supreme Court in 1937 for which of the following reasons?

   (A) He wanted to make sure that New Deal laws would be found constitutional.
   (B) He believed that additional conservative justices would balance the Court.
   (C) He owed favors to many political friends who were trained lawyers.
   (D) He wanted to increase minority representation on the Court.
   (E) He wanted socialists and communists to be represented on the Court.

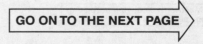

GO ON TO THE NEXT PAGE

By Permission of Chuck Asay and Creator's Syndicate, Inc.

9. The cartoon above makes which of the following points about federal aid policies in the years following the Second World War?

(A) The federal government has always been reluctant to offer financial aid to farmers.
(B) American farmers have never needed government support to maintain self-sufficiency.
(C) Much federal aid goes to individuals in forms other than welfare payments.
(D) Congress should cease paying both welfare and price supports.
(E) Price supports paid to farmers are not a significant percentage of the federal budget.

GO ON TO THE NEXT PAGE

10. The United States supported the Bay of Pigs invasion in 1961 in an attempt to overthrow

(A) Nikita Khrushchev
(B) Gamal Abdel Nasser
(C) Fidel Castro
(D) Chiang Kai-shek
(E) Ngo Dinh Diem

11. Single women and widows in the eighteenth-century British North American colonies had the legal right to

(A) hold political office
(B) serve as Protestant ministers
(C) vote
(D) own property
(E) serve on juries

12. Which of the following was most responsible for the repeal of the Stamp Act in 1766 ?

(A) The dumping of the East India Company's tea into Boston Harbor
(B) Petitions by the First Continental Congress to Parliament
(C) The boycott of British imports
(D) Acceptance by the Massachusetts colonists of alternate taxation
(E) Pressure on Parliament by the king

13. *Marbury* v. *Madison* was a significant turning point in the interpretation of the United States Constitution because it

(A) upheld the separation of church and state
(B) validated the principle of the free press
(C) established the practice of judicial review
(D) abolished the slave trade
(E) overturned the Alien and Sedition Acts

14. After the Civil War, sharecropping was an important element in the agricultural economy of which of the following regions?

(A) The Middle Atlantic states
(B) The South
(C) The Great Plains
(D) The West Coast
(E) New England

15. "Texas has been absorbed into the Union in the inevitable fulfillment of the general law which is rolling our population westward. . . . It was disintegrated from Mexico in the natural course of events, by a process perfectly legitimate on its own part, blameless on ours. . . . [Its] incorporation into the Union was not only inevitable, but the most natural, right and proper thing in the world."

The statement above is an expression of

(A) Social Darwinism
(B) antiabolitionism
(C) federalism
(D) Manifest Destiny
(E) self-determination

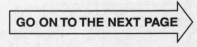

GO ON TO THE NEXT PAGE

Reprinted by permission of the New York Historical Society

16. The nineteenth-century cartoon above supports which of the following conclusions about the United States economy?

    (A) The emergence of strong unions resulted in loss of productivity.
    (B) The emergence of big government resulted in loss of liberties.
    (C) Railroad corporations wielded tremendous power in American society.
    (D) Southern planters wielded tremendous power in the Senate.
    (E) Rapid urbanization led to unsanitary conditions in many cities.

GO ON TO THE NEXT PAGE

17. "There was never the least attention paid to what was cut up for sausage; there would come all the way back from Europe old sausage that had been rejected, and that was moldy and white—it would be dosed with borax and glycerine, and dumped into the hoppers, and made over again for home consumption. . . . There would be meat stored in great piles in rooms; and the water from leaky roofs would drip over it, and thousands of rats would race about on it."

    The passage above is most likely excerpted from

    (A) John Steinbeck's *The Grapes of Wrath*
    (B) Theodore Dreiser's *An American Tragedy*
    (C) Jane Addams' *Twenty Years at Hull-House*
    (D) Lincoln Steffens' *The Shame of the Cities*
    (E) Upton Sinclair's *The Jungle*

MAJOR HOUSEHOLD EXPENDITURES, 1900 and 1928

1900	
2 Bicycles	$ 70
Wringer and washboard	$ 5
Brushes and brooms	$ 5
Sewing machine (mechanical)	$ 25
Total	$ 105
1928	
Automobile	$ 700
Radio	$ 75
Phonograph	$ 50
Washing machine	$ 150
Vacuum cleaner	$ 50
Sewing machine (electric)	$ 60
Other electrical equipment	$ 25
Telephone (year)	$ 35
Total	$1,145

18. The chart above shows the major household expenditures of a middle-class American family in 1900 and a similar family in 1928. Which of the following is an accurate statement supported by the chart?

    (A) Families needed more mechanical help with housework in 1928 than they did in 1900 because they had less domestic help.
    (B) Inflation caused a significant increase in the prices of most household goods by 1928.
    (C) Many families moved from rural to urban areas between 1900 and 1930 in search of employment opportunities.
    (D) By 1928 more consumer goods were available to families than had been available in 1900.
    (E) Increased consumer spending was a major cause of the stock market crash of 1929.

GO ON TO THE NEXT PAGE

19. "Rosie the Riveter" was a nickname given during the Second World War to

    (A) American women who did industrial work in the 1940's
    (B) American women who cared for soldiers wounded in battle
    (C) a machine that increased the speed of construction work
    (D) a woman who was a popular radio talk-show host of the 1940's
    (E) a woman who broadcast Japanese propaganda to American troops

GO ON TO THE NEXT PAGE

UPI/Corbis-Bettmann

20. The picture above illustrates efforts in the 1960's to organize a boycott that focused attention on the

    (A) long hours of grocery clerks and stock clerks
    (B) problems of Mississippi Valley fruit growers
    (C) labor shortages in produce transport companies
    (D) plight of migrant farmworkers
    (E) problems of West Coast wineries

GO ON TO THE NEXT PAGE

21. Which of the following statements best describes the response of Native Americans to the continued settlement of Europeans in North America during the eighteenth century?

    (A) Native Americans traded with the French and the English as a means of maintaining their autonomy.
    (B) Native Americans in the southern part of New France negotiated treaties with the French that allowed the peaceful expansion of the European timber trade.
    (C) Some Native Americans created a horse-based nomadic culture in the Northeast.
    (D) Native Americans in the Great Plains assimilated with the European settlers.
    (E) The Iroquois did not adopt European firearms and metal tools, in an effort to maintain their own traditions.

22. In the seventeenth century, the British colonies in the Chesapeake Bay region became economically viable due to the

    (A) adoption of representative government
    (B) introduction of tobacco cultivation
    (C) flourishing trade with American Indians
    (D) export of dried cod and whale tallow
    (E) cultivation of cotton

23. All of the following were aspects of the Constitution that was submitted to the states for ratification in 1787 EXCEPT

    (A) the ability to levy taxes
    (B) congressional authority to declare war
    (C) a two-term limit for Presidents
    (D) provision for impeachment of the President
    (E) provision for presidential State of the Union messages

GO ON TO THE NEXT PAGE

The St. Louis Art Museum. Gift Bank of America

24. The painting above, which shows an antebellum election site, supports which of the following statements?

    (A) Women were equal participants in the voting process.
    (B) The sale and provision of liquor was prohibited on election day.
    (C) Party workers had to remain at least 50 yards away from the polling place.
    (D) There were no property restrictions for male voters.
    (E) Elections were a welcome social event as well as a political obligation.

---

25. The introduction of canals, railroads, and new factory technology in the mid-nineteenth century affected which of the following regions LEAST?

    (A) New England
    (B) New York and Pennsylvania
    (C) New Jersey and Delaware
    (D) The South
    (E) The Midwest

GO ON TO THE NEXT PAGE

Questions 26-27 are based on the passage below.

"Unsanitary housing, poisonous sewage, contaminated water, infant mortality, the spread of contagion, adulterated food, impure milk, smoke-laden air, ill-ventilated factories . . . unwholesome crowding, prostitution and drunkenness are the enemies which the modern cities must face and overcome, would they survive. Logically their electorate should be made up of those who . . . have at least attempted to care for children, to clean houses, to prepare foods, to isolate the family from moral dangers. . . . To test the elector's fitness to deal with this situation by his ability to bear arms is absurd. . . . City housekeeping has failed partly because women, the traditional housekeepers, have not been consulted as to its multiform activities. The men have been carelessly indifferent to much of this civic housekeeping, as they have been carelessly indifferent to the details of the household."

Jane Addams, 1906.

26. Which of the following best reflects the main argument of the passage?

(A) Men should spend less time away from home and participate more fully in domestic life.
(B) Women should be able to vote in order to apply their proven housekeeping abilities to the civic sphere.
(C) Military solutions to social problems are ineffective because they ignore moral issues.
(D) Solving the problems of cities mostly depends on providing for poor children.
(E) Modern cities have been saved from ruin only by the involvement of women in civic issues.

27. The passage above suggests that Jane Addams would probably have supported all of the following EXCEPT

(A) military preparedness
(B) woman suffrage
(C) prohibition
(D) settlement houses
(E) the Pure Food and Drug Act

McCLURE'S
MAGAZINE
MAY
LINCOLN STEFFENS'S exposure of another type of municipal grafting; how Pittsburg differs from St. Louis and Minneapolis.
THE END OF THE WORLD, by Professor Newcomb. A powerful story, yet a scientific prediction; pictures by the famous French artist, Henri Lanos.
IDA M. TARBELL on the Standard tactics which brought on the famous oil crisis of 1878.
SIX SHORT STORIES

Culver Pictures, Inc.

28. The articles appearing in this 1905 issue of *McClure's Magazine* illustrate all of the following trends in the early twentieth-century United States EXCEPT:

    (A) Popular magazines were beginning to turn their attention to issues of reform.
    (B) Reform of municipal city governments was a growing concern.
    (C) Exposure of monopolistic business practices was beginning to draw public attention.
    (D) Scientific methods were increasingly called on to lend credibility to all sorts of theories.
    (E) Reformers of both government and society enjoyed widespread support among leading industrialists.

GO ON TO THE NEXT PAGE

Questions 29-30 are based on the chart below.

IMMIGRATION TO THE UNITED STATES BY AREA OF ORIGIN

Year	All Countries	Europe	Asia	Americas	Africa	Australasia
1921	805,228	652,364	25,034	124,118	1,301	2,281
1922	309,556	216,385	14,263	77,448	520	915
1924	706,896	364,339	22,065	318,855	900	679
1925	294,314	148,366	3,578	141,496	412	462
1927	335,175	168,368	3,669	161,872	520	746
1928	307,255	158,513	3,380	144,281	475	606
1929	279,678	158,598	3,758	116,177	509	636

29. Which of the following areas of origin showed the greatest percentage decline in the number of immigrants to the United States between 1921 and 1929 ?

(A) Europe
(B) Asia
(C) The Americas
(D) Africa
(E) Australasia

30. Which of the following best accounts for the trend in immigration shown in the chart?

(A) Improved economic conditions in many areas of origin
(B) Warfare in several areas of the world during this period
(C) New United States immigration legislation
(D) Economic instability in the United States
(E) Increased immigration to other areas of North America

GO ON TO THE NEXT PAGE

31. In the seventeenth century, some Pueblo Indians of the desert Southwest adopted Christianity as

    (A) an added dimension to their own religious culture, adding the Christian God as another deity
    (B) evidence of an ancient European culture that they were willing to embrace
    (C) a means of improving their agricultural practices
    (D) a means of establishing greater equality within their community
    (E) a means of direct communication with the afterlife through the practice of Christian prayer

32. Of the following, who challenged the religious establishment in Puritan New England?

    (A) Cotton Mather
    (B) Thomas Hutchinson
    (C) Anne Hutchinson
    (D) John Winthrop
    (E) Abigail Adams

33. Henry Clay's "American System" included which of the following?

    (A) A protective tariff that would fund internal improvements
    (B) Restriction on the use of federal money for national defense
    (C) Restriction on immigration from Asian countries
    (D) Elimination of the national bank
    (E) Protection of the property rights of Native Americans

34. In 1860 a southern writer, D. R. Hundley, wrote: "Know, then, that the Poor Whites of the South constitute a separate class to themselves; the Southern Yeomen are as distinct from them as the Southern Gentleman is from the Cotton Snob."

    Which of the following characterizations would Hundley probably accept as best describing the southern yeoman?

    (A) A class of White plantation employees who oversaw slave labor
    (B) A group of landowners who generally owned more than 100 slaves and who formed the elite of southern society
    (C) A group of independent farmers who owned small plots and few, if any, slaves
    (D) A small group of farmers who believed that there were few, if any, class distinctions in the South
    (E) A class of people known for their poor manners and lack of education

35. The Exclusion Act of 1882 prohibited the immigration of which of the following groups?

    (A) Irish
    (B) Mexicans
    (C) Eastern European Jews
    (D) Japanese
    (E) Chinese

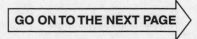

GO ON TO THE NEXT PAGE

MONTHLY WAGES AND SEXUAL COMPOSITION OF THE WORKFORCE IN SELECTED TRADES IN NEW YORK CITY, 1850

Trade	Average Male Wage	Average Female Wage	Percent Male	Percent Female
Clothing and tailors	$ 9.75	$ 6.99	48.5	51.5
Hats and millinery	27.51	17.14	43.5	56.5
Shoes and boots	24.32	10.43	75.2	24.8
Printing	36.28	14.48	71.3	28.7

36. Which of the following statements about the trades listed above is supported by the data in the table?

(A) The majority of female workers were in the hats and millinery trade.
(B) Both men and women received wages that were inadequate to support their families.
(C) In trades where women were in the majority, the difference between men's and women's wages was less than in trades where women were in the minority.
(D) The trades in which women were most highly represented had the lowest wages in the economy.
(E) The most skilled female workers were paid less than unskilled male workers.

GO ON TO THE NEXT PAGE

37. All of the following statements about the American home front during the Second World War are correct EXCEPT:

(A) The government instituted direct price controls to halt inflation.
(B) The Supreme Court upheld the forced relocation of Japanese Americans on the West Coast.
(C) Black workers migrated in large numbers from the rural South to the industrial cities of the North and West.
(D) Unemployment continued at Depression-era levels.
(E) Business leaders served as heads of the federal war-mobilization programs.

38. Which of the following events of the civil rights movement best illustrates the concept of "nonviolent civil disobedience"?

(A) The *Brown* v. *The Board of Education of Topeka* case of 1954
(B) The lunch-counter sit-ins of the early 1960's
(C) The March on Washington, D.C., in 1963
(D) The formation of the Black Panther party in 1966
(E) The desegregation of Little Rock, Arkansas, Central High School

39. In the 1950's John Kenneth Galbraith's *The Affluent Society* and W. H. Whyte's *The Organization Man* were significant because they

(A) criticized American conformity and the belief that economic growth would solve all problems
(B) challenged the American view that the Soviet Union was responsible for the Cold War
(C) advocated the nationalization of basic industries to increase production and profits
(D) were novels describing life among the "beat generation"
(E) urged a greater role for religion in American life and acceptance of Christian ethics by business executives

The Odd Couple

Reprinted by permission of Bill Mauldin and the Watkins/Loomis Agency.

40. Which of the following policies is the subject of the cartoon above?

(A) Vietnamization
(B) Containment
(C) Détente
(D) Interventionism
(E) Isolationism

41. The Halfway Covenant adopted by many Puritan congregations in the late seventeenth century did which of the following?

(A) Strengthened the Anglican church in New England
(B) Undermined religious toleration in New England
(C) Promoted Christianity among American Indians in New England
(D) Eased the requirements for church membership
(E) Encouraged belief in the doctrine of predestination

GO ON TO THE NEXT PAGE

42. At the time of the American Revolution, the most valuable cash crop produced in the southern states was

(A) cotton
(B) corn
(C) sugar
(D) wheat
(E) tobacco

43. The War of 1812 resulted in

(A) an upsurge of nationalism in the United States
(B) the acquisition of territories from Great Britain
(C) the strengthening of Napoleon in Europe
(D) the large-scale emigration of Europeans to the United States
(E) the elimination of United States shipping from European waters

44. Which of the following provides the best evidence of Lincoln's talents as a political leader?

(A) His success in getting his Reconstruction policies passed by Congress
(B) His skill in getting the South to acknowledge responsibility for the outbreak of the Civil War
(C) His success in securing adoption of the Fifteenth Amendment
(D) His ability to keep his party relatively united despite its internal conflicts
(E) His success in winning public support for a military draft

45. All of the following situations contributed to agrarian discontent in the late nineteenth century EXCEPT:

(A) Cotton averaged 5.8 cents a pound between 1894 and 1898, whereas it had been 15.1 cents a pound between 1870 and 1873.
(B) Short-haul railroad rates rose 60 percent in the 1890's.
(C) Farmers borrowed more heavily from banks than they had before the Civil War.
(D) European countries raised duties on agricultural products in the 1880's.
(E) The wheat harvest in Europe declined 30 percent in 1897.

46. At the beginning of the twentieth century, critics labeled individuals who exploited workers, charged high prices, and bribed public officials as

(A) robber barons
(B) free silverites
(C) knights of labor
(D) captains of industry
(E) muckrakers

GO ON TO THE NEXT PAGE

DISTRIBUTION OF TOTAL PERSONAL INCOME AMONG THE UNITED STATES POPULATION, 1950–1970

Year	Poorest Fifth	Second Poorest Fifth	Middle Fifth	Second Wealthiest Fifth	Wealthiest Fifth
1950	3.1%	10.5%	17.3%	24.1%	45.0%
1960	3.2%	10.6%	17.6%	24.7%	44.0%
1970	3.6%	10.3%	17.2%	24.7%	44.1%

47. The chart above supports which of the following statements?

(A) Federal antipoverty programs in the 1960's had little impact on the national distribution of income.
(B) Between 1950 and 1970, children tended to remain in the same socioeconomic groups as their parents.
(C) The wealthiest people earned about the same amount of money in 1970 as they earned in 1960.
(D) The increased number of women in the labor force in the 1970's had little effect on the amount of total family income.
(E) The number of people in the "poorest fifth" remained about the same from 1950 to 1970.

GO ON TO THE NEXT PAGE

48. "One who breaks an unjust law must do so openly, lovingly, and with a willingness to accept the penalty. I submit that an individual who breaks the law that conscience tells him is unjust, and who willingly accepts the penalty of imprisonment in order to arouse the conscience of the community over its injustice, is in reality expressing the highest respect for the law."

The quotation above most clearly expresses the views of

(A) Malcolm X
(B) Phyllis Schlafly
(C) Martin Luther King, Jr.
(D) Douglas MacArthur
(E) Barry Goldwater

49. Rachel Carson's book *Silent Spring* was a

(A) forestry manual
(B) description of deaf people's perception of the changing seasons
(C) protest against noise pollution
(D) protest against overuse of chemical insecticides
(E) protest against the Vietnam War

50. Which of the following was a consequence of President Lyndon B. Johnson's Great Society program?

(A) An end to the urban population decline in the East and Midwest
(B) Full employment until the end of the 1960's
(C) The near elimination of urban and rural poverty
(D) A major redistribution of the income tax burden
(E) An increase in federal spending on social services

51. "For we must consider that we shall be as a city upon a hill, the eyes of all people are upon us. So that if we shall deal falsely with our God in this work we shall have undertaken, and so cause Him to withdraw His present help from us, we shall be made a story and a by-word through the world."

The statement above was made by

(A) Jonathan Edwards preaching to a congregation during the Great Awakening
(B) John Winthrop defining the purpose of the Puritan colony
(C) Thomas Jefferson on the adoption of the Declaration of Independence
(D) William Penn defining the purpose of the Pennsylvania colony
(E) Benjamin Franklin gathering support for the American Revolution

52. Which of the following best characterizes the Anti-Federalists?

(A) They wanted a strong executive branch.
(B) They were loyal supporters of the Crown.
(C) They drew support primarily from rural areas.
(D) They favored universal suffrage.
(E) They favored rapid industrial development.

53. The Missouri Compromise was, in part, an effort to maintain the balance between the number of northerners and southerners in which of the following United States institutions?

(A) The Senate
(B) The House of Representatives
(C) Congress
(D) The Supreme Court
(E) The electoral college

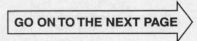

GO ON TO THE NEXT PAGE

54. Which of the following is true of the Black Codes of the Reconstruction era?

    (A) They promised every adult male former slave "forty acres and a mule."
    (B) They were Andrew Johnson's response to criticism that he was not doing enough for former slaves.
    (C) They were the result of joint actions by scalawags and carpetbaggers in the southern states.
    (D) They were passed by the Radical Republicans in Congress to ensure the rights of former slaves.
    (E) They were passed by Southern state legislatures to restrict the rights of former slaves.

55. Advocates of a free silver policy argued that the free coinage of silver would

    (A) increase the supply of money and end economic depressions
    (B) facilitate free trade between countries
    (C) limit the market power of farmers
    (D) stabilize the value of gold in relation to silver
    (E) increase the value of the dollar in relation to currencies of foreign countries

56. Skilled male workers felt threatened by all of the following changes that occurred in the United States economy between 1890 and 1920 EXCEPT the

    (A) arrival of large numbers of immigrants from southern Europe, eastern Europe, and Mexico
    (B) introduction of "scientific management" to increase factory production and lower labor costs
    (C) growing power of major corporations
    (D) increasingly widespread distribution of inexpensive consumer goods
    (E) growing presence of women workers in industry

57. Which of the following was demonstrated by the outcome of the presidential election of 1928 ?

    (A) The nation had become convinced of the futility of Prohibition.
    (B) "Republican prosperity" was a persuasive campaign slogan.
    (C) Ethnic and religious differences among Americans exerted little influence on their voting behavior.
    (D) Great numbers of ethnic minority-group voters switched from the Democratic to the Republican Party.
    (E) The Ku Klux Klan was the commanding force in United States politics during the 1920's.

58. "[The American] is intensely and cocksurely moral, but his morality and his self-interest are crudely identical. He is emotional and easy to scare, but his imagination cannot grasp an abstraction. He is a violent nationalist and patriot, but he admires rogues in office and always beats the tax-collector if he can. He is violently jealous of what he conceives to be his rights, but brutally disregardful of the other fellow's."

    The author of the quotation above is the noted journalist and satirist

    (A) Dorothy Thompson
    (B) Lillian Hellman
    (C) H. L. Mencken
    (D) Will Rogers
    (E) Pearl Buck

GO ON TO THE NEXT PAGE

59. Which of the following contributed most to ending the post-Second World War economic boom?

(A) Women leaving the workforce
(B) Development of the computer
(C) Consolidation of agriculture
(D) A shift in population to the Sunbelt
(E) The Arab oil embargo

60. The United States of the 1970's was characterized by an increase in all of the following EXCEPT

(A) computer technology and marketing
(B) an awareness of the rights of minorities
(C) the migration of Americans from the Frostbelt to the Sunbelt
(D) the strength of political party attachments
(E) the number of multinational corporations

61. Colonists in eighteenth-century South Carolina benefited from the knowledge of Africans about the cultivation of

(A) tobacco
(B) rice
(C) sugar
(D) cotton
(E) wheat

62. In the hundred years prior to 1776, which of the following had the LEAST influence on the emergence of the movement for independence in England's North American colonies?

(A) The control of money bills by colonial legislatures
(B) The long period of conflict between England and France
(C) The models provided by the autonomous governments of other English colonies
(D) The distance between England and its colonies
(E) Constitutional developments in England

63. "To maintain the existing relations between the two races, inhabiting that section of the Union, is indispensable to the peace and happiness of both. It cannot be subverted without drenching the country in blood, and extirpating one or the other of the races."

The statement above was most likely made by which of the following?

(A) John C. Calhoun to the United States Senate
(B) Frederick Douglass to the Anti-Slavery Society
(C) Daniel Webster to the South Carolina legislature
(D) John Brown at Harpers Ferry
(E) Abraham Lincoln in Springfield, Illinois

64. "In the late nineteenth century, the federal government followed a laissez-faire policy toward the economy."

A historian could argue against this thesis using all of the following pieces of evidence EXCEPT

(A) tariff laws protecting various industries from European competition
(B) laws granting land to the transcontinental railroad corporations
(C) government policy toward the unemployed during the depression of the 1890's
(D) the Bland-Allison Act of 1878 and the Sherman Silver Purchase Act of 1890
(E) the Interstate Commerce Act of 1887

65. Booker T. Washington encouraged Black people to pursue all of the following EXCEPT

(A) accommodation to White society
(B) racial solidarity
(C) industrial education
(D) economic self-help
(E) public political agitation

GO ON TO THE NEXT PAGE

66. "What we want to consider is, first, to make our employment more secure, and, secondly, to make wages more permanent. . . . I say the labor movement is a fixed fact. It has grown out of the necessities of the people, and, although some may desire to see it fail, still the labor movement will be found to have a strong lodgment in the hearts of the people, and we will go on until success has been achieved."

    The quotation above best reflects the philosophy of which of the following organizations around 1900 ?

    (A) Industrial Workers of the World
    (B) National Labor Union
    (C) American Federation of Labor
    (D) Congress of Industrial Organizations
    (E) Knights of Labor

67. Theodore Roosevelt issued his corollary to the Monroe Doctrine primarily because

    (A) Japan's actions in Manchuria had violated the "open door"
    (B) United States protection was needed by the colonies acquired in the Spanish-American War
    (C) the Filipino people revolted against United States rule
    (D) the financial difficulties of Caribbean nations threatened to bring about European intervention
    (E) the declining toll revenue from the Panama Canal threatened Panamanian stability

68. "The problem lay buried, unspoken, for many years in the minds of American women. It was a strange stirring, a sense of dissatisfaction, a yearning that women suffered in the middle of the twentieth century in the United States. Each suburban wife struggled with it alone. As she made the beds, shopped for groceries, ate peanut butter sandwiches with her children, chauffeured Cub Scouts and Brownies, she was afraid to ask even of herself the silent question—'Is this all?'"

    The passage above supports which of the following statements about women in the middle of the twentieth century?

    (A) Women were no longer interested in political activities.
    (B) Feminism tended to be a middle-class movement.
    (C) Feminism renewed interest in religion among women.
    (D) There were very few educational opportunities for women.
    (E) Most women supported the feminist movement.

69. "Government is not the solution to our problems. Government is the problem."

    The statement above was made by

    (A) John F. Kennedy, asserting that the government did not do enough for the people
    (B) Dwight D. Eisenhower, arguing that the government interfered with the military's operations
    (C) Jimmy Carter, claiming that the government was inefficient and unfair
    (D) Gerald Ford, charging that the government was corrupt
    (E) Ronald Reagan, contending that the government had taken on functions properly belonging to the private sector

GO ON TO THE NEXT PAGE

"I DON'T KNOW WHY THEY DON'T SEEM TO HOLD US IN AWE THE WAY THEY USED TO"

From Herblock At Large (Pantheon, 1987)

70. Which of the following best summarizes the idea expressed in the 1987 cartoon above?

(A) In the 1980's, budget and trade deficits and scandal undermined the international standing of the United States.
(B) President Reagan expected that an international economic summit would enable the United States to solve its financial problems.
(C) In the 1980's, the United States could not look to its economic partners for help in solving its economic problems.
(D) The economic problems of the United States in the 1980's resulted from European economic policies.
(E) Had it not been for the Iran-Contra scandal, the United States could have solved its economic problems.

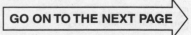

GO ON TO THE NEXT PAGE

71. "No man was a warmer wisher for reconciliation than myself, before the fatal nineteenth of April 1775, but the moment the event of that day was made known, I rejected the hardened, sullen tempered Pharaoh of England for ever; and disdain the wretch, that with the pretended title of FATHER OF HIS PEOPLE, can unfeelingly hear of their slaughter, and composedly sleep with their blood upon his soul."

The passage above comes from

(A) the Declaration of Independence
(B) *The Federalist* papers
(C) *Letters from a Farmer in Pennsylvania*
(D) the Virginia Resolves against the Stamp Act
(E) *Common Sense*

72. Alexander Hamilton's plan for stimulating economic growth in the United States included all of the following EXCEPT

(A) acquisition of additional territory
(B) a protective tariff
(C) expansion of manufacturing
(D) establishment of a national bank
(E) federal assumption of debts incurred by states during the Revolutionary War

73. The first American party system, which developed in the 1790's, maintained party discipline at the federal level primarily by means of

(A) caucuses
(B) nominating conventions
(C) rotation in office
(D) restrictive primaries
(E) "pork barrel" legislation

74. Which of the following was true of the Jacksonian Democrats in the 1830's?

(A) They were the minority party in the nation.
(B) They opposed a national bank.
(C) They supported South Carolina's nullification of the protective tariff.
(D) They were stronger in New England than in the West.
(E) They generally repudiated the ideas of the Jeffersonian Republicans.

75. "We hold these truths to be self-evident: that all men and women are created equal. . . . The history of mankind is a history of repeated injuries and usurpations on the part of man toward woman, having in direct object the establishment of an absolute tyranny over her."

The quotation above is excerpted from the

(A) Seneca Falls Declaration of Sentiments and Resolutions
(B) United States Declaration of Independence
(C) United States Constitution
(D) Declaration of Rights and Grievances
(E) Equal Rights Amendment (ERA)

76. Which of the following is true of the Pullman strike of 1894 ?

(A) It brought a substantial portion of American railroads to a standstill.
(B) It started when Pullman workers were fired after the Haymarket riot.
(C) It was caused by grievances about unsafe working conditions.
(D) It ended when the government forced management to settle with the union.
(E) It ended when the courts issued a blanket injunction against management.

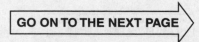

GO ON TO THE NEXT PAGE

77. "We must be the great arsenal of democracy. For this is an emergency as serious as war itself. We must apply ourselves to our task with the same resolution, the same sense of urgency, the same spirit of patriotism, and sacrifice, as we would show were we at war."

    The emergency to which the speaker refers was

    (A) German U-boat attacks in 1917
    (B) the Spanish Civil War in 1936
    (C) German warfare against Britain in 1940
    (D) the Berlin Blockade of 1948
    (E) the Cuban missile crisis of 1962

78. The legislation passed between 1935 and 1937 dealing with the role of the United States in future wars seemed to reflect a belief that

    (A) totalitarianism directly threatened the security of the United States
    (B) the United States should quickly intervene in any future world wars
    (C) the United States had made a mistake in not joining the League of Nations
    (D) the United States should not have become involved in the First World War
    (E) the United States should take a position of leadership in world affairs

79. Civil rights organizations in the 1950's and 1960's based their court suits primarily on the

    (A) five freedoms of the First Amendment
    (B) Fourteenth Amendment
    (C) Thirteenth Amendment
    (D) "necessary and proper" clause of the Constitution
    (E) Preamble to the Constitution

80. The Nixon administration differed from previous administrations in adopting which of the following Vietnam War policies?

    I. The bombing of North Vietnam
    II. The use of American combat troops
    III. The invasion of Cambodia
    IV. The mining of North Vietnamese harbors

    (A) I only
    (B) I and III only
    (C) II and III only
    (D) II and IV only
    (E) III and IV only

81. Which of the following political ideas or philosophies inspired the American revolutionaries of the eighteenth century?

    (A) Progressivism
    (B) Populism
    (C) Manifest Destiny
    (D) Republicanism
    (E) The Social Gospel

82. The first major nineteenth-century political conflict over the issue of slavery was settled by the

    (A) Alien and Sedition Acts
    (B) Kentucky and Virginia Resolutions
    (C) Missouri Compromise
    (D) Kansas-Nebraska Act
    (E) *Dred Scott* decision

GO ON TO THE NEXT PAGE

83. During the 1850's, Kansas became a significant issue for which of the following reasons?

    (A) The territory was an important way station in the Underground Railroad.
    (B) Northern and southern states vied to establish the first transcontinental railway through Kansas.
    (C) Kansas served as a center for the Peoples (Populist) Party's agitation against railroads and banks.
    (D) John Quincy Adams invoked the gag rule to prevent the discussion of slavery in the Senate.
    (E) It led to a divisive debate over the expansion of slavery into the territories.

84. Which of the following was a significant movement in American literature during the late nineteenth century?

    (A) Creationism
    (B) Modernism
    (C) Romanticism
    (D) Classicism
    (E) Realism

85. Edward Bellamy's *Looking Backward*, written in the 1880's, was a utopian reaction to which of the following?

    (A) The disillusionment with an increasingly competitive and industrial society
    (B) The plight of farmers who were driven off their land during the Great Depression
    (C) The disillusionment of the planter aristocracy in the post-Civil War era
    (D) The growing number of immigrants who regretted leaving their homes in Europe
    (E) Increasing concerns over the growth and power of labor unions in the railroad industry

86. The Harlem Renaissance refers to

    (A) Marcus Garvey's "back to Africa" crusade
    (B) the reemergence of the Ku Klux Klan as a force in American politics
    (C) writers and artists in New York who expressed pride in their African American culture
    (D) American expatriate writers living in Paris who wrote critically of American society
    (E) the political success of the Democratic Party in northern urban neighborhoods

87. The Federal Reserve Act of 1913 established a

    (A) single central bank like the Bank of England
    (B) method of insuring bank deposits against loss
    (C) system to guarantee the continued existence of the gold standard
    (D) system of local national banks
    (E) system of district banks coordinated by a central board

88. The Korean War and the Vietnam War differed in that only one involved

    (A) a formal declaration of war
    (B) a communist-led government
    (C) troops under United Nations auspices
    (D) Soviet arms support to one of the belligerents
    (E) United States air and ground forces

GO ON TO THE NEXT PAGE

From Herblock On All Fronts (New American Library, 1980)

89. Which of the following best summarizes the idea expressed in the cartoon above?

(A) Most people are too dependent on computers in their daily lives.
(B) The amount of information available via computers is so overwhelming that people are no longer able to use the information effectively.
(C) Individual privacy is being threatened by the computerization of personal information.
(D) Many industries in the United States are threatened with significant layoffs as computers replace workers.
(E) People in the United States have been more reluctant to begin using computers than have people in other parts of the world.

GO ON TO THE NEXT PAGE

90. Which of the following is an accurate statement about the Equal Rights Amendment to the Constitution proposed in the 1970's?

    (A) It was opposed primarily by those who feared a loss of political power.
    (B) It guaranteed equal opportunity for women in the workplace.
    (C) It became a part of the Constitution in 1978.
    (D) It represented the first effort to enfranchise women.
    (E) It failed to gain the necessary votes for ratification within the constitutional time limit.

STOP

IF YOU FINISH BEFORE TIME IS CALLED, YOU MAY CHECK YOUR WORK ON THIS TEST ONLY.
DO NOT TURN TO ANY OTHER TEST IN THIS BOOK.

How to Score the SAT Subject Test in United States History

When you take an actual SAT Subject Test in United States History, your answer sheet will be "read" by a scanning machine that will record your responses to each question. Then a computer will compare your answers with the correct answers and produce your raw score. You get one point for each correct answer. For each wrong answer, you lose one-quarter of a point. Questions you omit (and any for which you mark more than one answer) are not counted. This raw score is converted to a scaled score that is reported to you and to the colleges you specify.

Worksheet 1. Finding Your Raw Test Score

STEP 1: Table A on the following page lists the correct answers for all the questions on the Subject Test in United States History that is reproduced in this book. It also serves as a worksheet for you to calculate your raw score.

- Compare your answers with those given in the table.
- Put a check in the column marked "Right" if your answer is correct.
- Put a check in the column marked "Wrong" if your answer is incorrect.
- Leave both columns blank if you omitted the question.

STEP 2: Count the number of right answers.

Enter the total here: ________________

STEP 3: Count the number of wrong answers.

Enter the total here: ________________

STEP 4: Multiply the number of wrong answers by .250.

Enter the product here: ________________

STEP 5: Subtract the result obtained in Step 4 from the total you obtained in Step 2.

Enter the result here: ________________

STEP 6: Round the number obtained in Step 5 to the nearest whole number.

Enter the result here: ________________

The number you obtained in Step 6 is your raw score.

Table A

Answers to the Subject Test in United States History – Practice Test 1 and Percentage of Students Answering Each Question Correctly

Question Number	Correct Answer	Right	Wrong	Percentage of Students Answering the Question Correctly*	Question Number	Correct Answer	Right	Wrong	Percentage of Students Answering the Question Correctly*
1	A			71	33	A			43
2	C			85	34	C			38
3	B			89	35	E			42
4	C			64	36	C			46
5	B			92	37	D			64
6	B			80	38	B			64
7	E			62	39	A			32
8	A			77	40	C			29
9	C			74	41	D			37
10	C			77	42	E			54
11	D			72	43	A			52
12	C			61	44	D			37
13	C			61	45	E			33
14	B			77	46	A			57
15	D			80	47	A			32
16	C			74	48	C			48
17	E			69	49	D			30
18	D			83	50	E			57
19	A			69	51	B			39
20	D			53	52	C			47
21	A			41	53	A			28
22	B			55	54	E			63
23	C			71	55	A			49
24	E			90	56	D			39
25	D			56	57	B			32
26	B			53	58	C			19
27	A			83	59	E			27
28	E			36	60	D			29
29	B			57	61	B			15
30	C			60	62	C			23
31	A			31	63	A			18
32	C			43	64	C			25

Table A continued on next page

Table A continued from previous page

Question Number	Correct Answer	Right	Wrong	Percentage of Students Answering the Question Correctly*	Question Number	Correct Answer	Right	Wrong	Percentage of Students Answering the Question Correctly*
65	E			41	78	D			30
66	C			26	79	B			26
67	D			29	80	E			11
68	B			32	81	D			23
69	E			29	82	C			33
70	A			40	83	E			64
71	E			38	84	E			35
72	A			36	85	A			23
73	A			28	86	C			82
74	B			36	87	E			16
75	A			31	88	C			18
76	A			24	89	C			68
77	C			12	90	E			24

* These percentages are based on an analysis of the answer sheets of a representative sample of 8,509 students who took the original administration of this test and whose mean score was 534. They may be used as an indication of the relative difficulty of a particular question.

Finding Your Scaled Score

When you take SAT Subject Tests, the scores sent to the colleges you specify are reported on the College Board scale, which ranges from 200 to 800. You can convert your practice test raw score to a scaled score by using Table B. To find your scaled score, locate your raw score in the left-hand column of Table B; the corresponding score in the right-hand column is your scaled score. For example, a raw score of 39 on this particular edition of the SAT Subject Test in United States History corresponds to a scaled score of 560.

Raw scores are converted to scaled scores to ensure that a score earned on any one edition of a particular Subject Test is comparable to the same scaled score earned on any other edition of the same Subject Test. Because some editions of the tests may be slightly easier or more difficult than others, College Board scaled scores are adjusted so that they indicate the same level of performance regardless of the edition of the test taken and the ability of the group that takes it. Thus, for example, a score of 400 on one edition of a test taken at a particular administration indicates the same level of achievement as a score of 400 on a different edition of the test taken at a different administration.

When you take the SAT Subject Tests during a national administration, your scores are likely to differ somewhat from the scores you obtain on the tests in this book. People perform at different levels at different times for reasons unrelated to the tests themselves. The precision of any test is also limited because it represents only a sample of all the possible questions that could be asked.

Table B

Scaled Score Conversion Table
Subject Test in United States History – Practice Test 1

Raw Score	Scaled Score	Raw Score	Scaled Score	Raw Score	Scaled Score
90	800	52	630	14	430
89	800	51	630	13	430
88	800	50	620	12	420
87	800	49	620	11	420
86	800	48	610	10	410
85	800	47	610	9	410
84	800	46	600	8	400
83	800	45	600	7	400
82	800	44	590	6	390
81	800	43	590	5	390
80	800	42	580	4	380
79	800	41	580	3	380
78	790	40	570	2	370
77	780	39	560	1	370
76	780	38	560	0	360
75	770	37	550	-1	360
74	760	36	550	-2	350
73	750	35	540	-3	350
72	750	34	540	-4	340
71	740	33	530	-5	330
70	730	32	530	-6	330
69	730	31	520	-7	320
68	720	30	520	-8	310
67	710	29	510	-9	310
66	710	28	510	-10	300
65	700	27	500	-11	290
64	700	26	490	-12	290
63	690	25	490	-13	280
62	680	24	480	-14	270
61	680	23	480	-15	270
60	670	22	470	-16	260
59	670	21	470	-17	260
58	660	20	460	-18	250
57	660	19	460	-19	250
56	650	18	450	-20	240
55	650	17	450	-21	230
54	640	16	440	-22	230
53	640	15	440		

How Did You Do on the Subject Test in United States History?

After you score your test and analyze your performance, think about the following questions:

Did you run out of time before reaching the end of the test?

If so, you may need to pace yourself better. For example, maybe you spent too much time on one or two hard questions. A better approach might be to skip the ones you can't answer right away and try answering all the remaining questions on the test. Then if there's time, go back to the questions you skipped.

Did you take a long time reading the directions?

You will save time when you take the test by learning the directions to the Subject Test in United States History ahead of time. Each minute you spend reading directions during the test is a minute that you could use to answer questions.

How did you handle questions you were unsure of?

If you were able to eliminate one or more of the answer choices as wrong and guess from the remaining ones, your approach probably worked to your advantage. On the other hand, making haphazard guesses or omitting questions without trying to eliminate choices could cost you valuable points.

How difficult were the questions for you compared with other students who took the test?

Table A shows you how difficult the multiple-choice questions were for the group of students who took this test during its national administration. The right-hand column gives the percentage of students that answered each question correctly.

A question answered correctly by almost everyone in the group is obviously an easier question. For example, 85 percent of the students answered question 2 correctly. However, only 19 percent answered question 58 correctly.

Keep in mind that these percentages are based on just one group of students. They would probably be different with another group of students taking the test.

If you missed several easier questions, go back and try to find out why: Did the questions cover material you haven't yet reviewed? Did you misunderstand the directions?

Answer Explanations for United States History – Practice Test 1

1. Choice (A) is the correct answer. In the seventeenth and eighteenth centuries, the English colonial system was based largely on the principles of mercantilism, the theory that a nation's prosperity depends upon its supply of capital and the purpose of colonies is to enrich the home country. The English government implemented in its colonies such measures as the Navigation Acts, a series of acts intended to restrict England's carrying trade to English ships. Some of these acts enumerated colonial products, such as sugar, tobacco, indigo, rice, and molasses, that could only be shipped directly to England or to another English colony. These acts contributed to the unrest that led to the rebellion of the American colonies.

2. Choice (C) is the correct answer. The term "separation of powers" refers to the framers' division of governmental authority among the legislative, executive, and judicial branches of the government. This division of authority allows each branch to check the actions of the others, more or less balancing the powers of each branch.

3. Choice (B) is the correct answer. As a result of the enforcement of the Treaty of New Echota, Native American land in the East was exchanged for lands west of the Mississippi River. The Trail of Tears refers to the forced removal of the Cherokee tribe in 1838-39. Almost 17,000 tribe members were rounded up in camps and forced to relocate to the West. An estimated 4,000 Cherokees died during the relocation.

4. Choice (C) is the correct answer. Harriet Beecher Stowe, the author of *Uncle Tom's Cabin*, advocated the abolition of slavery. She was not involved with prohibition.

5. Choice (B) is the correct answer. The diagram indicates that the ratio of black males to black females remained fairly constant during the period from 1820 to 1850.

6. Choice (B) is the correct answer. The cartoon's caption ("Man Is But a Worm") and the portrayal of human figures alongside monkeys and other animals refer to Darwin's theory of evolutionary progress through natural selection.

7. Choice (E) is the correct answer. In the early twentieth century, young and unmarried women became more likely to work outside of the home. It was unusual for women who were married or had been married to work outside the home in the early years of the twentieth century.

8. Choice (A) is the correct answer. President Franklin D. Roosevelt initiated the New Deal programs in 1933 to provide economic relief during the Great Depression, but in the following year the Supreme Court began to find significant parts of the New Deal unconstitutional. In 1937, Roosevelt proposed the Judiciary Reorganization Bill, also known as the Court-packing Bill, which would allow him to increase the number of Supreme Court judges. He proposed this measure in order to appoint justices who would uphold the New Deal legislation.

9. Choice (C) is the correct answer. The cartoon depicts an individual portrayed as a farmer refusing welfare packets, while joyously accepting the same measures when they are called "price supports." This is a reference to the New Deal measures that guaranteed farmers a minimum price for their products in order to encourage the flow of production during the Great Depression.

10. Choice (C) is the correct answer. In 1959, Fidel Castro overthrew the regime of Fulgencio Batista and oversaw Cuba's transformation into a Communist state. In January 1961, President Dwight D. Eisenhower broke diplomatic ties with Cuba and, in April, newly inaugurated President John F. Kennedy approved and enacted an invasion of Cuba. The Bay of Pigs invasion was undertaken in an attempt to overthrow Castro.

11. Choice (D) is the correct answer. In colonial America, women could not hold political office, serve as clergy, vote, or serve as jurors, but single women and widows did have the right to own property.

12. Choice (C) is the correct answer. In 1765, the British Parliament passed the Stamp Act, an act that implemented direct taxation of legal documents, permits, commercial contracts, newspapers, pamphlets, and playing cards in the American colonies by requiring that they carry a tax stamp. The Stamp Act was protested by the colonists, who refused to use the stamps and boycotted imports from British merchants and manufacturers.

13. Choice (C) is the correct answer. The decision in *Marbury v. Madison* is significant because it asserted the principle of judicial review, or the power of the judiciary branch—in particular, the Supreme Court—to determine the constitutionality of legislation passed by Congress.

14. Choice (B) is the correct answer. Sharecropping was a system that evolved after the abolition of slavery in the South. Former slaves used their crops to pay for their rent, while planters provided cash advances to secure labor for their lands. It was a system that provided a source of labor for planters and a meager source of income for poor laborers.

15. Choice (D) is the correct answer. "Manifest Destiny," a term coined in the 1840s, refers to the belief that the United States has a destiny to expand its territorial borders and to spread its ideals of democracy and freedom. The quote discusses the annexation of Texas and expansion as a preordained ideal ("the most natural, right and proper thing in the world").

16. Choice (C) is the correct answer. The cartoon depicts the growing power of railroads, represented by the figure of a steam engine. People watch fearfully as the giant figure symbolizing the railroad walks through a ravaged area carrying a club labeled "CAPITAL." The cartoon suggests that the financial interests of the railroads were taking precedence over all other cultural values.

17. Choice (E) is the correct answer. *The Jungle*, a book written in 1906 by Upton Sinclair, was concerned with issues of food processing such as those listed in the passage. Sinclair, a socialist, wrote the book to elicit sympathy for workers but was ultimately successful in securing government legislation regarding food. The uproar caused by *The Jungle* aided the passage of the Meat Inspection Act and the Pure Food and Drug Act in 1906.

18. Choice (D) is the correct answer. The chart indicates that by 1928 many consumer goods not available to middle-class American families in 1900—including automobiles, radios, vacuum cleaners, and telephones—had become available.

19. Choice (A) is the correct answer. The nickname "Rosie the Riveter" referred to women who went to work in United States factories during the Second World War. Many women were employed by manufacturing plants to fill the positions left empty by men who were fighting in the war.

20. Choice (D) is the correct answer. The picture depicts striking migrant workers. The captions in the placards held by the workers refer to the NFWA, the National Farm Workers Association, which was founded by César Chávez in 1962. In 1965, Chávez and the NFWA led a strike by California grape pickers and a boycott of California grapes.

21. Choice (A) is the correct answer. In response to the continued settlement of Europeans in North America during the eighteenth century, Native Americans sought to establish trading relations with the French and the English.

22. Choice (B) is the correct answer. The Chesapeake Bay colonies began to thrive economically only after the cultivation of tobacco as a cash crop.

23. Choice (C) is the correct answer. The Twenty-second Amendment, proposed in 1947 and ratified in 1951, limits the president to two terms in office. The amendment was passed after President Franklin D. Roosevelt had been elected to a fourth term.

24. Choice (E) is the correct answer. The painting depicts men socializing at an election site in the mid-nineteenth century.

25. Choice (D) is the correct answer. New England, New York and Pennsylvania, New Jersey and Delaware, and the Midwest saw tremendous economic growth with the mid-nineteenth-century introduction of canals, railroads, and new factory technology. The South was the area that was least advanced in transportation and industry, and thus saw the least economic growth from the expansion in modes of transportation and industrial production.

26. Choice (B) is the correct answer. The quotation implies that women, who have proven their abilities in the domestic sphere ("those who . . . have at least attempted to care for children, to clean houses, to prepare foods"), should be allowed to vote in order to extend their helpful influence into the political sphere ("civic housekeeping").

27. Choice (A) is the correct answer. Jane Addams was a pacifist and the passage does not indicate her support for war. As her statement suggests ("To test the elector's fitness . . . by his ability to bear arms is absurd"), Addams thought society valued military prowess too highly. Moreover, choices (B), (C), (D), and (E) all describe reforms that Addams seems to think are necessary, given the information in the passage.

28. Choice (E) is the correct answer. The articles in this issue of *McClure's Magazine* illustrate the nature and some of the tactics of Progressive reform. Progressives sought to reform municipal governments ("exposure of another type of municipal grafting") and business practices of monopoly ("famous oil crisis of 1878"), and to emphasize scientific investigations ("A powerful story, yet a scientific prediction"). Progressives also attempted to regulate business and therefore were not always looked on favorably by industrialists, so it is incorrect to suggest that the reformers enjoyed widespread support among industrialists.

29. Choice (B) is the correct answer. Asia shows the sharpest drop in immigration during this period. The enforcement of the Chinese Exclusion Act coupled with the passage of the National Origins Act in 1924 resulted in a sharp decline in Asian immigration during this period.

30. Choice (C) is the correct answer. The chart shows declining immigration due to the passage of the National Origins Act, which restricted immigration in 1924 by establishing a system of national quotas. The Act, which strengthened legislation passed in 1921 and virtually barred immigration from Asia, severely limited immigration from southern and eastern Europe.

31. Choice (A) is the correct answer. Upon contact with Christianity, which had spread into South and Central America through the influence of the Spanish, some Pueblo Indians incorporated elements of Christianity into their own religious beliefs. This incorporation of Christian features into traditional belief systems occurred among native groups throughout the Americas.

32. Choice (C) is the correct answer. This question is about dissent in seventeenth-century Puritan New England. Anne Hutchinson challenged the authority of the clergy. Choices (A) and (D) are incorrect, as Cotton Mather and John Winthrop were leading members of the Puritan clergy. Choices (B) and (E) are incorrect, as both Thomas Hutchinson and Abigail Adams lived during a later time period.

33. Choice (A) is the correct answer. Henry Clay's "American System" was proposed during a period of heightened nationalism after the War of 1812. The American System was designed to promote national economic growth through high tariffs, internal improvements, western settlement, and reconciliation of regional differences. The other options were not aspects of Clay's system.

34. Choice (C) is the correct answer. The quotation suggests that "yeomen" are neither "Poor Whites" nor "Southern Gentlemen." Choices (A), (B), (D), and (E) do not describe southern yeomen.

35. Choice (E) is the correct answer. This question tests knowledge of immigration policy in the nineteenth century. The Exclusion Act of 1882 was passed as a reaction to Chinese immigration in the late nineteenth century. Many Chinese had come to the United States during the Gold Rush, and tended to work hard for low wages. When the United States economy suffered instability in the 1870s, Chinese immigrants were singled out.

36. Choice (C) is the correct answer. The chart indicates that the gap between the wages of men and women was far smaller in clothing, tailoring, hats, and millinery—jobs in which women were in the majority. None of the other statements are supported by the data in the table.

37. Choice (D) is the correct answer. Statement (D) is inaccurate. There was a sharp decrease in unemployment due to wartime industrial production. The need for workers was so great that thousands of women were employed in factories for the first time. All of the other statements are accurate.

38. Choice (B) is the correct answer. Nonviolent civil disobedience is the protest act of breaking laws in a peaceful manner and without any harm to others. The lunch-counter sit-ins were such an example, as African American students entered restaurants and cafes that were segregated and sat in areas marked for "Whites only," despite the fact that there were laws supporting segregation. Choice (A) is incorrect. This was a Supreme Court ruling that overturned school segregation and was not a protest. Choices (C) and (D) are incorrect. They refer to protests and events that were legal. Choice (E) is incorrect. This is a reference to a government initiative that was implemented through the use of military force.

39. Choice (A) is the correct answer. John Kenneth Galbraith and W. H. Whyte were two prominent social critics who criticized the American emphasis on materialism and conformity in the 1950s. The other choices do not describe Galbraith's and Whyte's books.

40. Choice (C) is the correct answer. Détente was a policy of peaceful coexistence of the United States and the Soviet Union. The cartoon depicts the American eagle and the Russian bear and symbolizes the two countries in harmony and united as a family. Choice (A) is incorrect. Vietnamization referred to the escalating conflict in Vietnam and the cartoon indicates harmony. Choice (B) is incorrect. Containment was a policy that sought to check the spread of communism pitting the United States against the Soviet Union. Choice (D) is incorrect. It refers to intervention in the internal affairs of another country. Choice (E) is incorrect. Isolationism did not mean harmony and cooperation, but rather an effort to exclude the outside world.

41. Choice (D) is the correct answer. The Halfway Covenant was adopted to address the problem of declining church membership in the late seventeenth century. Under this covenant, adults who had been baptized into the church as children but who had not yet experienced the conversion necessary for full membership could nonetheless have their children baptized. The other choices are incorrect.

42. Choice (E) is the correct answer. Tobacco was the most valuable export crop that was produced in the South on the eve of the Revolution in the 1770s. Cotton, choice (A), did not surpass tobacco as the South's chief crop until the 1800s. Choices (B), (C), and (D) are incorrect.

43. Choice (A) is the correct answer. The War of 1812 did lead to a rising spirit of nationalism. Choice (B) is incorrect. The war did not lead to the acquisition of territories. Choice (C) is incorrect. The war did not strengthen Napoleon. Choice (D) is incorrect. There was no large-scale emigration from Europe after the war. Choice (E) is incorrect. U.S. shipping and trade with Europe resumed after the war.

44. Choice (D) is the correct answer. Lincoln displayed remarkable political skills in holding the Republican Party together during the Civil War period, as radicals and moderates contended to shape policy. The other choices are incorrect.

45. Choice (E) is the correct answer. A declining wheat harvest in Europe did not contribute to agrarian discontent in the United States in the late nineteenth century. It helped to raise farm prices, relieving U.S. farmers. Each of the other choices did contribute to the economic depression suffered by American farmers in the 1890s.

46. Choice (A) is the correct answer. Critics called wealthy industrialists who engaged in exploitative practices "robber barons." Choice (D) was not a term of criticism that was applied to these individuals, and choices (B), (C), and (E) are terms that applied to those who opposed the practices described in the question.

47. Choice (A) is the correct answer. The chart shows that despite the passage of Great Society programs in the 1960s, the distribution of income remained relatively unchanged in 1970. One possible explanation may be due to the difficulty of promoting political and economic change through federal initiatives. Another reason may be due to the fact that in the 1970s technological change and economic growth had raised everyone's standard of living, minimizing the potential for wealth to be redistributed. The other statements are not supported by the information in the chart.

48. Choice (C) is the correct answer. The quotation is an excerpt from the "Letter from a Birmingham Jail" by Martin Luther King, Jr., in which he expresses his philosophy of civil disobedience. The other choices are not correct.

49. Choice (D) is the correct answer. This question concerns Rachel Carson's work on environmental pollution and its effects. Rachel Carson's book documented the harmful effects of chemicals. The other choices are incorrect.

50. Choice (E) is the correct answer. This question asks about the effects of the Great Society programs. The programs, which included Head Start, Job Corps, and VISTA, did increase federal spending on social services. Choice (A) is incorrect. The Great Society programs did not lead to a decline in urban population. Choice (B) is incorrect. There was no full employment during this period. Choice (C) is incorrect. The Great Society programs did not eliminate poverty, although they made efforts to provide assistance to the poor. Choice (D) is incorrect. The programs did not change the income tax structure.

51. Choice (B) is the correct answer. The quotation is an excerpt of John Winthrop's address to his Puritan congregation. The idea of "a city upon a hill," or a community that is an example to others, has been invoked by politicians, including Ronald Reagan, to describe the nation as a whole. The other choices are incorrect.

52. Choice (C) is the correct answer. The Anti-Federalists, persons who opposed ratification of the U.S. Constitution in 1787-89, drew their support primarily from farmers in rural areas. Choice (A) is incorrect. The Anti-Federalists feared a strong central government. Choice (B) is incorrect. The Anti-Federalists were not supporters of the Crown. Choice (D) is incorrect. The Anti-Federalists did not favor universal suffrage. Choice (E) is incorrect. The Anti-Federalists were opposed to industrial development and favored an agrarian economy.

53. Choice (A) is the correct answer. This question asks for an identification of one of the goals of the Missouri Compromise of 1820. The Compromise was an effort to maintain the balance between slave states and free states in the Senate, which in 1819 had senators from 11 free states and 11 slave states, by admitting Maine (free) and Missouri (slave) at the same time. Choices (B) and (C) are incorrect, as the Compromise did not change the House of Representatives. The other choices are incorrect, as the Compromise did not affect the balance in any of the other agencies of government.

54. Choice (E) is the correct answer. This question asks about the purpose of the Black Codes. The Black Codes were laws passed by Southerners to restrict the freedom of former slaves. Choices (A) and (B) are incorrect, as the Black Codes restricted the rights of former slaves. Choice (C) is incorrect, as Southerners, not carpetbaggers, passed the Codes. Choice (D) is incorrect, as the measures passed by Radical Republicans were intended to help former slaves (or freed slaves) and the Black Codes had the opposite effect.

55. Choice (A) is the correct answer. Advocates of free silver argued that the United States' tight domestic monetary policies were the cause of the economic depressions of the late nineteenth century. They believed that increasing the circulation of silver would help farmers by raising crop prices and allow farmers and others to pay their debts more easily. The other choices are incorrect.

56. Choice (D) is the correct answer. Although consumerism began in the 1870s with catalog buying, it did not become widespread until the mid-twentieth century. Skilled male workers were not threatened by consumerism during this period. Each of the other choices reflects a specific threat to skilled male workers around the turn of the century.

57. Choice (B) is the correct answer. In 1928, Republican Herbert Hoover, bolstered by years of economic prosperity under Republican administrations, defeated Alfred E. Smith, a Catholic who suffered from anti-Catholic prejudice.

58. Choice (C) is the correct answer. The quote is an excerpt from the work of H. L. Mencken, a satirist and critic of American social and cultural weaknesses. As the quote suggests, Mencken was famous for exposing American pretensions and hypocrisy.

59. Choice (E) is the correct answer. The question asks about the primary reason for the end of the post–Second World War boom. The 1973 oil embargo led to a huge increase in oil prices, inflation, and the end of the economic boom. The other choices are incorrect.

60. Choice (D) is the correct answer. The election of 1972 was the first presidential election in which most of the Southern states broke ranks with the Democratic Party and voted Republican. This shift in allegiances contradicted traditional party affiliations and also changed Southern politics.

61. Choice (B) is the correct answer. Colonists in South Carolina gained knowledge of rice cultivation from slaves from the "Rice Coast," the traditional rice-growing region of West Africa.

62. Choice (C) is the correct answer. The colonists were not influenced by autonomous governments in other English colonies because there were no autonomous governments in other English colonies. All the other choices refer to factors that contributed to the emergence of an independence movement.

63. Choice (A) is the correct answer. This is an excerpt from an address by John C. Calhoun to the United States Senate. This speech reflects Calhoun's anti-abolitionist views.

64. Choice (C) is the correct answer. The government provided no support for the unemployed during the 1890s. All other choices refer to intervention by the government to help particular interests and therefore could be used to disprove the statement that the government followed a laissez-faire, or "hands off," policy.

65. Choice (E) is the correct answer. Booker T. Washington never advocated direct political activism for black people. Washington believed that black people would be best served by pursuing the goals listed in the other choices.

66. Choice (C) is the correct answer. The quote represents the position of the American Federation of Labor, the sole unifying agency of the American labor movement in the early twentieth century.

67. Choice (D) is the correct answer. Theodore Roosevelt responded to a crisis in the Caribbean, where the Dominican Republic stopped payments on its debts to various nations, by issuing a corollary to the Monroe Doctrine. This statement reasserted the intention of the United States to prevent European intervention in Latin America, as established by the Monroe Doctrine.

68. Choice (B) is the correct answer. The passage is a quote from Betty Friedan and describes the frustrations of suburban middle-class women in the 1950s who generated the modern feminist movement. The other choices are not supported by the passage.

69. Choice (E) is the correct answer. This statement expresses Ronald Reagan's policy of small government: cutting taxes, scaling back government intervention, and letting the market and the private sector attempt to solve domestic social problems. This attitude toward government is a hallmark of the Reagan Revolution.

70. Choice (A) is the correct answer. The cartoon depicts the United States, symbolized by Ronald Reagan and Uncle Sam, afflicted by debt and scandals and no longer able to command respect from other nations.

71. Choice (E) is the correct answer. This is an excerpt from Thomas Paine's *Common Sense*, a pamphlet published in January 1776 that sold 150,000 copies and helped inflame the American Revolution. Paine was referring to the day of fighting between colonists and British soldiers at Lexington and Concord, during which several colonists were killed.

72. Choice (A) is the correct answer. Hamilton did not consider territorial acquisition as a primary factor in developing the economy and was a strong proponent of developing the manufacturing and mercantile base. The other choices represent aspects of his plan.

73. Choice (A) is the correct answer. The caucus was the apparatus for selecting political candidates during this period. In every election from 1800 to 1824, members of Congress from each party met in a caucus to choose the party's candidates for president and vice president.

74. Choice (B) is the correct answer. Jacksonian Democrats were vehemently opposed to a national bank, which they viewed as an instrument of mercantile interests. The other choices are inaccurate statements about the Jacksonian Democrats.

75. Choice (A) is the correct answer. The quote is an excerpt from the Seneca Falls Declaration. This Declaration, which was drawn up at a meeting in Seneca Falls, New York, in 1848, uses the language and the logic of the Declaration of Independence to make the case for women's rights.

76. Choice (A) is the correct answer. The Pullman strike was a major strike begun by Pullman rail workers who were angry about reduced wages. When sympathetic railway workers agreed to boycott all trains carrying Pullman cars, rail service was disrupted nationwide. Federal troops ended the strike and arrested the organizers.

77. Choice (C) is the correct answer. This is a quote from Franklin D. Roosevelt's speech after Germany's attack on Britain in 1940, before the United States entered the Second World War. Roosevelt appealed to factory owners and workers to turn their efforts to weapons production to aid in the fight against Germany.

78. Choice (D) is the correct answer. The neutrality acts passed between 1935 and 1937 sought to keep the United States out of the coming Second World War and were based on the belief that the United States' involvement in the First World War was a mistake. The other choices are incorrect.

79. Choice (B) is the correct answer. Civil rights organizations used the "due process" and "equal protection" clause of the Fourteenth Amendment, which guarantees equal rights under the law to all Americans, to force changes in existing laws. In *Brown v. Board of Education of Topeka*, for example, the Supreme Court held that segregated schools were unconstitutional under the Fourteenth Amendment.

80. Choice (E) is the correct answer. The invasion of Cambodia and the mining of North Vietnamese harbors were policies that were initiated by the Nixon administration. Previous administrations had sent thousands of combat troops to Vietnam and engaged in bombing the North.

81. Choice (D) is the correct answer. The eighteenth-century revolutionaries were inspired by the principles of republicanism, which emphasized popular sovereignty, equality, and liberty. The other terms are all associated with later periods in American history.

82. Choice (C) is the correct answer. The Missouri Compromise of 1820, which admitted Maine into the Union as a free state and Missouri as a slave state (but with some restrictions), solved the first major political conflict over slavery in the nineteenth century. The Missouri Compromise did not last; it was superceded by the Kansas-Nebraska Act of 1854. The other choices are incorrect.

83. Choice (E) is the correct answer. The Kansas-Nebraska Act of 1854 allowed people in the territories of Kansas and Nebraska to decide for themselves whether to allow slavery. Rival groups of settlers, some pro-slavery and some anti-slavery, moved into Kansas and fought with one another to determine the future of the state. After seven years of well-publicized bitter conflict, Kansas entered the Union as a free state in January 1861. The conflict in Kansas reverberated throughout the country and set the stage for the Civil War.

84. Choice (E) is the correct answer. This was a period when writers like William Dean Howells and Theodore Dreiser tried to portray the challenges posed by social and economic realities.

85. Choice (A) is the correct answer. Edward Bellamy's novel imagines a plan for repairing the problems of industrial society. The novel's main character awakes in the year 2000 after 113 years of sleep and is pleased to find himself living in an organized utopian society under wise government control.

86. Choice (C) is the correct answer. The term "Harlem Renaissance" refers to an outpouring of artistic and literary work by African American writers and artists centered in Harlem, in New York City, during the 1920s. The other choices are incorrect.

87. Choice (E) is the correct answer. The Federal Reserve Act created a network of regional Federal Reserve banks. The Federal Reserve System includes 12 Federal Reserve banks, a governing board, and several thousand member banks.

88. Choice (C) is the correct answer. The Korean War was supported by a United Nations resolution and involved United Nations troops. No U.N. troops participated in the Vietnam conflict. The other choices are incorrect.

89. Choice (C) is the correct answer. The cartoon depicts Americans living in a fishbowl, symbolizing the loss of privacy that comes with the storing of personal information on computers. The 1978 cartoon reflects early fears about the security of computer technology. The other choices are incorrect.

90. Choice (E) is the correct answer. The Equal Rights Amendment never gained sufficient votes for ratification. The amendment led to deep divisions within the feminist movement and was perceived by some opponents as a threat to family values.

United States History – Practice Test 2

Practice Helps

The test that follows is an actual, previously administered SAT Subject Test in United States History. To get an idea of what it's like to take this test, practice under conditions that are much like those of an actual test administration.

- Set aside an hour when you can take the test uninterrupted.
- Sit at a desk or table with no other books or papers. Dictionaries, other books, or notes are not allowed in the test room.
- Tear out an answer sheet from the back of this book and fill it in just as you would on the day of the test. One answer sheet can be used for up to three Subject Tests.
- Read the instructions that precede the practice test. During the actual administration, you will be asked to read them before answering test questions.
- Use a clock or kitchen timer to time yourself.
- After you finish the practice test, read the sections "How to Score the SAT Subject Test in United States History" and "How Did You Do on the Subject Test in United States History?"
- The appearance of the answer sheet in this book may differ from the answer sheet you see on test day.

UNITED STATES HISTORY TEST

The top portion of the page of the answer sheet that you will use to take the United States History Test must be filled in exactly as illustrated below. When your supervisor tells you to fill in the circle next to the name of the test you are about to take, mark your answer sheet as shown.

○ Literature	○ Mathematics Level 1	○ German	○ Chinese Listening	○ Japanese Listening
○ Biology E	○ Mathematics Level 2	○ Italian	○ French Listening	○ Korean Listening
○ Biology M	● U.S. History	○ Latin	○ German Listening	○ Spanish Listening
○ Chemistry	○ World History	○ Modern Hebrew		
○ Physics	○ French	○ Spanish	Background Questions: ①②③④⑤⑥⑦⑧⑨	

After filling in the circle next to the name of the test you are taking, locate the Background Questions section, which also appears at the top of your answer sheet (as shown above). This is where you will answer the following Background Questions on your answer sheet.

BACKGROUND QUESTIONS

Please answer the two questions below by filling in the appropriate circle in the Background Questions box on your answer sheet. The information you provide is for statistical purposes only and will not affect your test score.

Question I

How many semesters of United States History have you taken from grade 9 to the present? (If you are taking United States History this semester, count it as a full semester.) Fill in only one circle of circles 1-4.

- One semester or less —Fill in circle 1.
- Two semesters —Fill in circle 2.
- Three semesters —Fill in circle 3.
- Four or more semesters —Fill in circle 4.

Question II

Which, if any, of the following social studies courses have you taken from grade 9 to the present? (Fill in ALL circles that apply.)

- One or more semesters of government —Fill in circle 5.
- One or more semesters of economics —Fill in circle 6.
- One or more semesters of geography —Fill in circle 7.
- One or more semesters of psychology —Fill in circle 8.
- One or more semesters of sociology or anthropology —Fill in circle 9.

If you have taken none of these social studies courses, leave the circles 5 through 9 blank.

When the supervisor gives the signal, turn the page and begin the United States History Test. There are 100 numbered circles on the answer sheet and 90 questions in the United States History Test. Therefore, use only circles 1 to 90 for recording your answers.

UNITED STATES HISTORY TEST

Directions: Each of the questions or incomplete statements below is followed by five suggested answers or completions. Select the one that is best in each case and then fill in the corresponding circle on the answer sheet.

1. Indentured servitude in the British colonies of North America was primarily a

(A) method by which the colonies initially secured a workforce
(B) device for preventing the emancipation of slaves
(C) technique for regulating the size of the lower classes
(D) means by which England rid itself of criminals
(E) process by which young people learned skills

2. "My master used to ask us children, 'Do your folks pray at night?' We said 'No,' 'cause our folks had told us what to say. But the Lord have mercy, there was plenty of that going on. They'd pray, 'Lord, deliver us from under bondage.' "

The statement above was probably made by a

(A) Lowell mill worker who had escaped the poverty of a family farm
(B) former indentured servant recalling praying for the end of the term of servitude
(C) former slave criticizing the lack of religious worship in the quarters
(D) former slave remembering the need to conceal one's thoughts under slavery
(E) southern minister giving a sermon on prayer in the antebellum era

3. Which of the following was a major issue dividing the political parties during Andrew Jackson's presidency?

(A) A national bank
(B) Extension of the suffrage
(C) Immigration
(D) Military expenditures
(E) Railroad construction

4. All of the following were true of the industrial working class of late-nineteenth-century America EXCEPT:

(A) It was composed of native-born as well as immigrant workers.
(B) Working-class neighborhoods were sometimes segregated ethnically.
(C) Women and children frequently worked in factories.
(D) Most workers belonged to unions.
(E) Immigrants were hired primarily as unskilled and semiskilled workers.

5. The chief reason given by Woodrow Wilson for requesting a declaration of war against Germany in 1917 was the

(A) refusal of Germany to accept the Fourteen Points as a basis for peace negotiations
(B) need to establish a League of Nations after the war
(C) resumption of unrestricted submarine warfare by Germany
(D) economic rivalry between the United States and Germany
(E) cultural ties between the United States and England

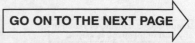

GO ON TO THE NEXT PAGE

6. "I have no doubt young criminals got their ideas of the romance of crime from moving pictures. I believe moving pictures are doing as much harm today as saloons did in the days of the open saloon, especially to the young. Movies are running day and night, Sunday and every other day, the year round, and in most jurisdictions without any regulation by censorship."

   The speaker quoted above would most likely agree with which of the following statements?

   (A) Blue laws should be repealed as unnecessary censorship.
   (B) The content of movies needs to be monitored to prevent the corruption of youth.
   (C) The censorship of technologies like radio and movies is not feasible.
   (D) The culture of the 1920's was a vast improvement over the decadent "Gay Nineties."
   (E) Outlawing movies would only cause a crime wave similar to that following Prohibition.

7. In the 50 years following the Second World War, inflation has meant a continuous increase in

   (A) tax rates
   (B) purchasing power
   (C) exports
   (D) prices
   (E) stock market activity

8. Which of the following statements about social trends in the United States between 1945 and 1970 is INCORRECT?

   (A) There was an overall increase in college enrollment.
   (B) The proportion of blue-collar jobs in the economy decreased.
   (C) Increasing numbers of African American children attended racially integrated schools.
   (D) There was an exodus of population from the cities to the suburbs.
   (E) More and more women abandoned paid employment in order to return to the home.

9. Which of the following was the stated reason for the Supreme Court ruling in the 1960's that prayer and formal religious instruction could not be required in public schools?

   (A) Atheism and agnosticism had spread throughout American society.
   (B) Church membership in America had declined rapidly.
   (C) Prayer was no longer a significant way in which Americans expressed their religious faith.
   (D) Prayer in public schools violated the principle of separation of church and state.
   (E) Prayer in public schools encouraged the renewal of religious tests for public office.

GO ON TO THE NEXT PAGE

10. Which of the following best summarizes the idea expressed in the 1991 cartoon above?

(A) Although the President claimed otherwise, the primary interest of the United States in the Persian Gulf War was access to oil.
(B) The United States government was worried about the ecological impact of the oil spills that occurred during the Persian Gulf War.
(C) The United States was justified in using military force because doing so was necessary to keep the price of oil low.
(D) A glut of oil production in the Middle East was the main cause of the Persian Gulf War.
(E) The United States should avoid involvement in disputes between governments in the Middle East.

GO ON TO THE NEXT PAGE

11. Which of the following actions would be INCONSISTENT with the English policy of mercantilism as it was applied to the North American colonies?

    (A) Requiring the colonists to export specified products only to England
    (B) Encouraging the colonies to produce articles that England otherwise would have to import from Europe
    (C) Encouraging the settlement of colonies suitable for the growing of tropical and semitropical staple crops
    (D) Encouraging the colonies to produce articles also produced in England
    (E) Prohibiting the importation of goods into the colonies except in English ships

12. The Great Awakening was a movement that

    (A) strengthened the position of the established clergy
    (B) appealed only to the lower classes
    (C) denied individual responsibility
    (D) excluded women and African Americans from religious services
    (E) emphasized inner experience as the principal way of discovering truth

13. In the first half of the nineteenth century, all of the following goals had widespread support among women reformers EXCEPT the

    (A) abolition of slavery
    (B) right of women to vote
    (C) liberalization of abortion laws
    (D) passage of temperance laws
    (E) right of married women to own property

14. In the United States all of the following changed in significant ways between 1850 and 1900 EXCEPT the

    (A) scale of business enterprise
    (B) election of women to national office
    (C) legal status of the African American population
    (D) technology of communication
    (E) religious affiliation of the total population

15. The Interstate Commerce Act of 1887 sought to prevent

    (A) discrimination by the railroads against small customers
    (B) publication of railroad rate schedules
    (C) transportation of children across state lines for immoral purposes
    (D) shipment across state lines of goods produced in sweatshops
    (E) use of the federal mails for the dissemination of birth control information

16. Which of the following statements best represents the nativist attitude toward the influx of immigrants around 1900 ?

    (A) Slavs and Italians will be assimilated as easily into the American way of life as were earlier immigrant groups.
    (B) Ellis Island should be enlarged to accommodate the huge influx of immigrants who do not speak English.
    (C) Immigrants will work for low wages and break strikes, which will hurt all American workers.
    (D) Native-born Americans should organize to help find jobs and homes for new immigrants so that they can become citizens as quickly as possible.
    (E) Political machines in the large cities must be responsible for providing immigrants with food, shelter, and jobs in return for their votes.

17. Which statement best describes the treatment of Black soldiers in the United States Army during the First World War?

    (A) Black soldiers were integrated into White units on a basis of full military equality.
    (B) Black soldiers served in segregated units often commanded by White officers.
    (C) Black Americans were drafted into the armed forces but not allowed to enlist.
    (D) Black Americans were not allowed in the armed forces but were encouraged to move to factory jobs.
    (E) Because Black leaders opposed the war, the government placed Black soldiers only in noncombat positions.

GO ON TO THE NEXT PAGE

18. Which of the following had the widest audience among Americans in the 1920's?

(A) Jazz festivals
(B) Professional football
(C) Television
(D) Movies
(E) Circuses

19. The economic policies of the New Deal are best described as a

(A) carefully designed plan to change the United States business system from capitalism to socialism
(B) series of hastily conceived temporary measures that pulled the economy out of the Depression by the start of President Franklin D. Roosevelt's third term
(C) mixture of partly effective short-run measures against the Depression and enduring changes in the role of the federal government
(D) program designed to equalize income for all Americans
(E) political response to the demand for federal deficit spending voiced by Democratic party platforms since the candidacy of Woodrow Wilson

20. Which of the following did most to broaden participation in the political process?

(A) The success of the States' rights movement
(B) The Supreme Court decision in the case of *Brown* v. *Board of Education of Topeka*
(C) The election of Franklin D. Roosevelt
(D) The decline of the Ku Klux Klan
(E) The Voting Rights Act of 1965

21. In the past 50 years in the House of Representatives, which of the following issues would most likely have resulted in a vote along party lines?

(A) Federal aid to education
(B) Civil rights legislation
(C) Election of the Speaker of the House
(D) Appropriations for foreign aid
(E) Agricultural subsidies

22. From the sixteenth through the eighteenth century, the cultural patterns of the American Indians of the western plains were most dramatically influenced by

(A) major changes in ecological conditions
(B) contact with tribes from eastern coastal areas
(C) the adoption of European military weaponry
(D) the adoption of European agricultural techniques
(E) the introduction of the horse by Spanish explorers

23. Many Americans believed the Articles of Confederation had which of the following problems?

(A) They gave insufficient power to the central government.
(B) They did not provide for a national legislature.
(C) They could not be amended.
(D) They were too long and complicated for the average person to understand.
(E) They lacked a Bill of Rights.

24. An important reason why Thomas Jefferson recommended the purchase of Louisiana from France was his wish to

(A) stimulate American manufacturing
(B) enhance the role of Congress in acquiring new territories
(C) embarrass the Federalists
(D) secure western territory to help fulfill his ideal of an agrarian republic
(E) follow advice given to him by Alexander Hamilton

25. In his book *Walden*, Henry David Thoreau did which of the following?

(A) Described the unspoiled innocence of the American West
(B) Recorded his thoughts concerning the value of a life of simplicity and contemplation
(C) Argued that such modern inventions as the telegraph and the railroad were bringing about a higher quality of cultural life in America
(D) Offered his impressions of southern plantation life
(E) Portrayed a fictional utopian community where all live in peace and harmony

GO ON TO THE NEXT PAGE

26. The primary reason the United States advanced the Open Door policy in 1899 was to

(A) consolidate good relations between the United States and European countries holding leases in China
(B) encourage Asian nations to protect Chinese interests
(C) expand the effort of European nations to Westernize China
(D) protect United States missionaries in China
(E) protect United States trading opportunities in China

27. A major difference between the Ku Klux Klan of the Reconstruction period and the Klan of the 1920's was that the Klan of the 1920's

(A) was hostile toward immigrants, non-Protestants, and African Americans
(B) was not particularly hostile toward African Americans
(C) expressed hostility only toward African Americans
(D) practiced vigilantism
(E) was confined to the South in its activities and membership

28. Which of the following contributed LEAST to the Great Depression?

(A) Weaknesses in the banking system
(B) Inflationary wage settlements
(C) The depressed agricultural sector
(D) Production in excess of consumption
(E) The stock market crash

29. Prior to its declaration of war in December 1941, the United States government gave help to the Allies by

(A) supplying war materials to the rebel forces in the Spanish Civil War
(B) placing an embargo on the export of oil and metal to Fascist Italy
(C) providing Lend-Lease aid
(D) denying aid to the Soviet Union
(E) encouraging the efforts of the America First Committee

30. Senator I: This amendment removes the incentive system from industry.

Senator II: This amendment will abolish capitalism.

Senator III: This amendment helps the worst elements in the country at the expense of the best elements in the country.

This discussion would most likely have taken place during the debate on which of the following constitutional amendments?

(A) Granting the vote to women
(B) Extending due process of law to all citizens
(C) Instituting direct election of senators
(D) Creating a federal income tax
(E) Abolishing slavery and indentured servitude

GO ON TO THE NEXT PAGE

Hy Rosen, in Albany *Times-Union*

31. Which of the following international incidents is the subject of the cartoon above?

(A) The Soviet invasion of Finland in 1939
(B) The Soviet blockade of Berlin in 1948
(C) The Hungarian Revolution of 1956
(D) The U-2 affair of 1960
(E) The Cuban missile crisis of 1962

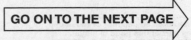

GO ON TO THE NEXT PAGE

32. Highly developed astronomy, mathematics, calendar systems, and agricultural techniques characterized the pre-Columbian cultures of

(A) Mesoamerica
(B) the Great Plains
(C) the Eastern Woodlands
(D) California
(E) the Subarctic

33. The first decade of the English settlement at Jamestown is most notable for the

(A) discovery of gold and precious metals
(B) successful cultivation and export of tobacco
(C) violent struggles between English and Spanish forces
(D) harmonious relations between the native inhabitants and settlers
(E) high mortality rate among the settlers

34. A principal consequence of the Northwest Ordinance of 1787 was that it

(A) terminated the earlier system of land surveying established by the federal government for the territories
(B) established a procedure for bringing new states into the Union as the equals of the older states
(C) stimulated the formation of the first political parties organized on a national basis
(D) encouraged the drafting of a new treaty with England on the disposition of the western territories
(E) strengthened the role of the thirteen original states in Congress

35. As chief justice of the Supreme Court, John Marshall issued significant opinions on all of the following EXCEPT

(A) judicial review
(B) federal *versus* state power
(C) the sanctity of contracts
(D) the rights of slaves as persons
(E) congressional control of interstate commerce

36. Of the following, which author was the first to create a western hero?

(A) Mark Twain
(B) Edgar Allan Poe
(C) James Fenimore Cooper
(D) Helen Hunt Jackson
(E) Willa Cather

37. "If the Creator had separated Texas from the Union by mountain barriers, the Alps or the Andes, there might be plausible objections; but He has planed down the whole [Mississippi] Valley including Texas, and united every atom of the soil and every drop of the water of the mighty whole. He has linked their rivers with the great Mississippi, and marked and united the whole for the dominion of one government, the residence of one people."

This quotation from the 1840's can be viewed as an expression of

(A) the New Nationalism
(B) popular sovereignty
(C) Manifest Destiny
(D) the Good Neighbor policy
(E) the frontier thesis

38. At the start of the Civil War, the North had all of the following advantages EXCEPT

(A) better military leaders
(B) a more extensive railroad network
(C) a larger population
(D) more heavy industry
(E) more abundant food resources

39. "Let it be understood that we cannot go outside of this alternative: liberty, inequality, survival of the fittest; not-liberty, equality, survival of the unfittest. The former carries society forward and favors all its best members; the latter carries society downward and favors all its worst members."

These sentiments are most characteristic of

(A) the Social Gospel
(B) Social Darwinism
(C) Socialism
(D) Progressivism
(E) Neoorthodoxy

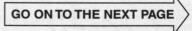

GO ON TO THE NEXT PAGE

40. The participation of women in the labor force between 1880 and 1930 rose primarily because

(A) most married women sought employment outside the home
(B) new jobs for women were created in offices, stores, and factories
(C) domestic service jobs increased
(D) discrimination against women in professions such as medicine and law declined
(E) equal pay acts encouraged more women to enter the workforce

41. All of the following accurately characterize the United States during the Second World War EXCEPT:

(A) Some consumer goods were rationed.
(B) Women entered the paid workforce in record numbers.
(C) Southerners migrated to industrial cities in increased numbers.
(D) The size and power of the federal government increased.
(E) The gross national product and wage levels declined.

42. During the period from 1492 to 1700, French activity in the Americas was primarily directed toward

(A) establishing trade with American Indians
(B) plundering American Indian settlements for gold and silver
(C) conquering Spanish and English colonies
(D) encouraging the growth of permanent settlements
(E) discovering a new route to Africa

43. During the years 1565-1763, Spanish Florida was important to Spain for which of the following reasons?

(A) It was a major source of valuable tropical produce.
(B) It was the center of the Catholic mission system in the New World.
(C) It retarded English colonial expansion southward from the Carolinas.
(D) It helped supply Spain with precious metals.
(E) It shielded converted Catholic Indians from Protestant missionaries.

44. Colonists supported the American Revolution for all of the following reasons EXCEPT

(A) the desire to preserve their local autonomy and way of life from British interference
(B) strong resentment against the quartering of British troops in colonial homes
(C) the desire for greater political participation in policies affecting the colonies
(D) a strong interest in achieving a more even distribution of income among the colonists
(E) a conviction that British ministers and other government officials were a corrupting influence on the colonists

45. The Supreme Court's dependency on the President to enforce its decisions is demonstrated by President Andrew Jackson's refusal to uphold

(A) the right of antislavery societies to send abolitionist publications through the mail
(B) land claims of the Cherokee in Georgia
(C) women's right to vote
(D) a slave's right to freedom after being in free territory
(E) payments made in paper money for public lands

GO ON TO THE NEXT PAGE

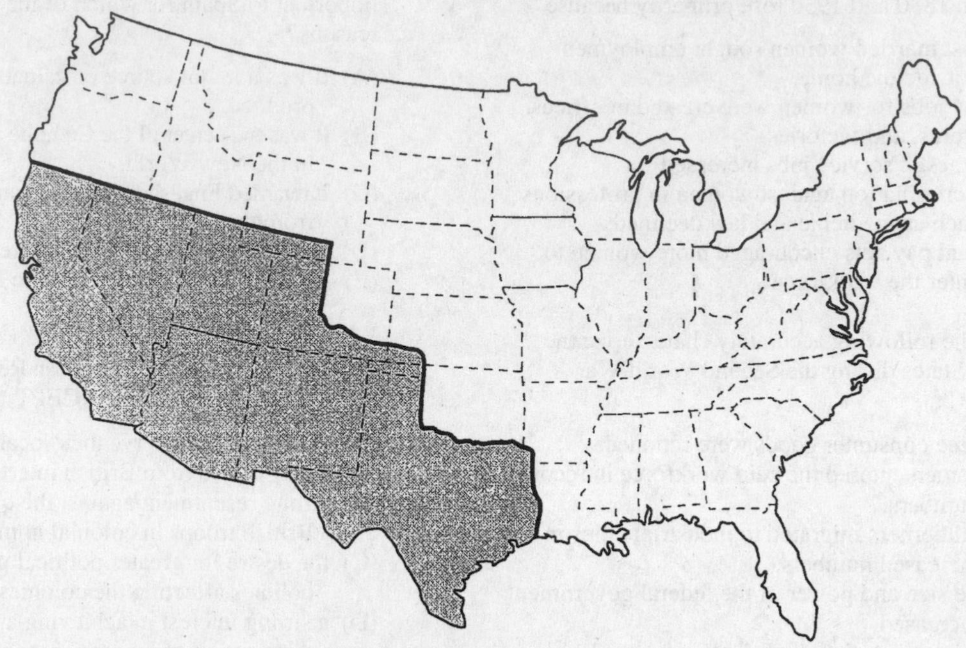

46. The entire shaded area in the map above was

    (A) ceded by Spain to the United States
    (B) once part of Mexico
    (C) claimed by the Confederacy
    (D) claimed by the Bear Flag Republic
    (E) known as the Gadsden Purchase

GO ON TO THE NEXT PAGE

47. Which of the following best describes the role played by the People's (Populist) party during the 1890's?

(A) An instrument to protect small businesses from governmental regulation
(B) An organization foreshadowing the subsequent socialist movement
(C) A vehicle for agrarian protest against the economic system
(D) The political arm of the new labor movement
(E) The medium through which urban ethnic groups entered national politics

48. "It seems to me . . . that the vital consideration connected with this problem of the trust is its effect upon our middle class — the independent, individual business person and the skilled artisan and mechanic. How does the trust affect them? . . . Their personal identity is lost. They become cogs and little wheels in a great complicated machine . . . . I favor complete and prompt annihilation of the trust — with due regard for property rights, of course."

The author of this statement would be likely to favor which of the following measures?

(A) Nationalization of industry
(B) A 100 percent inheritance tax
(C) The rapid diffusion of mass-production techniques
(D) Extensive distribution of free homestead land
(E) Strict application of the Sherman Act

GO ON TO THE NEXT PAGE

Puck/Rothco Cartoons

49. The cartoon above is making the point that Woodrow Wilson

(A) was the heir to the Populist tradition
(B) was the last in a line of reform-minded Presidents that included William Howard Taft and Theodore Roosevelt
(C) had a political philosophy that combined the tenets of the Republican and Progressive (Bull Moose) parties
(D) owed his election to the presidency in 1912 to the split in the Republican party
(E) owed his reelection to the presidency in 1916 to crossover votes by Republicans

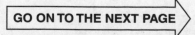

GO ON TO THE NEXT PAGE

50. The primary purpose of the National Origins Act of 1924 was to

(A) enumerate the populations of ethnic groups in the United States
(B) limit immigration to the United States
(C) help preserve American Indian culture
(D) fund archaeological expeditions
(E) support historical and genealogical research

51. Under Franklin D. Roosevelt's Good Neighbor policy, the United States stated its intention to refrain from intervening in the affairs of

(A) Latin America
(B) Europe
(C) Canada
(D) China
(E) Japan

52. President Truman's foreign policy after the Second World War had as its expressed aim

(A) preventive war
(B) atomic proliferation
(C) liberation of peoples under communist rule
(D) massive retaliation against Soviet aggression
(E) containment of international communism

53. The intellectual justification for revolutionary action contained in the Declaration of Independence was derived most directly from the work of

(A) Rousseau
(B) Locke
(C) Montesquieu
(D) Hobbes
(E) Voltaire

GO ON TO THE NEXT PAGE

SLAVE IMPORTATIONS, 1500 – 1810

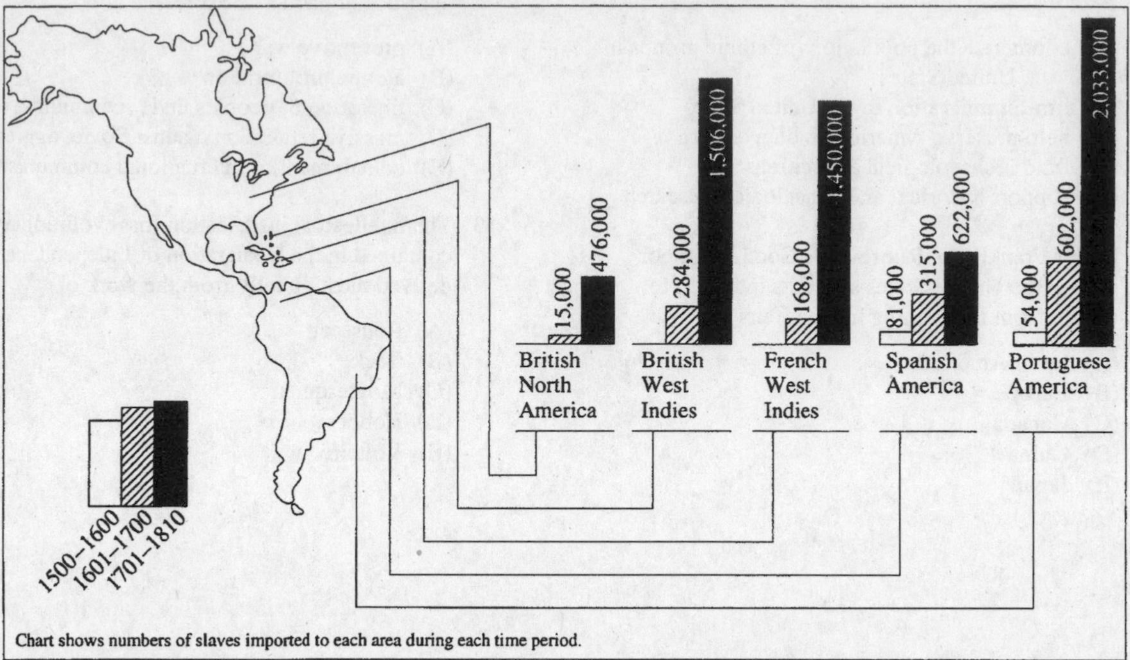

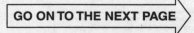

Chart shows numbers of slaves imported to each area during each time period.

Philip Curtin, *The Atlantic Slave Trade: A Census.*

54. The chart above lends support to which of the following statements about slave importations between 1500 and 1810 ?

(A) Sugar-growing regions imported more slaves than did any other region.
(B) The British imported more slaves to mainland colonies than to island colonies.
(C) The British monopolized the African slave trade in the eighteenth century.
(D) The importation of slaves decreased in proportion to the increase in native-born slave populations.
(E) The importation of slaves increased at the same rate in each region represented.

GO ON TO THE NEXT PAGE

55. "What then is the American, this new man? . . . I could point out to you a family whose grandfather was an Englishman, whose wife was Dutch, whose son married a French woman, and whose present four sons have now four wives of different nations. He is an American who, leaving behind him all his ancient prejudices and manners, receives new ones from the new mode of life he has embraced. . . . "

Which of the following is being described in this statement by an eighteenth-century observer of American life?

(A) Social stratification
(B) Nativism
(C) Anglicization
(D) Acculturation
(E) Denominationalism

56. The meaning of the Monroe Doctrine of 1823 is best summarized by which of the following statements?

(A) The United States would not permit the continuance of the African slave trade.
(B) The United States proclaimed its right to interfere in the internal affairs of neighboring nations.
(C) The United States would fight the creation of new colonies in the Western Hemisphere, although it would not interfere with existing ones.
(D) The United States would insist on a policy of equal treatment in trade with the Far East.
(E) The United States would not extend diplomatic recognition to any foreign government that came to power by force.

57. All of the following are correct statements about religious thought and expression in the nineteenth century EXCEPT:

(A) The religions of American Indians emphasized the sanctity of nature.
(B) The religion of slaves drew heavily on the Old Testament story of the Exodus.
(C) Catholic priests worked to establish parochial schools for the education of parish children.
(D) Deism and freethinking attracted wider support among Protestants than did evangelicalism.
(E) Most Protestant denominations supported the development of the temperance movement.

58. Which of the following is true about the Roosevelt Corollary to the Monroe Doctrine?

(A) It proclaimed a policing role for the United States in Latin America.
(B) It prohibited European loans to Latin America.
(C) It permitted temporary European armed interventions to collect debts in the Caribbean.
(D) It resulted from Japanese attempts to lease territory in Lower California.
(E) It met with general approval in Latin America.

59. All of the following were enacted into law during the New Deal EXCEPT

(A) a social security program
(B) a national health insurance program
(C) a federal work-relief program
(D) protection of collective bargaining
(E) federal regulation of stock exchanges

60. One purpose of the Marshall Plan of 1948 was to

(A) rebuild European economies through a joint recovery program
(B) aid the depressed agricultural economies of Latin American nations
(C) aid communist nations that would agree to embrace democracy
(D) give military aid to those nations resisting communist subversion
(E) help the peoples of Asia establish heavy industries

61. The decline of sharecropping and of the crop-lien system in the South after 1940 was due primarily to which of the following?

(A) The New Deal's establishment of an agricultural credit system for sharecroppers
(B) The political and social gains achieved by Black people through the civil rights movement
(C) The rise in cotton prices that freed sharecroppers from debt
(D) The closing of many southern banks during the Depression of the 1930's
(E) The increase in mechanization and the declining demand for cotton

GO ON TO THE NEXT PAGE

62. Economic inequality in colonial North America was greatest
    (A) in the Carolina backcountry
    (B) in inland towns
    (C) in seaboard cities
    (D) among the Pennsylvania Dutch
    (E) in the Shenandoah Valley

63. All of the following were basic to seventeenth-century New England Puritanism EXCEPT
    (A) belief in the innate goodness of human nature
    (B) belief in the general principles of Calvinism
    (C) intolerance of outspoken religious dissenters
    (D) the necessity for a trained and educated ministry
    (E) the duty of merchants to sell wares at a just price

64. As a diplomat during the American Revolution, Benjamin Franklin played a part in which of the following?
    (A) Preventing the French government from joining with the British against the United States
    (B) Bringing Spain into the Revolutionary War on the side of the United States
    (C) Concluding a peace between Britain and France, thereby ending the war in Europe
    (D) Concluding an alliance between France and the United States
    (E) Preserving French neutrality during the war

65. All of the following were among the causes of the War of 1812 EXCEPT
    (A) British Orders-in-Council
    (B) British monopoly of the Atlantic slave trade
    (C) British violations of United States territorial waters
    (D) British impressment of United States seamen
    (E) the desire of some United States citizens to annex Canada

66. Which of the following was NOT prominently advocated during the reform era of the 1830's and 1840's?
    (A) Trust-busting
    (B) Temperance
    (C) Abolitionism
    (D) Free public education
    (E) Utopian communitarianism

67. Which of the following most accurately characterizes the slave system in the South between 1820 and 1860 ?
    (A) Slaves were so restricted that they were unable to develop their own social life and culture.
    (B) The high mortality and low birthrates of the slaves necessitated large slave importations.
    (C) Slaves were assisted in their work by substantial numbers of White wage earners, most of whom were foreign immigrants.
    (D) Slaves worked in a wide variety of skilled and unskilled occupations.
    (E) Slave owners had little incentive to keep their slaves healthy.

68. The first free immigrants whose right of entry into the United States was curtailed by federal legislation were
    (A) Africans
    (B) Asians
    (C) Latin Americans
    (D) Eastern and Southern Europeans
    (E) Western and Northern Europeans

69. The rapid rise in labor union membership in the late 1930's was mainly a result of the
    (A) spread of assembly-line production
    (B) merger of the AFL and the CIO
    (C) opposition of labor to Franklin D. Roosevelt's New Deal policies
    (D) organizing efforts of the Knights of Labor
    (E) passage of the Wagner Act

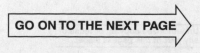

GO ON TO THE NEXT PAGE

THE SHIFTING FRONT IN KOREA*

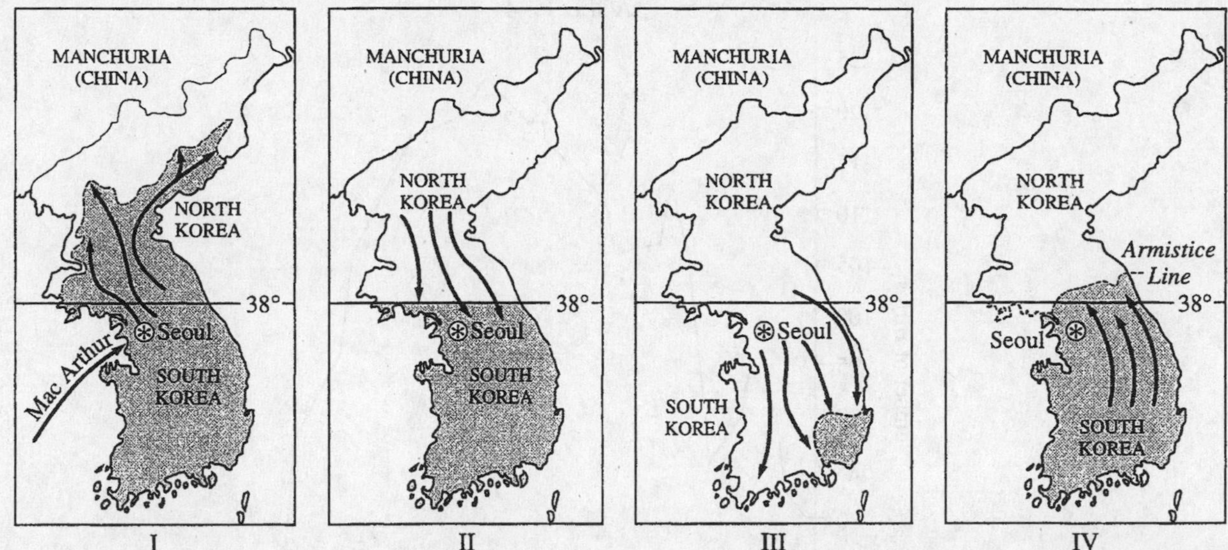

*Shaded areas represent position of UN forces.

70. Which of the following is the correct chronological sequence of the maps above?

(A) I, II, IV, III
(B) I, III, IV, II
(C) II, III, I, IV
(D) III, II, I, IV
(E) IV, II, III, I

GO ON TO THE NEXT PAGE

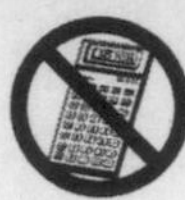

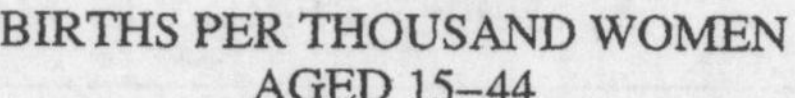
BIRTHS PER THOUSAND WOMEN
AGED 15–44

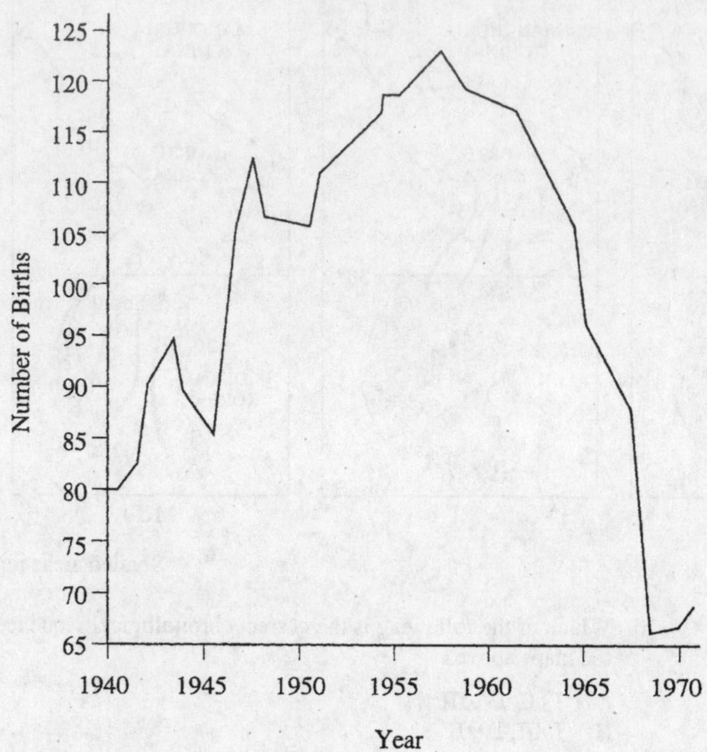

71. Which of the following statements is consistent with the data in the graph above?

    (A) The number of women having children rose during the Depression.
    (B) The wide availability of contraceptives led to a sharp decline in the birthrate during the 1960's.
    (C) Between 1955 and 1960 the United States had more women aged 15 to 44 than at any other time.
    (D) The number of single women having babies peaked in the 1960's.
    (E) The birthrate rose consistently between 1945 and 1960.

GO ON TO THE NEXT PAGE

72. In the 1700's the southern Appalachian region was distinguished by

(A) reliance on plantation agriculture
(B) the absence of indentured servitude
(C) numerous textile mills
(D) large numbers of Scots-Irish and German settlers
(E) high population densities

73. Anti-Federalist objections to ratification of the Constitution expressed all of the following fears EXCEPT:

(A) Congress would levy heavy taxes.
(B) The government would raise a standing army.
(C) The Bill of Rights was too broad.
(D) The President would have almost as much power as a king.
(E) State governments would wither away.

74. A broad discussion of the significance of the Missouri Compromise, the Tariff of 1833, and the Compromise of 1850 would necessarily mention which of the following?

(A) National debt
(B) Religious conflict
(C) The suffrage
(D) The Monroe Doctrine
(E) Sectional conflict

75. The Radical Republicans of America's post-Civil War period were radical in the sense that they favored

(A) civil and political rights for Black people
(B) the Reconstruction policies of President Andrew Johnson
(C) nationalization of the railroad and coal industries
(D) a government representing economic interests rather than geographical units
(E) a guaranteed minimum income for former slaves

76. When American reformers in the late nineteenth century claimed that "the tariff is the mother of trusts," they were arguing

(A) for a protective tariff and for an improvement in business ethics
(B) for a protective tariff and against monopolies
(C) for lower tariffs and against monopolies
(D) against monopolies and against the sales tax
(E) against monopolies and against taxes on exports

77. Which of the following events best supports a "class conflict" interpretation of American history?

(A) The nationwide railroad strike of 1877
(B) The Nullification crisis
(C) The rise of the Know-Nothing party
(D) The Supreme Court's decision in *Plessy* v. *Ferguson*
(E) Theodore Roosevelt's "taking" of the Panama Canal Zone

78. The year 1890 is significant in the history of the American West because the

(A) last major gold strike occurred in the Black Hills
(B) last massacre of American Indians occurred at Sand Creek
(C) most devastating blizzard ever to hit the Great Plains ended the long cattle drives
(D) transcontinental railroad was officially completed
(E) federal Census Office reported that a frontier line no longer existed

79. Organized labor opposed which of the following laws?

(A) The Social Security Act
(B) The Wagner Act
(C) The Fair Labor Standards Act
(D) The Taft-Hartley Act
(E) The Employment Act of 1946

GO ON TO THE NEXT PAGE

80. During the 1930's, which of the following was a fundamental political change that occurred among Black Americans?

(A) A shift of Black voters from the two major parties to the minor parties
(B) A shift of Black voters from the Republican party to the Democratic party
(C) A great increase in the proportion of Black people who registered to vote
(D) An increase in the importance of the Black vote in local elections in the South
(E) A decrease in the participation of Black voters in federal elections

81. The United Nations was designed to maintain peace in the post-Second World War period through the implementation of

(A) principles of free trade
(B) bipolarity
(C) collective security
(D) bilateral treaties
(E) regional pacts

82. Which of the following congressional actions resulted from an alleged attack on United States warships by North Vietnamese gunboats in 1964 ?

(A) A declaration of war against North Vietnam
(B) Passage of the War Powers Act
(C) Authorization for air attacks against selected targets in China as well as in North Vietnam
(D) A resolution urging the President to withdraw United States naval forces from Southeast Asian waters
(E) The Tonkin Gulf Resolution

83. In the early decades of the republic, the intentions and expectations of the authors of the United States Constitution were most fully realized in the

(A) respective roles of the executive and the legislative branches in conducting foreign policy
(B) extensive role of the executive branch in drafting legislation
(C) method of electing vice presidents
(D) formation of political parties
(E) elimination of property qualifications for voting

84. As Secretary of the Treasury, Alexander Hamilton did which of the following?

(A) Sought to avoid a centralized banking system that could control the nation's currency
(B) Sought to link the interests of the national government and monied people
(C) Proposed to tax domestic manufactures to discourage the growth of factory towns
(D) Proposed to require the state governments to pay off the national debt
(E) Proposed to give away western land to small farmers to encourage settlement

85. One of the goals of the Populist movement was

(A) government control of railroads
(B) collective ownership of farms
(C) a strengthened electoral college
(D) legislation to raise tariffs
(E) abolition of income taxes

86. In *How the Other Half Lives*, Jacob Riis revealed the plight of

(A) Black sharecroppers in the Deep South
(B) Chinese workers in the railroad gangs of the West
(C) European immigrants in the tenements of New York City
(D) young boys in the Pennsylvania coal mines
(E) American Indians in the Southwest

87. All of the following statements about the American economy during the First World War are correct EXCEPT:

(A) Government boards were organized to manage crucial sectors of the economy.
(B) Members of minority groups, especially Black people, moved into northern industrial cities to work in war factories.
(C) The number of unionized workers increased.
(D) The federal government expanded its prosecution of antitrust suits against large corporations.
(E) Taxes were increased for corporations and wealthy individuals to help finance the war.

GO ON TO THE NEXT PAGE

88. At the Yalta Conference in February 1945, Franklin D. Roosevelt's options were limited most seriously by which of the following?

    (A) Winston Churchill's suspicions of Roosevelt's motives and friendship
    (B) The poor health of Joseph Stalin
    (C) The rising tide of criticism of Roosevelt's leadership at home
    (D) The presence of Soviet troops in the Far East
    (E) The presence of Soviet troops in Poland

89. The American counterculture of the 1960's opposed

    (A) left-wing ideals of the 1930's and 1940's
    (B) modernist art and literature
    (C) the conservation movement
    (D) the materialism of American society
    (E) trade unionism

90. In the United States, the largest growth in population during the 1970's occurred in which of the following?

    (A) The Northeast Corridor from Boston to Washington, D.C.
    (B) States below the 37th parallel from Virginia to California
    (C) States of the upper Midwest from Ohio to Minnesota
    (D) The most heavily populated states, including New York, Pennsylvania, Illinois, and California
    (E) The regions concentrating on mature industries such as steel, automobiles, and major appliances

STOP

IF YOU FINISH BEFORE TIME IS CALLED, YOU MAY CHECK YOUR WORK ON THIS TEST ONLY. DO NOT TURN TO ANY OTHER TEST IN THIS BOOK.

How to Score the SAT Subject Test in United States History

When you take an actual SAT Subject Test in United States History, your answer sheet will be "read" by a scanning machine that will record your responses to each question. Then a computer will compare your answers with the correct answers and produce your raw score. You get one point for each correct answer. For each wrong answer, you lose one-quarter of a point. Questions you omit (and any for which you mark more than one answer) are not counted. This raw score is converted to a scaled score that is reported to you and to the colleges you specify.

Worksheet 1. Finding Your Raw Test Score

STEP 1: Table A on the following page lists the correct answers for all the questions on the SAT Subject Test in United States History that is reproduced in this book. It also serves as a worksheet for you to calculate your raw score.

- Compare your answers with those given in the table.
- Put a check in the column marked "Right" if your answer is correct.
- Put a check in the column marked "Wrong" if your answer is incorrect.
- Leave both columns blank if you omitted the question.

STEP 2: Count the number of right answers.

Enter the total here:________________

STEP 3: Count the number of wrong answers.

Enter the total here:________________

STEP 4: Multiply the number of wrong answers by .250.

Enter the product here: ________________

STEP 5: Subtract the result obtained in Step 4 from the total you obtained in Step 2.

Enter the result here:________________

STEP 6: Round the number obtained in Step 5 to the nearest whole number.

Enter the result here:________________

The number you obtained in Step 6 is your raw score.

Table A

Answers to the Subject Test in United States History – Practice Test 2 and Percentage of Students Answering Each Question Correctly

Question Number	Correct Answer	Right	Wrong	Percentage of Students Answering the Question Correctly*	Question Number	Correct Answer	Right	Wrong	Percentage of Students Answering the Question Correctly*
1	A			66	32	A			70
2	D			85	33	E			45
3	A			69	34	B			45
4	D			71	35	D			45
5	C			74	36	C			45
6	B			95	37	C			65
7	D			78	38	A			57
8	E			63	39	B			69
9	D			96	40	B			51
10	A			90	41	E			54
11	D			68	42	A			47
12	E			54	43	C			51
13	C			68	44	D			62
14	B			76	45	B			56
15	A			65	46	B			61
16	C			86	47	C			26
17	B			83	48	E			42
18	D			35	49	D			49
19	C			58	50	B			53
20	E			79	51	A			61
21	C			59	52	E			54
22	E			56	53	B			57
23	A			54	54	A			58
24	D			67	55	D			40
25	B			57	56	C			45
26	E			73	57	D			51
27	A			59	58	A			65
28	B			33	59	B			34
29	C			73	60	A			37
30	D			74	61	E			41
31	E			69	62	C			32

Table A continued on next page

Table A continued from previous page

Question Number	Correct Answer	Right	Wrong	Percentage of Students Answering the Question Correctly*	Question Number	Correct Answer	Right	Wrong	Percentage of Students Answering the Question Correctly*
63	A			34	77	A			31
64	D			61	78	E			22
65	B			32	79	D			34
66	A			34	80	B			40
67	D			33	81	C			45
68	B			35	82	E			42
69	E			19	83	A			37
70	C			36	84	B			31
71	B			56	85	A			27
72	D			28	86	C			44
73	C			47	87	D			37
74	E			64	88	E			36
75	A			43	89	D			51
76	C			40	90	B			24

* These percentages are based on an analysis of the answer sheets of a representative sample of 2,993 students who took the original administration of this test and whose mean score was 556. They may be used as an indication of the relative difficulty of a particular question.

Finding Your Scaled Score

When you take SAT Subject Tests, the scores sent to the colleges you specify are reported on the College Board scale, which ranges from 200 to 800. You can convert your practice test raw score to a scaled score by using Table B. To find your scaled score, locate your raw score in the left-hand column of Table B; the corresponding score in the right-hand column is your scaled score. For example, a raw score of 60 on this particular edition of the SAT Subject Test in United States History corresponds to a scaled score of 680.

Raw scores are converted to scaled scores to ensure that a score earned on any one edition of a particular Subject Test is comparable to the same scaled score earned on any other edition of the same Subject Test. Because some editions of tests may be slightly easier or more difficult than others, College Board scaled scores are adjusted so that they indicate the same level of performance regardless of the edition of the test taken and the ability of the group that takes it. Thus, for example, a score of 400 on one edition of a test taken at a particular administration indicates the same level of achievement as a score of 400 on a different edition of the test taken at a different administration.

When you take the SAT Subject Tests during a national administration, your scores are likely to differ somewhat from the scores you obtain on the tests in this book. People perform at different levels at different times for reasons unrelated to the tests themselves. The precision of any test is also limited because it represents only a sample of all the possible questions that could be asked.

Table B

Scaled Score Conversion Table
Subject Test in United States History – Practice Test 2

Raw Score	Scaled Score	Raw Score	Scaled Score	Raw Score	Scaled Score
90	800	52	630	14	420
89	800	51	630	13	420
88	800	50	620	12	410
87	800	49	610	11	410
86	800	48	610	10	400
85	800	47	600	9	400
84	800	46	600	8	390
83	800	45	590	7	390
82	800	44	580	6	380
81	800	43	580	5	380
80	790	42	570	4	370
79	790	41	570	3	370
78	780	40	560	2	360
77	780	39	560	1	360
76	770	38	550	0	350
75	770	37	540	-1	350
74	760	36	540	-2	340
73	760	35	530	-3	340
72	750	34	530	-4	330
71	740	33	520	-5	330
70	740	32	520	-6	320
69	730	31	510	-7	320
68	730	30	510	-8	310
67	720	29	500	-9	310
66	720	28	490	-10	300
65	710	27	490	-11	300
64	700	26	480	-12	290
63	700	25	480	-13	280
62	690	24	470	-14	280
61	690	23	470	-15	270
60	680	22	460	-16	270
59	670	21	460	-17	260
58	670	20	450	-18	250
57	660	19	450	-19	250
56	660	18	440	-20	240
55	650	17	440	-21	230
54	640	16	430	-22	230
53	640	15	430		

How Did You Do on the Subject Test in United States History?

After you score your test and analyze your performance, think about the following questions:

Did you run out of time before reaching the end of the test?

If so, you may need to pace yourself better. For example, maybe you spent too much time on one or two hard questions. A better approach might be to skip the ones you can't answer right away and try answering all the remaining questions on the test. Then if there's time, go back to the questions you skipped.

Did you take a long time reading the directions?

You will save time when you take the test by learning the directions to the Subject Test in United States History ahead of time. Each minute you spend reading directions during the test is a minute that you could use to answer questions.

How did you handle questions you were unsure of?

If you were able to eliminate one or more of the answer choices as wrong and guess from the remaining ones, your approach probably worked to your advantage. On the other hand, making haphazard guesses or omitting questions without trying to eliminate choices could cost you valuable points.

How difficult were the questions for you compared with other students who took the test?

Table A shows you how difficult the multiple-choice questions were for the group of students who took this test during its national administration. The right-hand column gives the percentage of students that answered each question correctly.

A question answered correctly by almost everyone in the group is obviously an easier question. For example, 96 percent of the students answered question 9 correctly. However, only 19 percent answered question 69 correctly.

Keep in mind that these percentages are based on just one group of students. They would probably be different with another group of students taking the test.

If you missed several easier questions, go back and try to find out why: Did the questions cover material you haven't yet reviewed? Did you misunderstand the directions?

Answer Explanations for United States History – Practice Test 2

1. Choice (A) is the correct answer. In colonial America, one of the biggest problems faced by large landowners was the need of laborers to work their land. Indentured servitude was a method by which these landowners paid for the passage of young men and women from Europe in return for their labor for a fixed period of time.

2. Choice (D) is the correct answer. Most American slave owners feared any kind of thinking, religious or political, on the part of their slaves and would punish slaves for having any ideas of their own. Slaves had learned to keep their thoughts—and their prayers—concealed from their owners. This quotation is evidently from a former slave who had learned this lesson even as a young child.

3. Choice (A) is the correct answer. One of the major issues between political parties during Andrew Jackson's presidency was the national bank. Jackson and the Jacksonian Democrats were against a bank that had control over public (government) finances and little regulation by the government. The National Republicans wanted the charter for the bank renewed. The issue led to the end of the national bank. Voting rights for anyone except white adult males, immigration to the United States, military expenditures, and railroad construction did not become major political issues until after Jackson's presidency.

4. Choice (D) is the correct answer. Of all the choices, this statement is the only one that is not true. Although labor unions emerged during the second half of the nineteenth century, only a small percentage of workers belonged to unions.

5. Choice (C) is the correct answer. Although Germany had slowed its submarine warfare after the sinking of the *Lusitania*, it reinstated unrestricted submarine warfare not only against British ships, but also against American merchant ships.

6. Choice (B) is the correct answer. The speaker states that young people who have entered a life of crime were persuaded to do so by the romanticized portrayal of crime in the

movies. The speaker would certainly agree that the content of movies needs to be monitored and censored to protect young people from such undesirable influence.

7. Choice (D) is the correct answer. Although the economic factors mentioned in the other choices—tax rates, purchasing power, exports, and stock market activity—also increased during the last half of the twentieth century, inflation refers to the general rise in the prices of consumer goods.

8. Choice (E) is the correct answer. The statement in choice (E) is not true. In fact, the opposite is true. After the Second World War, more and more American women entered the workforce.

9. Choice (D) is the correct answer. The Supreme Court would base its ruling on constitutional law, not on religious trends of Americans. One of the fundamental principles of the Constitution is the separation of church and state. The Supreme Court ruled that prayer and religious instruction—aspects of "church"—could not be required by public schools—an aspect of "state."

10. Choice (A) is the correct answer. In the cartoon the speaker is from the United States White House; the implication is that the speaker is the president. Oil is dripping off the other side of the globe; nothing else, such as people, foreign government buildings, or war machinery (tanks, jets), is depicted. Although the president is saying that the Persian Gulf War is not about oil, the *only* thing pictured in the Persian Gulf area of the globe is oil.

11. Choice (D) is the correct answer. Under mercantilism, England would not want competition for articles produced in England, even from articles produced in its own colonies. Such competition would not benefit England. All of the activities mentioned in choices (A), (B), (C), and (E) ensured that colonial economic activities would benefit England, which was the purpose of mercantilism.

12. Choice (E) is the correct answer. The Great Awakening was a religious movement by revivalists who preached that the individual must make a personal commitment to Christ, that the individual was responsible. The movement weakened the established colonial clergy (A), appealed to all classes of people (B), and welcomed women and African Americans (D).

13. Choice (C) is the correct answer. In the first half of the nineteenth century, there were no laws regarding abortion. All of the other movements—abolition of slavery, women's suffrage, temperance laws, and property ownership—were widely supported by women reformers.

14. Choice (B) is the correct answer. In the last half of the nineteenth century, most states did not allow women to vote, much less to run for office, despite the movement for women's rights during this time. Significant changes did occur in all of the other areas—business, legal status of African Americans (men), communication technology, and the diversification of religious affiliation.

15. Choice (A) is the correct answer. The Interstate Commerce Act of 1887 was one of the first attempts by the federal government to regulate commerce. It required railroads to publish their rate schedules (prices for passengers and freight) so that railroads could not charge small shippers higher prices than they charged the larger companies. The activities mentioned in choices (C), (D), and (E) were not yet issues in the United States.

16. Choice (C) is the correct answer. Nativists were native-born American citizens who viewed new immigrants as a threat to the American way of life. Included in this anti-immigrant view was the belief that immigrants would take away jobs from American workers. With these views, nativists were unlikely to help immigrants or to view them in any favorable way.

17. Choice (B) is the correct answer. Although African American men were both drafted and allowed to enlist during the First World War, they were assigned to segregated units commanded by white officers. Progress toward racial desegregation of the United States military did not begin until 1948, after the Second World War.

18. Choice (D) is the correct answer. Although the 1920s was known as the "Jazz Age," festivals were little known. Television was still in experimental stages, and professional football was only beginning. Although circuses were still popular, especially in rural areas, the moving pictures—and the new "talkies"—appealed to vast urban audiences.

19. Choice (C) is the correct answer. Becoming president for the first of his four terms in 1933, Franklin Delano Roosevelt instituted the New Deal, a series of federal programs intended to pull the United States out of the Great Depression. Although short-lived, many of the measures were effective in providing employment and relief to millions

of Americans. The New Deal also permanently extended the federal government's role in regulating business, industry, commerce, banking, and labor.

20. Choice (E) is the correct answer. Although the States' rights movement (A) and the presidency of Franklin D. Roosevelt (C) created interest on the part of voters, neither extended political participation to disenfranchised sectors of the American population. Certainly, the Supreme Court ruling in *Brown v. Board of Education of Topeka* (B) and the decline of the Ku Klux Klan (D) helped African Americans gain momentum in the Civil Rights Movement but, again, neither extended political participation. The Civil Rights Act of 1965 did away with practices, such as literacy tests, that made voting by some people almost impossible, thereby ensuring participation in the political process, through voting, of African Americans and other minority groups.

21. Choice (C) is the correct answer. During the last 50 years, members of opposing political parties have been on the same side of the issues listed in choices (A), (B), (D), and (E), and members of the same political party have opposed each other on these same issues. The Speaker of the House is elected by the members of the House and is the most likely issue to be voted on according to party affiliation. Usually, the Speaker is a member of the majority party.

22. Choice (E) is the correct answer. Before the eighteenth century, the most dramatic influence on the culture of the American Plains Indians was the introduction of the horse by Spanish explorers. The horse increased their mobility so that they could more easily follow the herds of buffalo on which their lives depended. It also increased their ability to make war on neighboring tribes and to expand their control over vast areas.

23. Choice (A) is the correct answer. The major problem with the Articles of Confederation was the insufficient power of the central government. Although the new government could deal with foreign countries and settle disputes between or among states, it had very few powers. Most of the powers of government remained with the states. Basically, the Articles created a very loose confederation of very independent states.

24. Choice (D) is the correct answer. Thomas Jefferson's ideal nation was an agrarian republic. He did not push for the purchase of the Louisiana Territory to embarrass the Federalists (C), whom he said all lived in cities, or to follow the advice of Alexander Hamilton (E), his political opponent, or to stimulate manufacturing (A), which he despised. Instead, he advocated the purchase in order to mold the United States into his ideal.

25. Choice (B) is the correct answer. In *Walden*, Thoreau recounts his experiences during his two years living in near seclusion in the woods of Massachusetts, not the American West (A) or a Southern plantation (C). Thoreau also expounded on his philosophy of individualism and living simply in harmony with nature, away from the noisy, industrialized, and densely populated cities.

26. Choice (E) is the correct answer. Although the United States might have stated other reasons for the Open Door Policy of 1899, its primary interest was economic—to protect U.S. trading opportunities in China and to prevent European and Asian countries from taking over all Chinese trade.

27. Choice (A) is the correct answer. In the 1920s, the Ku Klux Klan began to target anyone who was not a white, Protestant, native-born American—African Americans, Jews, immigrants, union workers, Catholics. As during the Reconstruction period, the Klan used vigilante tactics, not only in the South, but also in northern, midwestern, and western states.

28. Choice (B) is the correct answer. Inflationary wages were nonexistent before the 1930s. On the other hand, all of the factors mentioned in the other choices—a nonregulated banking system, low farm prices, overproduction of manufactured goods, and the stock market crash—did contribute to the Great Depression.

29. Choice (C) is the correct answer. Before it entered the Second World War, the neutral United States used the lend-lease policy to provide war materials, food, and other necessities to the Allied forces, without requiring the Allied nations to pay for those goods.

30. Choice (D) is the correct answer. Many viewed a tax on individual and corporate income as an end to capitalism and free enterprise. Choice (A) is incorrect. Women's suffrage was not associated with the economic issue discussed. Choice (B) is incorrect. Due process of law protected all citizens, the best and the worst, and had no direct effect on the economic system of the country. Choice (C) is incorrect. The method of electing senators would have no direct effect on the economy. Choice (E) is incorrect. Abolishing slavery and indentured servitude was not considered a threat to industrial capitalism.

31. Choice (E) is the correct answer. The political cartoon requires the reader to recognize Nikita Khrushchev, premier of the USSR, disguised as Napoleon Bonaparte, retreating on a horse made of missiles. In the background is Fidel Castro, leader of

Cuba, dressed as a peasant and waving the Cuban flag. With the word "retreat" at the top, the cartoon refers to the withdrawal of Soviet missiles from Cuba in 1962. The other choices are incorrect because neither Cuba nor Fidel Castro had anything to do with these other events.

32. Choice (A) is the correct answer. The technological and agricultural advances mentioned in this question were accomplishments of the Maya, Toltec, and Aztec who had empires throughout Mesoamerica (in Mexico and upper Central America) before the arrival of Spanish explorers. Although the Native Americans of the Eastern Woodlands had an advanced agricultural economy and some large cities, the peoples who populated the areas mentioned in the other choices did not have highly developed systems of astronomy, mathematics, or calendars.

33. Choice (E) is the correct answer. Although Jamestown was the first permanent English settlement in North America, nearly two-thirds of the first settlers died from disease (dysentery and typhoid fever) during the first year. At first, Native Americans were helpful; however, they soon began making war on the English settlers (D). Neither gold nor other precious metals were found here, as they had been in Mexico (A), and the cultivation and export of tobacco did not occur until more settlers and supplies arrived and the colony had been made a royal colony (B). Although the Spanish had claimed the land that would later become known as Florida, they had no interest in this area of North America (C).

34. Choice (B) is the correct answer. The Northwest Ordinance of 1787 set the guidelines for the government of the area known as the Northwest Territory and specified that the area would make up from three to five states. The Ordinance also set the minimum adult male population for each of these areas to become a territory and eventually a state, outlawed slavery, and granted its citizens the same rights as other American citizens had. Most important, these newly organized states would have the same status as the older states of the Union.

35. Choice (D) is the correct answer. John Marshall, Chief Justice of the Supreme Court from 1801 to 1833, led the Court in making numerous rulings that firmly established the Court's power of judicial review (*Marbury v. Madison*), strengthened the power of the federal government over the states, and affirmed congressional control of both the sanctity of contracts and interstate commerce. The question of a slave's rights did not come before the Supreme Court until 1857 in *Dred Scott v. Sandford.*

36. Choice (C) is the correct answer. In the five novels that compose *The Leatherstocking Tales*, published between 1823 and 1841, Cooper portrays Natty Bumppo, the hero, as

a noble frontiersman caught between two worlds—the natural, unsettled wilderness and the developing, growing settlements of the young nation. Although Twain and Cather both created western heroes and heroines, their works came much later. Poe wrote poetry and short stories of the macabre. Jackson's works focused on the cruel and unjust treatment of Native Americans.

37. Choice (C) is the correct answer. This quotation supports the idea of Manifest Destiny—that the expansion of the United States to include not only Texas but all of the lands leading to the Pacific Ocean was not only inevitable but also divinely ordained.

38. Choice (A) is the correct answer. Although the Union dominated the Confederacy in terms of railroads, population, industry, resources, wealth, and military force, the South had Robert E. Lee, a military genius, as leader of Virginia's military forces and eventually as chief of all the Confederate forces. The South also had a number of talented and highly trained military officers. The Union army had little effective military leadership until Lincoln appointed Ulysses S. Grant as military commander in 1864.

39. Choice (B) is the correct answer. This quotation reflects the concept of Social Darwinism, which held that government should not interfere in human interactions because political power and economic dominance would naturally fall to "the fittest."

40. Choice (B) is the correct answer. From 1880 through 1930, the growth of business and industry provided opportunities for women as office workers, store clerks, and factory workers. The other choices are incorrect. During this period, most married women were homemakers or worked in the home; women did not receive equal pay; and women faced increased restrictions on entering professions such as medicine and law.

41. Choice (E) is the correct answer. Rather than declining, both production and wages in the United States increased during the Second World War. Domestic factories and industries became "war" factories and industries, and workers were needed and paid to perform the jobs. Because of the war effort, some goods, such as gasoline and food, were rationed; women performed jobs once held only by men; Southerners, especially African Americans, migrated north in search of jobs and a better life; and the federal government became stronger and bigger.

42. Choice (A) is the correct answer. The main interest of France in establishing settlements in the Americas was trade with American Indians. In exchange for furs, especially beaver, the French gave metal products (pots and tools), decorated blankets, glass beads, and other goods that the native peoples did not make for themselves. The French established only a few permanent settlements, mostly along the St. Lawrence River and at the mouth of the Mississippi River, where there was easy access to shipping ports.

43. Choice (C) is the correct answer. To maintain its hold in the Americas, Spain needed Florida to prevent English colonial expansion into the area south of the Carolinas. Florida was neither a source of precious metals or tropical produce, nor a center of Catholicism.

44. Choice (D) is the correct answer. The colonists were not interested in achieving an even distribution of income. Instead, they supported the idea of independence from England because they wanted more say in how they were governed and in preserving their way of life.

45. Choice (B) is the correct answer. The state of Georgia had taken land owned by the Cherokee under a treaty with the United States. The Cherokee appealed to the Supreme Court, which ruled in their favor. However, Georgia ignored the ruling and continued to take the land. Jackson, as president, did not intervene to enforce the Supreme Court's decision, and the Cherokee were forced to leave their lands in Georgia and move to the Oklahoma Territory.

46. Choice (B) is the correct answer. The area shaded in the map was once part of Mexico. Although all of the land had once been part of the Spanish Empire, none of this area was ceded by Spain to the United States (A), and only Texas was part of the Confederacy (C). The Bear Flag Republic included only a small area in northern California (D), and the Gadsden Purchase included a small portion in southern Arizona and New Mexico (E).

47. Choice (C) is the correct answer. The Populist Party of the 1890s, supported by southern and western farmers, called for measures, such as abolishing the national banking system and nationalizing the railroads, to help them out of financial difficulties.

48. Choice (E) is the correct answer. Large trusts or monopolies were combinations of companies that gained control of the market and forced out any competition. The Sherman Antitrust Act of 1890 made such monopolies illegal.

49. Choice (D) is the correct answer. The cartoon requires the reader to recognize the symbols of the political parties in the 1912 election: the elephant symbolizes the Republican Party, the bull moose symbolizes the Progressive Party, and the donkey, ridden by Wilson, represents the Democratic Party. The mathematic division sign between the elephant and bull moose means "the Republican Party divided (or split) by the Progressive Party," and the equal sign means that this split resulted in the election of the Democratic Party's candidate, Woodrow Wilson.

50. Choice (B) is the correct answer. According to the National Origins Act of 1924, the number of immigrants from a certain country allowed into the United States was based on the proportion of the U.S. population with the number of people from that country already living in the United States in 1890. This Act was passed in order to exclude or minimize immigrants from different racial, ethnic, or religious backgrounds.

51. Choice (A) is the correct answer. In general, the Good Neighbor policy under Franklin D. Roosevelt meant that the United States would no longer interfere in Latin American countries. Previously, the United States had used economic, political, and military force in various Latin American countries in order to protect American business interests in those countries.

52. Choice (E) is the correct answer. To counteract the spread of communism, President Truman proposed the Truman Doctrine in 1947, by which the United States would aid any country threatened by communist takeover.

53. Choice (B) is the correct answer. The principles of government embodied in the Declaration of Independence and the U.S. Constitution are directly based on the political theories of John Locke. According to Locke's theory, government derived its power from the people who were governed, not by divine right; government had an obligation to protect the people's natural and property rights; and government that failed in this protection should be abolished.

54. Choice (A) is the correct answer. According to the chart, the highest numbers of slaves were imported to the British West Indies, French West Indies, and Portuguese America, all sugar-growing areas. British colonies in North America imported the

fewest number of slaves (B), and the Portuguese imported the highest number of slaves during all three periods (C). The information provided in the chart is insufficient to support the statements in choices (D) and (E).

55. Choice (D) is the correct answer. The statement focuses on the eighteenth-century cultural diversity of American families, which, in this quotation, are a mixture of English, Dutch, French, and other backgrounds. The statement does not mention social status (A) or religious faith (E). By implication, the statement indicates that the American family is opposite of the concepts of nativism (B) and Anglicization (C).

56. Choice (C) is the correct answer. According to the Monroe Doctrine, first proposed by James Monroe in 1823, the United States would not allow any European powers to establish new colonies on the American continents or to attempt to regain control of colonies that had won their independence.

57. Choice (D) is the correct answer. In the United States during the nineteenth century, the tenets of evangelicalism—that the individual must make a personal religious commitment and that the Bible is the authoritative source of religious knowledge—were widely supported by Protestant churches and continue to be represented in most Protestant denominations.

58. Choice (A) is the correct answer. Proposed by Theodore Roosevelt in 1904, the Roosevelt Corollary extended the Monroe Doctrine (which was meant to prevent European expansion in Latin America) and stated that the United States could intervene in the affairs of Latin American countries.

59. Choice (B) is the correct answer. Under the New Deal in the 1930s, laws to establish a social security program, set up a federal work-relief program, protect collective bargaining, and regulate stock exchanges were all enacted. A law to establish a national health insurance program was not enacted until 1966.

60. Choice (A) is the correct answer. Under the Marshall Plan, the United States would provide financial aid to rebuild the economy, agriculture, and industry of European countries, including Germany, that had been ravaged by the Second World War.

61. Choice (E) is the correct answer. After 1940, the increase in farming mechanization, such as cotton-picking machines, and a decrease in the cotton market meant that farmers no longer needed sharecroppers to help produce their crops.

62. Choice (C) is the correct answer. In most areas of colonial America, such as inland towns and farming backcountries, the people tended to be fairly equal economically. In the seaboard cities, however, export merchants became quite wealthy and composed an economic upper class. These wealthy merchants represented only a small percentage of the population of these cities, but they owned much of the total wealth. Their wealth was far greater than that of the middle class, which was composed of artisans and shopkeepers, and even greater than that of those who worked for wages.

63. Choice (A) is the correct answer. Rather than innate goodness of human nature, one of the principles of Puritanism is the basic sinfulness of human nature. Although Puritans believed that one's eternal fate was predetermined and could not be known for certain, they also believed that a person's conversion might indicate that he or she was chosen by God for salvation.

64. Choice (D) is the correct answer. Shortly after the Revolutionary War began in 1776, Franklin was able to convince the king of France to provide financial aid to the United States. Less than two years later, in February 1778, Franklin was able to establish an economic and military alliance between France and the United States.

65. Choice (B) is the correct answer. The slave trade had been outlawed by both Great Britain and the United States before the War of 1812. The United States entered a war against Great Britain because Great Britain had prohibited neutral countries from trading with France, with which it was at war (A), violated U.S. territorial waters by attacking and boarding American ships to look for deserters (C), and forced American sailors into military service (D). Some U.S. citizens also wanted to make Canada part of the United States (E).

66. Choice (A) is the correct answer. Trusts, or monopolies, did not become a factor in the American economy until the late nineteenth century. However, temperance, abolitionism, and free public education were widely supported by various segments of the American population. Utopian communitarianism resulted in communities such as the Oneida Community, where there was no government or any other restraints on individual behavior.

67. Choice (D) is the correct answer. In the four decades before the American Civil War, most slaves worked as field laborers on the plantations, but many also worked as housemaids, seamstresses, carpenters, blacksmiths, cooks, midwives, nurses, and gardeners. Even within the restricted environment, slaves developed their own social lives (A), and their population in the American South grew at a normal rate,

so importation, which had been outlawed in 1808, was not necessary (B). Because plantation owners depended almost entirely on slave labor (C), they had great incentive to keep the slaves healthy (E).

68. Choice (B) is the correct answer. With the enactment of the Chinese Exclusion Act of 1882, passed in response to growing feelings of nativism, Congress limited the number of new Chinese immigrants to almost none.

69. Choice (E) is the correct answer. The National Labor Relations Act (NLRA), also known as the Wagner Act, was passed by Congress in 1935. Its purpose was to govern relations between laborers and management in businesses involved in interstate commerce. The NLRA, along with other laws that supported workers, such as the Fair Labor Standards Act, was part of Roosevelt's Second New Deal.

70. Choice (C) is the correct answer. On June 25, 1950, fighting between North and South Korean troops broke out along the 38th parallel (Map II). Within three days, the North Koreans had taken Seoul and advanced quickly, taking all but a small area surrounding Pusan (Map III). United Nations troops led by General Douglas MacArthur pushed the North Koreans back all the way to the Chinese border (Map I). China sent troops to help the North Koreans retake the area that included Seoul, but an armistice between the U.N., China, and North Korea was signed, setting the North–South border at the 38th parallel (Map IV).

71. Choice (B) is the correct answer. From about 1962 to 1968, the number of births sharply dropped from about 117 to about 66 per 1,000 women. Although it is not shown, the wide availability of contraceptives during this time period would be consistent with the drop in number of births.

72. Choice (D) is the correct answer. Attracted by cheap land and relative freedom of religion, thousands of Germans and Scots-Irish immigrated to the Middle Colonies and settled in the Appalachian frontier of western Pennsylvania, Maryland, Virginia, and the Carolinas.

73. Choice (C) is the correct answer. The Anti-Federalists opposed the ratification of the new United States Constitution because it did not have a Bill of Rights. Despite the long and hard debate over this issue, each of the 13 states finally ratified the Constitution between 1787 and 1790. In 1791, the first 10 amendments to the Constitution were ratified and became the Bill of Rights.

74. Choice (E) is the correct answer. The Missouri Compromise, the Tariff of 1833, and the Compromise of 1850 all centered on the slavery issue, which divided the United States along sectional lines—North, South, and West. The Missouri Compromise dealt with the admission of new states as slave states or free states; the Tariff of 1833 dealt with high taxes on manufactured goods imported by Southern (slave) states; and the Compromise of 1850 dealt with the lands obtained from Mexico after the Mexican War and their admission as slave or free states.

75. Choice (A) is the correct answer. After the Civil War, the Radical Republicans favored punitive measures against the former Confederate states and leaders, and equal rights for former slaves. They opposed President Andrew Johnson's Reconstruction policy (B) because they believed it was not punitive enough against the Southern states and did not grant civil and political rights to black Americans.

76. Choice (C) is the correct answer. The late nineteenth century was the time of big business trusts, or monopolies, which knocked out competition from small businesses and controlled prices of goods. High tariffs, or taxes on imported goods, favored monopolies because they reduced competition from foreign businesses. Progressive reformers sought lower tariffs and the end of trusts.

77. Choice (A) is the correct answer. The railroad strike of 1877 started out as a local strike against a single railroad, but grew to involve workers and railroads across the country. The railroad workers represented the poor working class, who worked in dangerous conditions for low wages and no benefits. The railroads represented the wealthy owners.

78. Choice (E) is the correct answer. By 1890, the American frontier, in the common meaning of the word, no longer existed. The country from the Atlantic to the Pacific was settled, crisscrossed with railroads, spotted with booming towns, and most of the territories of the American West had been admitted as states into the Union. All parts of the country were linked geographically, economically, and politically.

79. Choice (D) is the correct answer. The Labor-Management Relations Act of 1947, also known as the Taft-Hartley Act, was unfavorable toward organized labor. It amended the National Labor Relations Act by limiting and regulating union activities, especially with regard to the right of workers not to belong to a union or to participate in collective bargaining. The acts mentioned in the other choices were all favorable to workers and were generally supported by organized labor.

80. Choice (B) is the correct answer. Since Reconstruction, black voters had supported the Republican Party, the party of Abraham Lincoln. During the 1930s, however, large numbers of black voters switched to the Democratic Party. This shift occurred as a result of the devastating effects of the Great Depression on the black population, the increased involvement of black workers in labor unions, and the Republican Party's recruitment of Southern segregationists.

81. Choice (C) is the correct answer. According to the doctrine of collective security, the nations of the world could unite into a federation that could protect its member countries and smaller countries against aggression by other countries. After the First World War, this idea took shape as the League of Nations, whose purpose was to prevent another world war. The League of Nations failed, unable to prevent the Second World War. At the end of the Second World War, the United Nations was created to achieve collective security.

82. Choice (E) is the correct answer. In response to alleged attacks on U.S. naval ships that were in North Vietnam's territorial waters, Congress passed the Tonkin Gulf Resolution. The Resolution granted President Lyndon Johnson war-making powers and, in effect, represented Congressional approval of U.S. involvement in the Vietnam War.

83. Choice (A) is the correct answer. Several events during the first few decades of the republic proved that the executive and legislative branches of the government could function in their respective roles in making and carrying out foreign policy. With the Louisiana Purchase, the War of 1812, and the proclamation of the Monroe Doctrine, the United States proved itself to be a strong, independent nation in its dealings with the other nations of the world.

84. Choice (B) is the correct answer. As part of his plan to organize the finances and solve the money problems of the new nation, Secretary of the Treasury Alexander Hamilton proposed a national bank that would hold the government's money and back its currency. The bank would be regulated by the government but would be privately financed and owned by wealthy financiers. This plan would have permanently tied the government to the bank's owners.

85. Choice (A) is the correct answer. The Populist movement, which had its roots in farmers' alliances and eventually formed the People's Party, embraced several reforms that would help farmers, including government control of the railroads to lower shipping costs for farmers.

86. Choice (C) is the correct answer. In *How the Other Half Lives*, Riis documented the conditions of tenements, schools, and neighborhoods of immigrants in New York City and was instrumental in bringing about needed reforms in the congested parts of the city.

87. Choice (D) is the correct answer. Although the federal government increased its control over big business through banking reforms, lower tariffs, and stricter antitrust laws, most of the big trusts and monopolies had already been "busted" before the First World War.

88. Choice (E) is the correct answer. By the time Roosevelt, Winston Churchill, and Joseph Stalin met at Yalta in February 1945, the Soviet Union had taken over Poland.

89. Choice (D) is the correct answer. Members of the American counterculture of the 1960s, sometimes called hippies, protested against many aspects of American society, including its materialism. Many members of the counterculture believed that Americans should be more concerned with the environment, civil rights, women's rights, and world peace than with material indulgences.

90. Choice (B) is the correct answer. During the 1970s, the greatest population growth occurred in the Sunbelt, the states south of the 37th parallel. This growth was a result of population migrations from the North and Northeast as well as immigration from Latin American and Asian countries.

World History

Purpose

The Subject Test in World History measures your understanding of the development of major world cultures and your use of historical techniques, including the application and weighing of evidence and the ability to interpret and generalize. The test covers all historical fields:

- political and diplomatic
- intellectual and cultural
- social and economic

Format

This one-hour test consists of 95 multiple-choice questions. Many of the questions are global in nature, dealing with issues and trends that have significance throughout the modern world.

The chart on the following page shows you what chronological and geographical materials are covered on the test and the approximate percentages of questions covering that content.

Content

The questions test your:

- familiarity with terms commonly used in the social sciences
- understanding of cause-and-effect relationships
- knowledge of the history and geography necessary for understanding major historical developments
- grasp of concepts essential to historical analysis
- capacity to interpret artistic materials
- ability to assess quotations from speeches, documents, and other published materials
- ability to use historical knowledge in interpreting data based on maps, graphs, and charts

Chronological Material Covered	Approximate Percentage of Test
Prehistory and Civilizations to 500 Common Era (C.E.)*	25
500–1500 C.E.	20
1500–1900 C.E.	25
Post-1900 C.E.	20
Cross-chronological	10
Geographical Material Covered	
Global or Comparative	25
Europe	25
Africa	10
Southwest Asia	10
South and Southeast Asia	10
East Asia	10
Americas	10

* The SAT Subject Test in World History uses the chronological designations B.C.E. (before common era) and C.E. (common era). These labels correspond to B.C. (before Christ) and A.D. (anno Domini), which are used in some world history textbooks.

How to Prepare

You can prepare academically for the test by taking a one-year comprehensive course in world or global history at the college-preparatory level and through independent reading of materials on historic topics. Because secondary school programs differ, the SAT Subject Test in World History is not tied to any one textbook or particular course of study. Familiarize yourself with the directions in advance. The directions in this book are identical to those that appear on the test.

Score

The total score is reported on the 200-to-800 scale.

Sample Questions

All questions on the Subject Test in World History are multiple choice, requiring you to choose the best response from five choices. The following sample questions illustrate the types of questions on the test, their range of difficulty, and the abilities they measure. Questions may be presented as separate items or in sets based on quotations, maps, pictures, graphs, or tables.

Directions: Each of the questions or incomplete statements below is followed by five suggested answers or completions. Select the one that is best in each case and then fill in the corresponding circle on the answer sheet.

1. The strongest evidence that the peoples of the Paleolithic Age believed in an afterlife is found in their

   (A) weapons and tools
   (B) ceremonial human sacrifices
   (C) cave paintings
   (D) stone sculptures
   (E) burial practices

Choice (E) is the correct answer to question 1. Evidence related to Paleolithic burial practices strongly suggests that peoples of the Paleolithic Age (2.5 million to 10,000 B.C.E.) believed in an afterlife. Paleolithic people were often buried with useful items indicating preparation for an afterlife. The other choices are incorrect. Paleolithic weapons and tools (A) provide information about how these people hunted and lived, but tell us little or nothing concerning their belief in an afterlife. There is not much evidence of human sacrifice (B) by Paleolithic peoples. The few surviving cave paintings from this era (C) reveal little about religious beliefs, focusing mostly on animals. Paleolithic stone sculptures (D) may suggest some religious belief, but they do not provide strong evidence of belief in an afterlife.

2. Which of the following adults had full citizenship in Athens in the fifth century B.C.E.?

   (A) All who spoke Greek
   (B) All freeborn men and women
   (C) Only adults of noble birth
   (D) Only land-owning free men and women
   (E) All free men of Athenian parentage

Choice (E) is the correct answer to question 2. All free men of Athenian parentage possessed full citizenship in Athens in the fifth century B.C.E. The other choices are incorrect. A majority of the population, including slaves, women, and resident aliens (choices A and B), was excluded from full citizenship. However, there were no property requirements for citizenship (D), and a citizen did not have to be of noble birth (C), as long as both his parents were Athenians.

3. The Chinese concept of the Mandate of Heaven included all of the following EXCEPT:

   (A) The people will naturally rebel against a government that does not follow the "way of heaven."

   (B) A ruler has a responsibility to be benevolent toward the people.

   (C) Natural disasters are a sign of heaven's displeasure with a country's rulers.

   (D) Heaven would bless the authority of a just ruler.

   (E) A legitimate ruler must be of noble birth.

Choice (E) is the correct answer to question 3. Choices (A), (B), (C), and (D) are all consistent with the concept of the Mandate of Heaven. Rulers of the Chinese Zhou dynasty in the eleventh century B.C.E. originated the concept to justify their overthrow of the previous dynasty. The concept states that heaven would bless a king who ruled justly (D), but would pass the Mandate to someone else if the king began to misuse his power. The Mandate of Heaven claimed that because the ruler's authority is granted by heaven, he had a responsibility to be benevolent toward the people (B). If the ruler abused the Mandate and strayed from the "way of heaven," natural disasters could be expected (C), and a revolution would be acceptable (A). Because the Mandate was based solely on the ruler's fair use of his power, a legitimate ruler did not necessarily have to be of noble birth; in fact, some of the most powerful Chinese dynasties were established and ruled by people of modest birth.

4. The ancient trade route known as the Silk Road facilitated the exchange of goods between

   (A) Japan and Portugal

   (B) Japan and Korea

   (C) China and the Roman Empire

   (D) China and Japan

   (E) China and Southeast Asia

Choice (C) is the correct answer to question 4. The ancient trade route known as the Silk Road facilitated the exchange of goods between China and the Roman Empire. This 4,000-mile trade route across central Asia connected China and Europe. Caravans traveled back and forth on the Silk Road, carrying silk from China and gold, silver, and other products from the Roman Empire. The other choices are incorrect. The Silk Road originated in China, not Japan (choices A and B), and went westward into Europe, not toward Japan (D) or Southeast Asia (E).

5. Filial piety and veneration of ancestors are central to the teachings of

   (A) Buddha
   (B) Confucius
   (C) Hammurabi
   (D) Krishna
   (E) Zoroaster

Choice (B) is the correct answer to question 5. Filial piety and veneration of ancestors are central to the teachings of Confucius. Chinese philosopher Confucius (circa 551–479 B.C.E.), whose teachings became the basis of Confucianism, stressed the importance of maintaining proper relationships within society, especially within families. According to Confucius, children should respect and obey their parents and elder family members ("filial piety"), while the elder members should love and nurture the younger members. Veneration for one's ancestors, those elder members who have died, follows from this principle. The other choices are incorrect. While the teachings of Buddha (A), Hammurabi (C), Krishna (D), and Zoroaster (E) may have touched on the importance of family relationships, the elements of filial piety and veneration of ancestors were central only to the teachings of Confucius.

6. In the thirteenth and fourteenth centuries, an important economic link between Europe and Africa was the export of

   (A) cotton from East Africa to Europe
   (B) gold from West Africa to Europe
   (C) grain from Europe to Egypt
   (D) timber from Europe to West Africa
   (E) grain from Europe to East Africa

Choice (B) is the correct answer to question 6. During the thirteenth and fourteenth centuries, the main export from Africa to Europe was gold. In the thirteenth century, the Mali Empire in West Africa took control of the lucrative trans-Saharan trade of gold and salt, sending gold north across the Sahara Desert to the Mediterranean Sea and Europe, and bringing salt and other goods south of the Sahara. As the Europeans had yet to discover the riches of the Americas, most gold circulating in Europe came from Africa. The other choices are incorrect since none of them describes a major pattern of trade between Europe and Africa.

7. The emergence of which of the following is most closely identified with the practice of manorialism?

   (A) Cities
   (B) Capitalism
   (C) The three-field system
   (D) Overseas expansion
   (E) Long-distance trade

Choice (C) is the correct answer to question 7. The European medieval social and economic system of manorialism is closely linked to the three-field system. Manorialism was the system in which the European countryside was divided into manors that were each controlled by a lord. The peasants on many of these manors used the three-field system of crop rotation. In the three-field system, the land was divided into thirds: one-third for fall crops, one-third for spring crops, and one-third left fallow or unused. The crops were then rotated each year, allowing the soil's nutrients time to regenerate and increasing agricultural productivity. The other choices are incorrect. Manorialism was a system of land use in the European countryside, not cities (A). Manorialism was an economic system that preceded the rise of capitalism throughout Europe (B). Manorialism is generally associated with locally self-sufficient economies and did not do much to generate overseas expansion (D) or long-distance trade (E).

8. Which of the following can be found as part of the original design of Gothic but not of Romanesque cathedrals?

   (A) Rounded arches
   (B) Flying buttresses
   (C) Windows
   (D) Transepts
   (E) Wooden pews

Choice (B) is the correct answer to question 8. Flying buttresses are found in Gothic cathedrals, not in Romanesque cathedrals. Flying buttresses are half arches on the outside of Gothic cathedrals that help hold up the weight of the buildings' stone ceilings. These external buttresses, by supporting part of the weight of the buildings' ceilings, lessen the need for thick walls, thus they make possible the large stained glass windows typical of Gothic cathedrals. The other choices are incorrect. Rounded arches (A) are typically found in Romanesque, not Gothic cathedrals. Windows (C), transepts (D), and wooden pews (E) are found in both types of cathedrals.

9. Most Africans taken to the Americas as slaves lost their freedom when they were
   (A) taken as prisoners in raids and wars among African states
   (B) captured by roving bands of European slave raiders
   (C) forced into indentured servitude by their relatives
   (D) taken captive resisting European infiltration
   (E) captured by Asian slave traders

Choice (A) is the correct answer to question 9. Most Africans taken to the Americas as slaves originally lost their freedom when they were taken as prisoners in raids and wars among African states. The practice of enslaving prisoners of war was common in Africa before colonization by Europeans. European slave traders gave African groups an opportunity to exchange their prisoners of war for manufactured goods and firearms at European slave-trading posts on the African coast. Occasionally, raids among African nations were undertaken for the sole purpose of capturing prisoners to be sold as slaves bound for America. The other choices are incorrect. Europeans rarely infiltrated (D) or raided (B) the African continent themselves in search of slaves. Africans were not generally offered the opportunity of indentured servitude in America (C). The African slaves bound for America were acquired by European, not Asian, slave traders (E).

10. By the seventeenth century, Spain's American colonies were governed by
   (A) papal nuncios
   (B) elected assemblies
   (C) private trading companies
   (D) a hierarchy of bureaucratic officials
   (E) native leaders under Spanish supervision

Choice (D) is the correct answer to question 10. By the seventeenth century, Spain's American colonies, known collectively as New Spain, were governed by a hierarchy of bureaucratic officials. The Spanish empire in the Americas was divided into regions called viceroyalties, each of which was governed by an appointed viceroy and his staff. The other choices are incorrect. The regions were governed by appointed officials from Spain or of Spanish descent, not native leaders (E), elected assemblies (B), or private trading companies (C). Although Catholicism was strictly enforced and used as a justification for exploitation of the colonies, church ambassadors known as papal nuncios (A) did not govern the colonies.

11. Which of the following statements is characteristic of Social Darwinist thinking?
    (A) Nature is not a useful model for human social organization.
    (B) Charity and government help for the poor only encourage the unfit to survive.
    (C) Society has an obligation to support writers and artists.
    (D) All persons have a natural right to existence by virtue of their shared humanity.
    (E) Laissez-faire economic policies are ruinous in the long run.

Choice (B) is the correct answer to question 11. Social Darwinism is a social theory that applies the idea of natural selection from Charles Darwin's theory of evolution to the development of human societies. In Darwin's writings, "survival of the fittest" describes how some organisms develop mutations that make them fitter for survival than others. These organisms survive while others die out. Similarly, according to Social Darwinism, some members of society, typically the rich, possess characteristics that cause them to "naturally" succeed and survive, while others, typically the poor, do not. According to the Social Darwinists, since the poor in society are inherently unfit to survive, it is improper to provide them charity and other assistance. The other choices are incorrect. Social Darwinism claims that human societies share the same organization as nature (A). Although Social Darwinism does not necessarily imply that writers and artists are unfit for survival, it would not hold society obliged to support any of its members (C). According to Social Darwinism, nobody has a natural "right" to exist (D). The principles of laissez-faire economics, which state that government should not restrict the natural competition of businesses, are generally in line with Social Darwinism and would not be considered ruinous (E).

"THE ANGEL IN 'THE HOUSE'": OR, THE RESULT OF FEMALE SUFFRAGE

12. The intent of the 1884 cartoon above was to

(A) attack women as too politically uninformed to be granted suffrage

(B) argue that women's suffrage would lead to a female majority in Parliament

(C) appeal for women's suffrage in order to raise the moral tone of parliamentary debate

(D) suggest that a political role for women is contrary to the virtues of femininity

(E) suggest that women would make just as effective legislators as men

Choice (D) is the correct answer to question 12. This 1884 cartoon is intended to suggest that a political role for women is contrary to the virtues of femininity. By the late ninteenth century, social movements in Great Britain calling for the right to vote and increased political involvement of women were becoming stronger. These movements, however, were met with opposition from those who felt women had specific abilities or virtues that were contrary to the tasks of politics. The caption of the cartoon is a play on words of the title of a popular mid-nineteenth century poem, "The Angel in the House," by Coventry Patmore, which argued that women had a moral role to play but one that should be confined to the domestic sphere. The cartoon suggests that women would be out of place in the political activity of the "House," or Parliament. The other choices are incorrect. The cartoon does not address the issue of women's knowledge of politics (A). Nothing in the cartoon suggests that women might achieve a political majority (B). The cartoon does not suggest that women would raise the moral tone of Parliament (C). The disarray of the domestic objects surrounding the woman in the cartoon does not suggest effectiveness (E).

13. "Imperialism is capitalism in that stage of development in which the dominance of monopolies and finance capital has established itself; in which the export of capital has acquired pronounced importance; in which the division of the world among the international trusts has begun; in which the division of all territories of the globe among the great capitalist powers has been completed."

    The definition of imperialism above was written by

    (A) Max Weber
    (B) Mary Wollstonecraft
    (C) Benito Mussolini
    (D) Arnold Toynbee
    (E) V. I. Lenin

Choice (E) is the correct answer to question 13. This definition of imperialism was written by V. I. Lenin and published in his 1917 pamphlet entitled "Imperialism, the Highest Stage of Capitalism." Lenin (1870–1924) helped lead the Russian Communist Revolution and eventually became the first premier of the Soviet Union. He published this pamphlet as part of his effort to educate revolutionaries and organize the Russian workers. By 1917, industrialization was increasingly allowing a few large companies to control the majority of production. Lenin thought that this concentration of power in capitalist economies, in which a few wealthy company owners would, in effect, control the lives of millions of workers, was a form of imperialism and must be resisted. The other choices are incorrect; none of the other people mentioned addressed capitalism and imperialism in this way.

14. Which of the following was an important component of India's foreign policy under Indira Gandhi?

    (A) The maintenance of a formal alliance with Great Britain
    (B) The formation of a military alliance with China
    (C) Support for United States policy in Southeast Asia
    (D) The maintenance of friendly relations with the Soviet Union
    (E) Advocacy of an armed invasion of Afghanistan

Choice (D) is the correct answer to question 14. Maintaining friendly relations with the Soviet Union was an important component of India's foreign policy under Indira Gandhi, who served as prime minister from 1966 to 1977 and from 1980 to 1984. Under Gandhi's leadership, India signed the Treaty of Peace, Friendship, and Cooperation with the Soviet Union in 1971. The support from the Soviet Union helped India defeat Pakistan in December 1971, and helped deter aggressive behavior by China towards India. The other choices are incorrect. Under Indira Gandhi, India was not formally aligned with Great Britain (A) or militarily aligned with China (B). The partnership with the Soviets clearly signaled a worsening of relations with the United States (C). Although the Soviet Union invaded Afghanistan during this time, India was not officially involved (E).

15. Which of the following led to one of the major crises of the Cold War era?

(A) The sinking of the *Lusitania*
(B) The Italian invasion of Ethiopia
(C) Gandhi's civil disobedience campaign
(D) The sentencing of Nelson Mandela to life imprisonment
(E) The installation of missiles with nuclear warheads in Cuba

Choice (E) is the correct answer to question 15. The installation of Russian nuclear missiles in Cuba led to one of the major crises of the Cold War. The Cold War refers to the geopolitical struggle between the United States and the Soviet Union that started at the end of World War II and ended with the collapse of the Soviet Union in 1991. The closest the United States and the Soviet Union came to actual war was in 1962, when the Soviet Union installed nuclear missiles in Cuba capable of hitting Washington, D.C., within twenty minutes from launch. President John F. Kennedy learned about the missile sites and announced a naval "quarantine" around Cuba to block the Soviets from reaching Cuba. Eventually the Soviet Union agreed to remove the missiles and the United States ended the quarantine and removed nuclear missiles they had installed in Turkey. The other choices are incorrect. The sinking of the *Lusitania* (A), the Italian invasion of Ethiopia (B), and Gandhi's civil disobedience campaign in India (C), all occurred before the Cold War. The sentencing of South African activist Nelson Mandela to life imprisonment (D) did not create a major crisis during the Cold War.

World History – Practice Test 1

Practice Helps

The test that follows is an actual, previously administered SAT Subject Test in World History. To get an idea of what it's like to take this test, practice under conditions that are much like those of an actual test administration.

- Set aside an hour when you can take the test uninterrupted.
- Sit at a desk or table with no other books or papers. Dictionaries, other books, or notes are not allowed in the test room.
- Tear out an answer sheet from the back of this book and fill it in just as you would on the day of the test. One answer sheet can be used for up to three Subject Tests.
- Read the instructions that precede the practice test. During the actual administration, you will be asked to read them before answering test questions.
- Use a clock or kitchen timer to time yourself.
- After you finish the practice test, read the sections "How to Score the SAT Subject Test in World History" and "How Did You Do on the Subject Test in World History?"
- The appearance of the answer sheet in this book may differ from the answer sheet you see on test day.

WORLD HISTORY TEST

Directions: Each of the questions or incomplete statements below is followed by five suggested answers or completions. Select the one that is best in each case and then fill in the corresponding circle on the answer sheet.

Note: The World History Test uses the chronological designations B.C.E. (before common era) and C.E. (common era). These labels correspond to B.C. (before Christ) and A.D. (anno Domini), which are used in some world history textbooks.

1. Which of the following was true of both Greece and China in the period around 500 B.C.E.?

   (A) Both fostered vibrant philosophical schools that debated the human condition.
   (B) Both were threatened by more powerful neighboring civilizations.
   (C) Both experienced economic revolutions brought on by the discovery of iron.
   (D) Both underwent social revolutions that led to the seclusion of women.
   (E) Both suffered from overpopulation that led to class warfare and massive emigration.

. Which of the following is true of the epic poems the *Mahabharata*, the *Iliad*, and the *Tales of the Heike* ?

) All three were influenced by Chinese literary forms.
   All three stress the exploits of a warrior elite.
   ll three were written down at first and later ransmitted orally.
   three stress humanity's independence n the influence of the gods.
   ians have conclusively identified the s of the three works.

3. Which of the following statements about the effects of Muhammad's teaching is true?

   (A) Islam initially attracted many followers, but gradually became less popular.
   (B) Muhammad believed that social differences needed to be preserved, which encouraged divisions in society.
   (C) Islam affected every aspect of life and encouraged unity among converts with widely diverse backgrounds.
   (D) Muhammad believed that wealth should be renounced; thus Islam did not attempt to expand.
   (E) Muslims set up a complex priesthood that mediated the contact between Allah and individual believers.

4. The military campaigns of the Huns under Attila contributed to which of the following?

   (A) The introduction of the bubonic plague to Asia
   (B) The fall of the western Roman Empire
   (C) The division of Charlemagne's empire
   (D) The introduction of horse domestication into western Europe
   (E) The defeat of the Muslims in Spain

WORLD HISTORY TEST

The top portion of the page of the answer sheet that you will use to take the World History Test must be filled in exactly as illustration below. When your supervisor tells you to fill in the circle next to the name of the test you are about to take, mark your answer sheet as shown.

○ Literature	○ Mathematics Level 1	○ German	○ Chinese Listening	○ Japanese Listening
○ Biology E	○ Mathematics Level 2	○ Italian	○ French Listening	○ Korean Listening
○ Biology M	○ U.S. History	○ Latin	○ German Listening	○ Spanish Listening
○ Chemistry	● World History	○ Modern Hebrew		
○ Physics	○ French	○ Spanish	Background Questions: ① ② ③ ④ ⑤ ⑥ ⑦ ⑧ ⑨	

After filling in the circle next to the name of the test you are taking, locate the Background Questions box on your answer sheet (as shown above). This is where you will answer the following Background Questions on your answer sheet.

BACKGROUND QUESTIONS

Please answer the two questions below by filling in the appropriate circle in the Background Questi… on your answer sheet. <u>The information you provide is for statistical purposes only and will not af… test score.</u>

<u>Question I</u>

How many semesters of world history, world cultures, or European hist… grade 9 to the present? (If you are taking a course this semester, cour… only <u>one</u> circle of circles 1- 4.

- One semester or less
- Two semesters
- Three semesters
- Four or more semesters

<u>Question II</u>

For the courses in world history, world… following geographical areas did yo…

- Africa
- Asia
- Europe
- Latin Ame…
- Middle…

When the supervisor … on the answer sheet and … answers.

WORLD HISTORY TEST

The top portion of the page of the answer sheet that you will use to take the World History Test must be filled in exactly as illustration below. When your supervisor tells you to fill in the circle next to the name of the test you are about to take, mark your answer sheet as shown.

○ Literature	○ Mathematics Level 1	○ German	○ Chinese Listening	○ Japanese Listening
○ Biology E	○ Mathematics Level 2	○ Italian	○ French Listening	○ Korean Listening
○ Biology M	○ U.S. History	○ Latin	○ German Listening	○ Spanish Listening
○ Chemistry	● World History	○ Modern Hebrew		
○ Physics	○ French	○ Spanish	Background Questions: ①②③④⑤⑥⑦⑧⑨	

After filling in the circle next to the name of the test you are taking, locate the Background Questions box on your answer sheet (as shown above). This is where you will answer the following Background Questions on your answer sheet.

BACKGROUND QUESTIONS

Please answer the two questions below by filling in the appropriate circle in the Background Questions box on your answer sheet. The information you provide is for statistical purposes only and will not affect your test score.

Question I

How many semesters of world history, world cultures, or European history have you taken from grade 9 to the present? (If you are taking a course this semester, count it as a full semester.) Fill in only one circle of circles 1- 4.

- One semester or less —Fill in circle 1.
- Two semesters —Fill in circle 2.
- Three semesters —Fill in circle 3.
- Four or more semesters —Fill in circle 4.

Question II

For the courses in world history, world cultures, or European history you have taken, which of the following geographical areas did you study? Fill in all of the circles that apply.

- Africa —Fill in circle 5.
- Asia —Fill in circle 6.
- Europe —Fill in circle 7.
- Latin America —Fill in circle 8.
- Middle East —Fill in circle 9.

When the supervisor gives the signal, turn the page and begin the World History Test. There are 100 numbered circles on the answer sheet and 95 questions in the World History Test. Therefore, use only circles 1 to 95 for recording your answers.

WORLD HISTORY TEST

Directions: Each of the questions or incomplete statements below is followed by five suggested answers or completions. Select the one that is best in each case and then fill in the corresponding circle on the answer sheet.

Note: The World History Test uses the chronological designations B.C.E. (before common era) and C.E. (common era). These labels correspond to B.C. (before Christ) and A.D. (anno Domini), which are used in some world history textbooks.

1. Which of the following was true of both Greece and China in the period around 500 B.C.E.?

   (A) Both fostered vibrant philosophical schools that debated the human condition.
   (B) Both were threatened by more powerful neighboring civilizations.
   (C) Both experienced economic revolutions brought on by the discovery of iron.
   (D) Both underwent social revolutions that led to the seclusion of women.
   (E) Both suffered from overpopulation that led to class warfare and massive emigration.

2. Which of the following is true of the epic poems the *Mahabharata*, the *Iliad*, and the *Tales of the Heike* ?

   (A) All three were influenced by Chinese literary forms.
   (B) All three stress the exploits of a warrior elite.
   (C) All three were written down at first and later transmitted orally.
   (D) All three stress humanity's independence from the influence of the gods.
   (E) Historians have conclusively identified the authors of the three works.

3. Which of the following statements about the effects of Muhammad's teaching is true?

   (A) Islam initially attracted many followers, but gradually became less popular.
   (B) Muhammad believed that social differences needed to be preserved, which encouraged divisions in society.
   (C) Islam affected every aspect of life and encouraged unity among converts with widely diverse backgrounds.
   (D) Muhammad believed that wealth should be renounced; thus Islam did not attempt to expand.
   (E) Muslims set up a complex priesthood that mediated the contact between Allah and individual believers.

4. The military campaigns of the Huns under Attila contributed to which of the following?

   (A) The introduction of the bubonic plague to Asia
   (B) The fall of the western Roman Empire
   (C) The division of Charlemagne's empire
   (D) The introduction of horse domestication into western Europe
   (E) The defeat of the Muslims in Spain

GO ON TO THE NEXT PAGE

5. After the fall of the Han dynasty, the nomadic peoples who invaded China did which of the following?

   (A) They attempted to restore the Han dynasty to power.
   (B) They tried unsuccessfully to convert the Chinese to Islam.
   (C) They outlawed the use of the Chinese language by governing officials.
   (D) They launched an invasion of Japan.
   (E) They adopted Chinese culture and customs.

6. Mahavira and Buddha were similar in that both

   (A) were successful military leaders who conquered most of India
   (B) resisted the spread of Islam in India
   (C) were theorists who pioneered new mathematical concepts
   (D) led religious movements that challenged the social order of Hinduism
   (E) were martyred for their beliefs

7. "Warfare in nineteenth-century southern Africa was revolutionized with the development of the short, stabbing spear, the body shield, and a tactical formation known as the ox's horns."

   The above describes innovations developed by the

   (A) Zulu
   (B) Xhosa
   (C) Sotho
   (D) Shona
   (E) Ibo

8. All of the following are central to the practice of Islam EXCEPT

   (A) Observation of Ramadan through fasting
   (B) Monotheism
   (C) Prayer five times a day facing Mecca
   (D) Making a pilgrimage to Mecca at least once
   (E) Realistic representations of people in art

9. Which of the following is a pair of neighboring countries both of which had acquired the capability of exploding nuclear weapons by the late 1990's?

   (A) Argentina and Chile
   (B) Mexico and the United States
   (C) The Czech Republic and Germany
   (D) India and Pakistan
   (E) North Korea and South Korea

10. Which of the following best describes the economic strategy of the Soviet Union under Stalin?

    (A) Development of a mixed economy
    (B) Creation of a landowning peasant class
    (C) Production for export
    (D) Centralized economic planning
    (E) Government encouragement of free enterprise

11. Historiography is

    (A) a single, accurate account of events in past time
    (B) the study of how historical accounts are produced
    (C) a chronological chart of historical events
    (D) a historical account based only on written records
    (E) the official record of past events, usually produced by a government

12. Which of the following describes the primary role of the scholar-gentry in imperial China?

    (A) The mainstay of the imperial bureaucracy
    (B) The development of political revolution
    (C) The education of China's peasantry
    (D) The dissemination of European culture in China
    (E) The advancement of engineering and agricultural science

GO ON TO THE NEXT PAGE

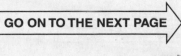

13. The Japanese victory in the Russo-Japanese War demonstrated to other non-Western peoples that

    (A) successful modernization was not a strictly Western phenomenon
    (B) countries that held traditional values could not defeat a European power
    (C) passive resistance could be effectively employed in the defeat of a European power
    (D) the distance between Asia and Europe would make Asian industrialization difficult
    (E) further expansion by Russia in Asia was inevitable

14. The defeat of the Umayyads by the Abbasids in 750 C.E. led to the relocation of the caliphate and of the primary center of Islamic culture from

    (A) Mecca to Medina
    (B) Jerusalem to Cairo
    (C) Damascus to Baghdad
    (D) Constantinople to Beirut
    (E) Córdoba to Alexandria

15. Which of the following is an example of an ancient megalithic structure?

    (A) Stonehenge
    (B) The Coliseum
    (C) Angkor Wat
    (D) The Acropolis
    (E) Great Zimbabwe

16. The Aztec viewed the Toltec as

    (A) barbarians who lacked culture
    (B) slaves, fit only for conquest
    (C) the givers of civilization
    (D) heretics who practiced a forbidden religion
    (E) the greatest rivals to the Aztec dominance of the valley of Mexico

17. The terms Indo-European and Bantu were created to describe

    (A) biological races
    (B) language groups
    (C) religious movements
    (D) artistic styles
    (E) ancient empires

18. According to one theory of state formation, large states first developed in river valleys because

    (A) coordination of large-scale irrigation projects created the need for more complex organizations
    (B) the healthier climates of river valleys allowed large populations to develop there
    (C) river valleys provided the best natural defensive barriers for growing states
    (D) river valleys were the only sources of drinking water large enough to support concentrated populations
    (E) river valleys were the best sources of metal ores for weapons and tools

19. In England in the late nineteenth century it was socially acceptable for young working-class women to take jobs as domestic servants because

    (A) many of their employers allowed them to do volunteer work among the urban poor on evenings and weekends
    (B) this work was believed to contribute to habits of hard work, cleanliness, and obedience, which were seen as good preparation for marriage
    (C) such jobs provided opportunities for them to meet and marry men from higher social classes
    (D) the training they received in household management provided them with skills needed for later careers in business
    (E) residence in middle- or upper-class homes contributed to their political education

20. In Chinese history, the phrase "Mandate of Heaven" refers to the

    (A) divine selection of China as the holiest place in the world
    (B) obligation of each individual to obey religious teachings
    (C) divine favor enjoyed by wise and benevolent rulers
    (D) Chinese version of the Ten Commandments
    (E) most important of the Confucian writings

GO ON TO THE NEXT PAGE

21. Which of the following is the commonly accepted meaning of the term *Homo sapiens* ?

(A) The southern apes
(B) The upright-walking humans
(C) The consciously thinking humans
(D) The animal with a large brain
(E) The missing link

22. In their original form, all of the following major religions focused on humanity's relationship to a god or gods EXCEPT

(A) Buddhism
(B) Christianity
(C) Hinduism
(D) Islam
(E) Judaism

23. Social Darwinism is most closely associated with the idea that

(A) government should provide support for disadvantaged members of society
(B) competition is natural to society
(C) revolution is inevitable
(D) imperialistic expansion will increase economic pressures on citizens
(E) technological development will decrease the gap between rich and poor

24. Which of the following led Great Britain and France to declare war on Germany in 1939 ?

(A) Hitler established a fascist dictatorship in Germany.
(B) Germany occupied France.
(C) Germany annexed Austria.
(D) Germany invaded Poland.
(E) Germany passed anti-Semitic laws.

25. The pyramids in ancient Egypt were built to function primarily as

(A) temples
(B) tombs
(C) watchtowers
(D) astronomical observatories
(E) sundials

26. In the Hindu caste system, members of the Brahman caste originally served as

(A) priests
(B) farmers
(C) warriors
(D) merchants
(E) herders

27. Which of the following is attributed to Alexander the Great?

(A) Three centuries of political stability in the Middle East
(B) The establishment of the basic political forms of the Roman Empire
(C) The concept of kingship limited by elected representatives
(D) The spread of Greek cultural forms into western Asia
(E) The extension of property and inheritance rights to women

28. Prior to the Roman conquests of Gaul, Spain, and Britain, these areas were inhabited primarily by

(A) Celts
(B) Goths
(C) Greeks
(D) Mongols
(E) Scythians

29. Which of the following major ancient civilizations did NOT originate along a river valley?

(A) Chinese
(B) Indian
(C) Egyptian
(D) Mesopotamian
(E) Greek

GO ON TO THE NEXT PAGE

30. Which of the following changes best characterizes the commercial revolution that accelerated during the 1400's and continued throughout the Age of Exploration?

(A) The growth of capitalism as an economic system
(B) The shift of the center of trading from the Mediterranean Sea to the Indian Ocean
(C) The development and application of communism
(D) The decline in the production of consumer goods
(E) The loss of overseas empires by western European nations

31. The words "alchemy," "algebra," "assassin," "sugar," "zenith," and "zero" entered the English language as a result of the influence on Europe of which of the following cultures?

(A) Arabic
(B) Turkish
(C) Indian
(D) Aramaic
(E) Hebrew

32. The principal development during the Neolithic Age was the

(A) disappearance of the Neanderthals
(B) invention of writing
(C) beginning of metallurgy
(D) domestication of animals and plants
(E) appearance of craft specialization

33. Cultivation of which of the following crops most drastically changed the geographical distribution of human populations?

(A) Sugar
(B) Opium
(C) Tobacco
(D) Tea
(E) Cotton

34. Which of the following crops originated in Mesoamerica and spread to South America and the present-day United States in the pre-Columbian period?

(A) Maize
(B) Oats
(C) Peanuts
(D) Potatoes
(E) Wheat

35. The African kingdoms of Mali and Ghana acquired much of their wealth from

(A) trade across the Sahara
(B) trade with Portuguese ships along the Atlantic coast
(C) trade across the Atlantic with the Maya and Aztec
(D) production of food for export to Europe
(E) tribute from the Islamic states north of the Sahara

GO ON TO THE NEXT PAGE

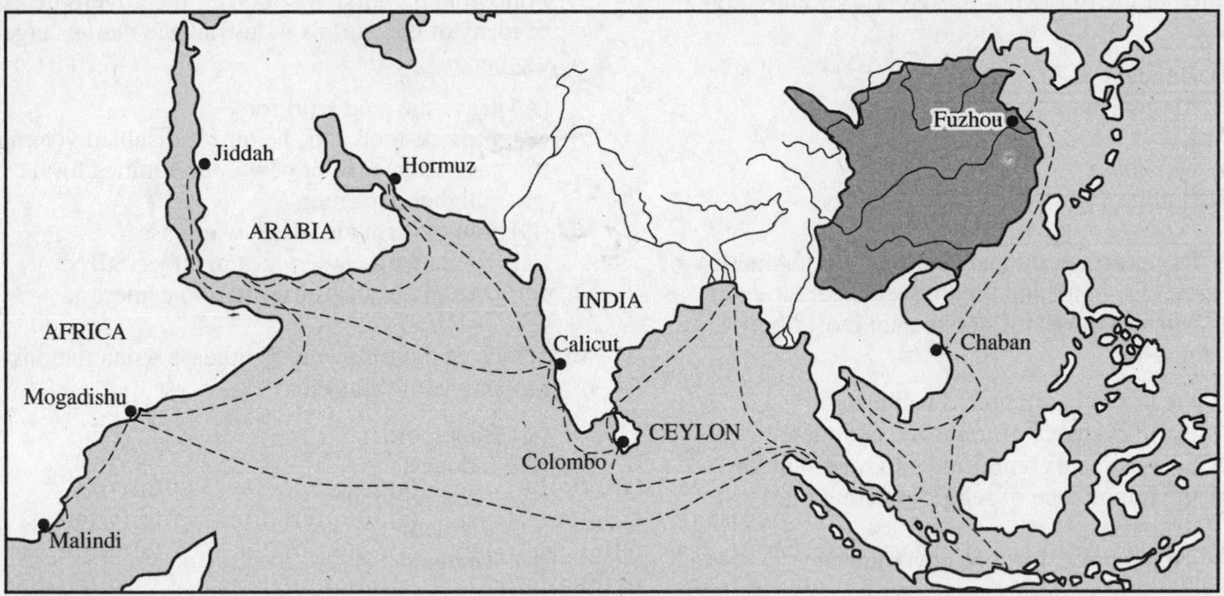

36. The map above shows the route of

(A) Marco Polo on his travels to the court of Kublai Khan
(B) Ibn Battutah on his travels through Dar al-Islam
(C) Zheng He in his seafaring voyages from China
(D) the Arab slave traders
(E) the Buddhist pilgrim Xuanzang

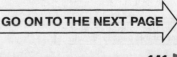

GO ON TO THE NEXT PAGE

37. Which of the following was NOT a Swahili city-state?

    (A) Zimbabwe
    (B) Mogadishu
    (C) Kilwa
    (D) Mombasa
    (E) Sofala

38. The large earthen mounds built in North America between the tenth and the thirteenth centuries C.E., such as those at Cahokia, are most likely evidence of

    (A) the use of communal dwellings
    (B) the importance of trade and commerce
    (C) a large-scale commitment to road-building
    (D) the importance of religious ceremonies and rituals
    (E) a democratic form of government

39. Following the First World War, the governments of many of the world's industrialized nations urged women to

    (A) leave the paid workforce
    (B) provide food and shelter for disabled veterans
    (C) take advantage of new opportunities for higher education
    (D) join the army to offset war losses
    (E) volunteer their services in understaffed hospitals and rehabilitation centers

40. Which of the following Southeast Asian nations has an Islamic majority?

    (A) Singapore
    (B) Indonesia
    (C) The Philippines
    (D) Vietnam
    (E) Thailand

GO ON TO THE NEXT PAGE

EURASIA, 1300 C.E.

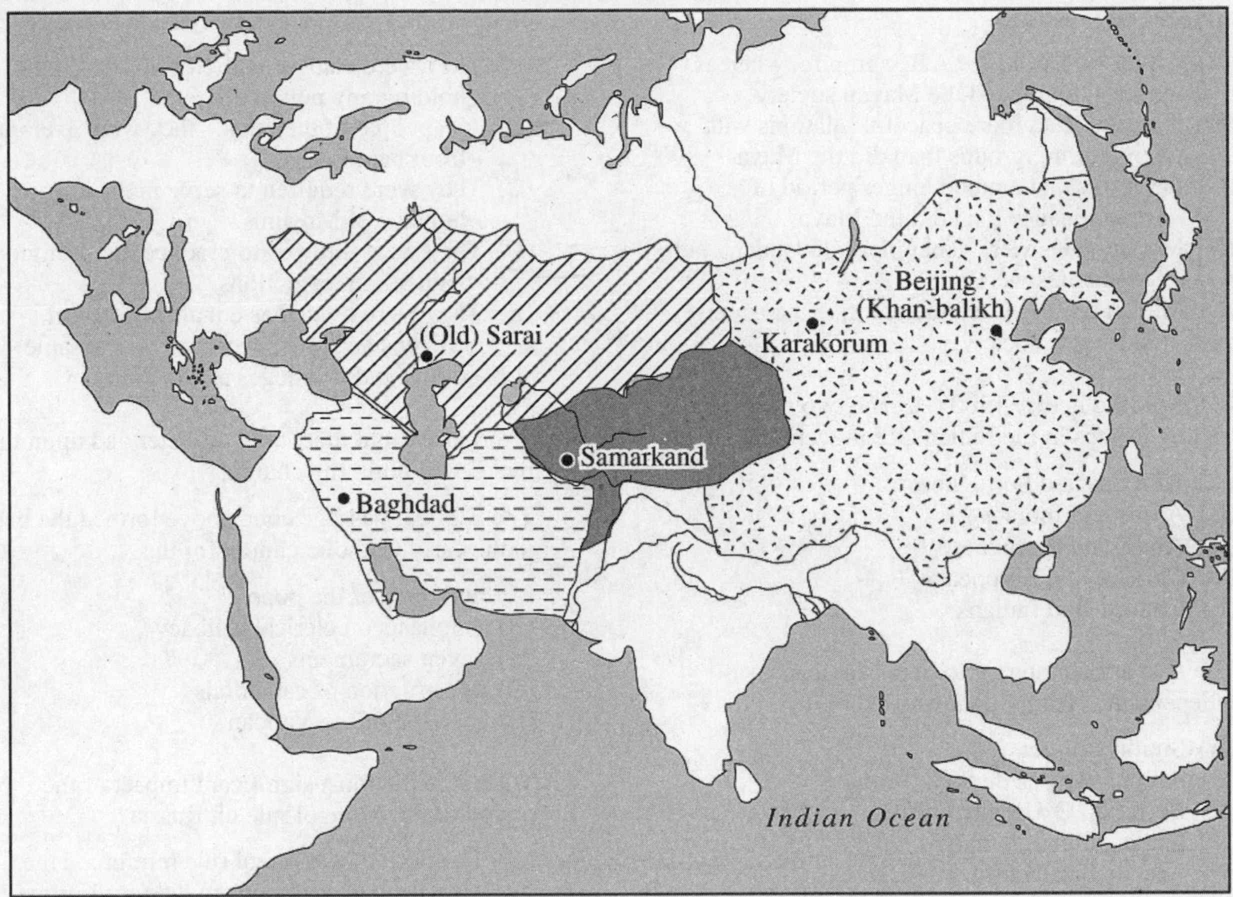

41. The four differently shaded land regions on the map above were collectively known as the

(A) Quadruple Alliance
(B) Hellenistic Kingdoms
(C) Mongol Khanates
(D) Mamluk Sultanates
(E) Tetrarchy

GO ON TO THE NEXT PAGE

42. Mayan civilization differed from Aztec civilization in that
    (A) nobles governed the Aztec empire, whereas priests dominated the Mayan society
    (B) the Aztec had more peaceful relations with neighboring groups than did the Maya
    (C) the Aztec had a much longer period of predominance than did the Maya
    (D) Mayan cities were generally independent, but Aztec cities were not
    (E) Mayan society was much more expansionist than Aztec society

43. In the period before 1500 C.E., the two primary trading groups in the Indian Ocean were the
    (A) Africans and Portuguese
    (B) Arabs and Indians
    (C) Arabs and Portuguese
    (D) Chinese and Europeans
    (E) Chinese and Indians

44. The first armed attempt to gain Mexican independence from Spain was led by
    (A) Simón Bolívar
    (B) Antonio López de Santa Anna
    (C) Bernardo O'Higgins
    (D) Father Miguel Hidalgo
    (E) José de San Martín

45. The feudal periods in Japan and western Europe were similar in that both
    (A) coincided with a period of growth in the money economy
    (B) were characterized by frequent warfare
    (C) saw the development of strong monarchies
    (D) were marked by greater freedom for women than had existed previously
    (E) were dominated by religious strife

46. Which of the following cities had the largest population in 1000 C.E.?
    (A) Constantinople
    (B) London
    (C) Paris
    (D) Rome
    (E) Toledo

47. Which of the following is true of the legal status of Jews and Christians in early Islamic society?
    (A) They were categorically forbidden from holding any public office.
    (B) As "people of the book," they were exempt from taxation.
    (C) They were required to serve in the army in place of Muslims.
    (D) They were allowed to practice their religions with some restrictions.
    (E) They were treated as equals of Muslim citizens and were accorded all the same rights and privileges as Muslims.

48. "And I say unto thee, thou art Peter and upon this rock I will build my church."

    The Biblical passage cited above formed the basis in the early Catholic church for the
    (A) authority of the pope
    (B) emphasis on clerical celibacy
    (C) seven sacraments
    (D) construction of cathedrals
    (E) location of the Vatican

49. What was the most significant impact of the period of the Mongol rule on Russia?
    (A) The period of Mongol rule reinforced the isolation of Russia from western Europe.
    (B) The Mongols aided the Russians in gaining political dominance over the peoples of the Central Asian steppes.
    (C) The period of Mongol rule introduced many Muslims into the region of Russia.
    (D) The Mongol domination resulted in the destruction of Eastern Orthodoxy and the rise of Nestorian Christianity.
    (E) Russians' admiration of Mongol culture led them to abandon their Byzantine roots.

GO ON TO THE NEXT PAGE

50. Which of the following was an important characteristic of the Inca road system?

(A) It was well equipped for even the heaviest wheeled wagons.
(B) It was kept up by privately owned commercial companies.
(C) It required frequent repair because of the high tides and salt water of the Pacific.
(D) It facilitated transportation among the towns of the high Andes mountains.
(E) It linked independent city-states.

51. As a result of the defeats of China in the first Anglo-Chinese war (1839-1842) and in later conflicts with Westerners, the Chinese were forced to do all of the following EXCEPT

(A) allow Western missionaries to seek converts in China
(B) cede Hong Kong territory to the British
(C) open numerous port cities to foreign traders
(D) grant Westerners in China the privilege of extraterritoriality
(E) ban the import of opium into China

52. In 750 C.E., a major political difference between China and Europe was that, unlike Europe, China

(A) was a unified empire
(B) was a theocracy
(C) was controlled by rulers who came from outside its borders
(D) was under threat of invasion from all sides
(E) had a republican form of government

53. "When the personal life is cultivated, the family will be regulated; when the family is regulated, the state will be in order; and when the state is in order, there will be peace throughout the world."

The quotation above reflects a key tenet of which of the following teachings?

(A) Taoism
(B) Zen Buddhism
(C) Mahayana Buddhism
(D) Shinto
(E) Confucianism

54. Early Roman religious ritual was heavily influenced by the religious practices of the

(A) Scythians
(B) Gauls
(C) Etruscans
(D) Carthaginians
(E) Druids

55. After amassing the largest land empire ever known, most of the Mongols and Turks who invaded central and south Asia converted to

(A) Confucianism
(B) Christianity
(C) Buddhism
(D) Judaism
(E) Islam

56. In the seventeenth century, European maritime trade was dominated by the

(A) English
(B) Dutch
(C) French
(D) Swedes
(E) Spanish

57. The failure of Europe's potato crop in the late 1840's spurred mass emigration from

(A) Sweden
(B) Spain
(C) Ireland
(D) Italy
(E) Russia

58. Which of the following became important New World contributions to the world's food crops?

(A) Wheat and barley
(B) Rice and sugarcane
(C) Oats and millet
(D) Corn and potatoes
(E) Bananas and melons

GO ON TO THE NEXT PAGE

59. Alexander II emancipated the serfs and introduced government reforms following Russia's defeat in the
    (A) Balkan Wars
    (B) Crimean War
    (C) First World War
    (D) Russo-Turkish Wars
    (E) Russo-Japanese War

60. After independence, India pursued a foreign policy that led to which of the following?
    (A) Its membership in the Soviet-backed Warsaw Pact
    (B) Its membership in the Southeast Asia Treaty Organization
    (C) Its signing of a mutual defense pact with the People's Republic of China
    (D) Its emergence as a leader of the Nonaligned Movement
    (E) Its avoidance of armed conflict with its neighbors

61. Which of the following best characterizes the classical economic theory of Adam Smith?
    (A) The demands of consumers are met most cheaply by competition among individual producers.
    (B) Since land is the source of value, the whole economy will benefit if small holdings are consolidated into large estates.
    (C) An increase in wages will increase the demand for manufactured goods, making the economy as a whole grow.
    (D) Since the interests of businessmen and workers are necessarily in conflict, the interests of one can thrive only at the expense of the other.
    (E) To encourage the growth of infant national industries, government should protect them from unfair foreign competition by imposing tariffs.

62. Which of the following countries are members of the Organization of Petroleum Exporting Countries (OPEC) ?
    (A) Argentina, Mexico, and Turkey
    (B) China, Egypt, and the United States
    (C) Great Britain, Canada, and Morocco
    (D) The Soviet Union, Syria, and Kenya
    (E) Venezuela, Nigeria, and Iraq

63. The navigator James Cook was most famous for
    (A) being the first to sail around the world
    (B) charting a northwest passage
    (C) exploring the Antarctic continent
    (D) scientific observation on Caribbean islands
    (E) charting the seas around Australia and New Zealand

64. In closing Japan to Europeans, the Tokugawa shogunate was motivated primarily by a desire to limit
    (A) the influence of Westerners on Japanese government and society
    (B) a large influx of European immigrants
    (C) widespread intermarriage between Japanese and Europeans
    (D) the despoiling of Japan's pristine natural environment by Europeans
    (E) the spread of industrialization to Japan

65. Which of the following was a major consequence of the opening of large silver mines in Spanish colonies in the Americas during the 1500's?
    (A) The production of goods in Spain for export to its colonies in America was greatly stimulated.
    (B) The increased wealth circulating in Spain's colonies fueled a resurgence of Native American culture.
    (C) The European economy experienced an extended period of price inflation.
    (D) The Spanish colonies where the mines were located were successful in declaring their independence from Spain.
    (E) Other European powers succeeded in capturing the mines from Spain.

GO ON TO THE NEXT PAGE

66. Which of the following societies was the LEAST dependent on livestock?

(A) Aztec society
(B) Chinese society
(C) Persian society
(D) Tartar society
(E) Roman society

67. Which of the following was called "the Sick Man of Europe" in the nineteenth century?

(A) Italy
(B) Spain
(C) The Netherlands
(D) The Ottoman Empire
(E) Russia

68. The eighteenth-century philosophy of Deism was strongly denounced by

(A) Voltaire and his followers
(B) the Roman Catholic church
(C) essayists in Diderot's *Encyclopédie*
(D) Locke and his followers
(E) Frederick the Great of Prussia

69. Which of the following was one of the major effects of the spread of gunpowder technology in Europe in the 1400's and 1500's C.E.?

(A) The superior firepower of European armies led to the reconquest of most lands that had been lost to the Ottoman Turks.
(B) The widespread use of guns in hunting led to a virtual extermination of game animals and game birds in Europe.
(C) The high cost of equipping armies with guns led to a strengthening of some centralized monarchies at the expense of feudal lords.
(D) Fear of the new technology led to religious revivals in many areas of Europe.
(E) Many European countries sought to avoid conflicts with each other because gunpowder made wars more destructive.

70. Which of the following factors contributed to the success of independence movements in Latin America during the early 1800's?

(A) Military and economic aid from the United States
(B) An increase in the production of precious metals from Latin American mines
(C) The establishment of universities throughout Latin America
(D) The drain on Spain's resources caused by the Napoleonic Wars
(E) Intervention by professional revolutionaries from France

71. In the sixteenth and seventeenth centuries, the primary interest of the European powers in the East Indies was to

(A) buy rice and other food grains
(B) obtain wood for shipbuilding
(C) obtain spices for trading
(D) seek markets for exports
(E) exploit silver mines in the area

72. The most characteristic feature of Enlightenment thought was

(A) opposition to slavery
(B) antimaterialism
(C) opposition to religious belief
(D) an emphasis on reason
(E) a belief in sexual equality

73. Mazzini, Cavour, and Garibaldi are most often associated with

(A) parliamentary democracy in Italy
(B) Italian unification
(C) the rebuilding of Rome
(D) Italian imperialism in Ethiopia
(E) Italian industrialization

GO ON TO THE NEXT PAGE

74. When Siddhartha Gautama (the Buddha) embarked on his spiritual quest in the sixth century B.C.E., his primary concern was

(A) whether there is one God or many
(B) whether there is life after death
(C) why humans suffer
(D) how to convert nonbelievers
(E) the relationship between religion and the state

75. Which of the following best explains ancient Egypt's ability to support a large population?

(A) Its strategic location on the Mediterranean Sea
(B) The approval its religious leaders gave to the concept of large families
(C) The yearly flooding of the Nile River
(D) The early introduction of technology from Mesopotamia
(E) The use of the three-field crop rotation system

76. Which of the following best characterizes demographic change in eighteenth century England?

(A) Destruction of the nuclear family during the Industrial Revolution caused the population to decline.
(B) Unhealthy conditions in crowded cities caused the population to decline.
(C) Pressures of the enclosure movement caused the population to decline.
(D) Dramatically rising birth rates caused the population to increase.
(E) Falling death rates caused the population to increase.

GO ON TO THE NEXT PAGE

77. The cartoon above shows President Gamal Abdel Nasser (1956-1970) encouraging Egyptians to see the advantages of

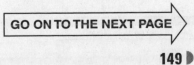

(A) maintaining equality in the workplace
(B) curbing population growth
(C) reducing consumption
(D) increasing savings
(E) legalizing unions

78. Of the following Southeast Asian countries, which is NOT matched with the colonial power that dominated it during the colonial period?

(A) Vietnam	France
(B) Burma	Germany
(C) Indonesia	the Netherlands
(D) Malaya	Great Britain
(E) The Philippines	the United States

79. The Boxer Rebellion was a revolt of

(A) Indian soldiers against British domination
(B) Vietnamese against French domination
(C) Arabs against the Ottoman Empire
(D) Chinese against Western imperialism
(E) Koreans against Japanese rule

Mansell Collection

80. The picture above, which depicts the symbolic crowning of a twelfth-century king of Sicily by Christ, reveals the cultural influence of

(A) Russia
(B) Scandinavia
(C) Spain
(D) Islam
(E) Byzantium

GO ON TO THE NEXT PAGE

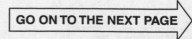

81. The political and religious center at Great Zimbabwe, which reached its height in the fifteenth century, was characterized by all of the following EXCEPT

(A) long-distance trading
(B) gold mining
(C) significant population expansion
(D) a written epic tradition
(E) copper and bronze ornament making

82. Which of the following art forms originated in the United States?

(A) Impressionism
(B) Surrealist poetry
(C) Social realism
(D) Jazz
(E) Atonal music

83. The Provisional Government failed to keep the support of the Russian people in 1917 because it

(A) executed the entire royal family
(B) collectivized agriculture and industry
(C) allowed Nicholas II to rule as a constitutional monarch
(D) suffered a humiliating defeat by the Japanese
(E) continued Russia's participation in the First World War

84. Which of the following best describes the Indian National Congress?

(A) The first national political organization in India to challenge British rule
(B) The first all-Indian legislative body formed after independence in 1947
(C) An organization formed by Hindus that primarily preached tolerance of Indian Muslims
(D) An organization formed by Hindus and Muslims that sought social reform within India
(E) A conference of Muslim religious leaders that convened to discuss Indian statehood

85. Of all the dictatorial regimes established in Europe between the First and Second World Wars, the one that held power the longest was that of

(A) Hitler
(B) Stalin
(C) Mussolini
(D) Pilsudski
(E) Franco

86. One of the principal strengths of the Byzantine empire was its

(A) constitutional monarchy
(B) sound economic base
(C) preference for decentralized government
(D) close relationship with the Roman Catholic church
(E) orderly system of succession to the throne

87. The first significant test of the ability of the League of Nations to respond when a major nation acted as an aggressor occurred when

(A) Japan invaded Manchuria
(B) the Soviet Union invaded Poland
(C) Japan declared war on China
(D) Franco's rebels attacked Spanish loyalists
(E) Hitler incorporated Austria into the Third Reich

88. In the 1980's, which of the following Muslim countries most actively promoted Islamic fundamentalism?

(A) Morocco
(B) Iran
(C) Iraq
(D) Indonesia
(E) Turkey

89. Mao Zedong revolutionized Chinese Marxist doctrine in the 1920's by advocating that the

(A) Chinese Communist Party sever its ties with the Soviet Union to preserve its independence
(B) Chinese Communist Party allow its rival, the Kuomintang, to reform a separate government on the island of Taiwan
(C) Chinese Communist Party renounce the use of violence to achieve revolution
(D) rural peasants, not the urban proletariat, lead the revolution in China
(E) landlord and capitalist classes be allowed to survive even after the communists took power

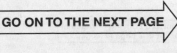

GO ON TO THE NEXT PAGE

90. The economies of China, North Korea, and North Vietnam were relatively isolated from the world economy during much of the third quarter of the twentieth century primarily because of their

(A) adherence to a planned Marxist economy
(B) inability to recover from the devastation of the Second World War
(C) subjection to a trade embargo enforced by the United Nations
(D) subjection to almost continual civil wars
(E) enduring extended droughts due to global climate change

91. The partition of Korea at the end of the Second World War in 1945 was primarily the result of

(A) rivalry between the United States and the Soviet Union
(B) Japanese dominance of important sectors of the Korean economy
(C) the emergence of China as a major world power
(D) the inability of the Koreans to agree on a form of government
(E) sharp cultural differences between northern and southern Korea

92. During the American occupation of Japan following the Second World War, authorities seeking to restructure Japanese society received the strongest support from which of the following Japanese groups?

(A) Socialist leaders
(B) Business leaders
(C) Military leaders
(D) Expatriates returning to Japan
(E) Members of the imperial court

93. Many historians believe that the end of the French Revolutionary era was the

(A) execution of King Louis XVI
(B) Reign of Terror
(C) storming of the Bastille prison
(D) defeat of Napoleon in Russia
(E) peace settlement at the Congress of Vienna

94. The nations that signed and confirmed the 1975 Helsinki Accords agreed to

(A) establish uniform prices for crude oil
(B) establish peace in the Middle East
(C) cooperate among themselves and respect human rights
(D) end the Vietnam conflict and withdraw all foreign troops
(E) end the Cold War

95. In the late twentieth century, experts began to question the value of building large dam projects in the developing world primarily because these projects tend to

(A) reduce the cost of electric power in the countries in which they are built
(B) displace people from their homes and disturb the ecology of the regions in which they are built
(C) encourage separatist movements in the areas in which they are built
(D) conflict with the development plans of the central governments of the countries in which they are built
(E) disrupt road and rail communications across the rivers on which the dams are built

STOP

If you finish before time is called, you may check your work on this test only. Do not turn to any other section in the test.

NO TEST MATERIAL ON THIS PAGE

How to Score the SAT Subject Test in World History

When you take an actual SAT Subject Test in World History, your answer sheet will be "read" by a scanning machine that will record your responses to each question. Then a computer will compare your answers with the correct answers and produce your raw score. You get one point for each correct answer. For each wrong answer, you lose one-quarter of a point. Questions you omit (and any for which you mark more than one answer) are not counted. This raw score is converted to a scaled score that is reported to you and to the colleges you specify.

Worksheet 1. Finding Your Raw Test Score

STEP 1: Table A on the following page lists the correct answers for all the questions on the Subject Test in World History that is reproduced in this book. It also serves as a worksheet for you to calculate your raw score.

- Compare your answers with those given in the table.
- Put a check in the column marked "Right" if your answer is correct.
- Put a check in the column marked "Wrong" if your answer is incorrect.
- Leave both columns blank if you omitted the question.

STEP 2: Count the number of right answers.

Enter the total here: ________________

STEP 3: Count the number of wrong answers.

Enter the total here: ________________

STEP 4: Multiply the number of wrong answers by .250.

Enter the product here: ______________

STEP 5: Subtract the result obtained in Step 4 from the total you obtained in Step 2.

Enter the result here: _______________

STEP 6: Round the number obtained in Step 5 to the nearest whole number.

Enter the result here: _______________

The number you obtained in Step 6 is your raw score.

TABLE A

Answers to the Subject Test in World History – Practice Test 1 and Percentage of Students Answering Each Question Correctly

Question Number	Correct Answer	Right	Wrong	Percentage of Students Answering the Question Correctly*	Question Number	Correct Answer	Right	Wrong	Percentage of Students Answering the Question Correctly*
1	A			66	33	A			41
2	B			59	34	A			64
3	C			76	35	A			50
4	B			49	36	C			52
5	E			65	37	A			24
6	D			79	38	D			59
7	A			61	39	A			33
8	E			93	40	B			71
9	D			57	41	C			69
10	D			76	42	D			19
11	B			35	43	B			37
12	A			54	44	D			37
13	A			80	45	B			55
14	C			41	46	A			67
15	A			51	47	D			51
16	C			21	48	A			36
17	B			43	49	A			60
18	A			29	50	D			55
19	B			81	51	E			69
20	C			71	52	A			65
21	C			47	53	E			65
22	A			73	54	C			45
23	B			85	55	E			62
24	D			82	56	B			32
25	B			95	57	C			89
26	A			73	58	D			65
27	D			68	59	B			43
28	A			46	60	D			35
29	E			77	61	A			46
30	A			48	62	E			65
31	A			73	63	E			46
32	D			56	64	A			83

Table A continued on next page

Table A continued from previous page

Question Number	Correct Answer	Right	Wrong	Percentage of Students Answering the Question Correctly*	Question Number	Correct Answer	Right	Wrong	Percentage of Students Answering the Question Correctly*
65	C			53	81	D			49
66	A			27	82	D			88
67	D			63	83	E			52
68	B			50	84	A			41
69	C			36	85	E			12
70	D			52	86	B			31
71	C			71	87	A			41
72	D			82	88	B			53
73	B			60	89	D			56
74	C			77	90	A			55
75	C			65	91	A			47
76	E			20	92	B			54
77	B			80	93	E			38
78	B			39	94	C			26
79	D			74	95	B			77
80	E			67					

* These percentages are based on an analysis of the answer sheets of a representative sample of 9,745 students who took the original administration of this test and whose mean score was 611. They may be used as an indication of the relative difficulty of a particular question.

Finding Your Scaled Score

When you take SAT Subject Tests, the scores sent to the colleges you specify are reported on the College Board scale, which ranges from 200 to 800. You can convert your practice test raw score to a scaled score by using Table B. To find your scaled score, locate your raw score in the left-hand column of Table B; the corresponding score in the right-hand column is your scaled score. For example, a raw score of 39 on this particular edition of the SAT Subject Test in World History corresponds to a scaled score of 580.

Raw scores are converted to scaled scores to ensure that a score earned on any one edition of a particular Subject Test is comparable to the same scaled score earned on any other edition of the same Subject Test. Because some editions of the tests may be slightly easier or more difficult than others, College Board scaled scores are adjusted so that they indicate the same level of performance regardless of the edition of the test taken and the ability of the group that takes it. Thus, for example, a score of 400 on one edition of a test taken at a particular administration indicates the same level of achievement as a score of 400 on a different edition of the test taken at a different administration.

When you take the SAT Subject Tests during a national administration, your scores are likely to differ somewhat from the scores you obtain on the tests in this book. People perform at different levels at different times for reasons unrelated to the tests themselves. The precision of any test is also limited because it represents only a sample of all the possible questions that could be asked.

Table B

Scaled Score Conversion Table Subject Test in World History Test – Practice Test 1					
Raw Score	Scaled Score	Raw Score	Scaled Score	Raw Score	Scaled Score
95	800	55	670	15	440
94	800	54	660	14	440
93	800	53	660	13	430
92	800	52	650	12	420
91	800	51	640	11	420
90	800	50	640	10	410
89	800	49	630	9	410
88	800	48	630	8	400
87	800	47	620	7	400
86	800	46	620	6	390
85	800	45	610	5	380
84	800	44	610	4	380
83	800	43	600	3	370
82	800	42	590	2	370
81	800	41	590	1	360
80	800	40	580	0	360
79	800	39	580	-1	350
78	800	38	570	-2	350
77	790	37	570	-3	340
76	790	36	560	-4	340
75	780	35	560	-5	330
74	770	34	550	-6	330
73	770	33	550	-7	330
72	760	32	540	-8	320
71	760	31	530	-9	320
70	750	30	530	-10	310
69	750	29	520	-11	310
68	740	28	520	-12	300
67	740	27	510	-13	300
66	730	26	510	-14	300
65	720	25	500	-15	290
64	720	24	490	-16	280
63	710	23	490	-17	280
62	710	22	480	-18	270
61	700	21	480	-19	260
60	690	20	470	-20	250
59	690	19	470	-21	250
58	680	18	460	-22	240
57	680	17	450	-23	230
56	670	16	450	-24	220

How Did You Do on the Subject Test in World History?

After you score your test and analyze your performance, think about the following questions:

Did you run out of time before reaching the end of the test?

If so, you may need to pace yourself better. For example, maybe you spent too much time on one or two hard questions. A better approach might be to skip the ones you can't answer right away and try answering all the remaining questions on the test. Then if there's time, go back to the questions you skipped.

Did you take a long time reading the directions?

You will save time when you take the test by learning the directions to the Subject Test in World History ahead of time. Each minute you spend reading directions during the test is a minute that you could use to answer questions.

How did you handle questions you were unsure of?

If you were able to eliminate one or more of the answer choices as wrong and guess from the remaining ones, your approach probably worked to your advantage. On the other hand, making haphazard guesses or omitting questions without trying to eliminate choices could cost you valuable points.

How difficult were the questions for you compared with other students who took the test?

Table A shows you how difficult the multiple-choice questions were for the group of students who took this test during its national administration. The right-hand column gives the percentage of students that answered each question correctly.

A question answered correctly by almost everyone in the group is obviously an easier question. For example, 82 percent of the students answered question 24 correctly. However, only 19 percent answered question 42 correctly.

Keep in mind that these percentages are based on just one group of students. They would probably be different with another group of students taking the test.

If you missed several easier questions, go back and try to find out why: Did the questions cover material you haven't yet reviewed? Did you misunderstand the directions?

Answer Explanations for World History – Practice Test 1

1. Choice (A) is the correct answer. Philosophical schools flourished in both Greece and China around 500 B.C.E. In Greece, during the sixth and fifth centuries B.C.E., many influential philosophers, including Pythagoras, Parmenides, Heraclitus, Socrates, and Plato debated the human condition. At the same time in China, Lao Tzu wrote *Tao Te Ching*, in which he outlined a new philosophical understanding and practice of human life, eventually known as Taoism. Also in China, the philosophy of Confucianism took shape at this time.

2. Choice (B) is the correct answer. The central characters of these three epic poems are all from the elite class of warriors of their respective civilizations. The *Mahabharata* recounts the battle between two branches of the same Indian warrior family, the Kauravas and the Pandavas. The *Iliad* focuses on the battle between the Trojan and the Achaean (or Greek) warriors. The *Tales of the Heike* is an account of the struggle between two Japanese samurai clans, the Taira and the Minamoto.

3. Choice (C) is the correct answer. Islam, founded on Muhammad's teaching, stresses the influence of Allah (God) on every aspect of human life. As such, Islam's teachings and decrees affected the entire life of its converts, thus establishing similarity and unity among followers of diverse backgrounds.

4. Choice (B) is the correct answer. Attila led his empire and armies of the Huns from 434 C.E. until his death in 453 C.E. Although he never gained full control over the area covered by the Western Roman Empire, in the 450s, Attila invaded and ravaged much of the Empire, entirely destroying several cities. This damage by Attila contributed to the deterioration of the Western Roman Empire and its eventual fall in 476.

5. Choice (E) is the correct answer. After the fall of the Han dynasty, northern China eventually came to be ruled by nomadic peoples. They were far fewer than the Chinese people they governed. As a result, they tended to assimilate or adopt the customs of the larger Chinese population.

6. Choice (D) is the correct answer. Both Mahavira and Buddha led religious movements in India sometime between the sixth and fourth centuries B.C.E. They both came from prominent families in Hindu society and developed religious systems that challenged that social order. Mahavira impoverished himself and spread teachings that became the basic tenets of Jainism. Buddha developed the religious system that has come to be known as Buddhism.

7. Choice (A) is the correct answer. In 1816, Shaka took over leadership of the Zulu. Shaka reorganized the Zulu army and instituted the use of short spears that forced close warfare. He also developed military tactics that utilized several groups of warriors, some of which encircled the foe from the sides like a set of ox's horns. Under Shaka, the Zulu were incredibly successful warriors who dominated southern Africa throughout the nineteenth century.

8. Choice (E) is the correct answer. Realistically representing people in art is not central to Islamic faith and is generally considered to go against the teachings of Muhammad. The five central pillars of Islam are fasting during Ramadan (A); professing faith in the one God, Allah (B); praying five times daily facing Mecca (C); making a pilgrimage to Mecca at least once (D); and giving alms to the poor.

9. Choice (D) is the correct answer. In the late 1990s, Pakistan acquired the capability of exploding nuclear weapons. India had acquired this capability in 1974. The two countries share their western and eastern borders, respectively, and historically have a strained relationship, especially with respect to the disputed territory of Kashmir, so the acquisition of nuclear weapons by both countries is a matter of global concern.

10. Choice (D) is the correct answer. The main tenet of Stalin's governing strategy was to centralize as much control of the Soviet Union as possible. A major strategy for achieving strong central control was to centralize economic planning. Soviet economic decisions under Stalin were made by a central State authority; companies were not allowed to make private economic decisions.

11. Choice (B) is the correct answer. Historiography is the study of different ways historical events are interpreted and recorded, not the study of the events themselves. Historiography is also the study of the methodology and practices used when writing history. Its elements include inquiry into the nature and credibility of the source, evolving views of history, and the specific perspective from which a particular history or historical narrative has been written.

12. Choice (A) is the correct answer. In imperial China, the scholar-gentry (sometimes referred to as scholar-officials or mandarins) composed the most important part of the official bureaucracy. The members of the scholar-gentry usually came from landowner families and were the imperial civil servants. They were well educated and, by the Tang dynasty (618–907 C.E.), had to pass civil service exams to receive a position. At this time, wealthy merchants paid to educate their sons so they could pass the exam and become imperial bureaucrats.

13. Choice (A) is the correct answer. Japan's defeat of Russia in the Russo-Japanese War (1904–1905) demonstrated that modernization was not limited to Western nations. Japan was able to defeat the massive Russian navy and much of the Russian army. By using its newly modernized forces, Japan's victory established it as a world power in the modern era and was a source of inspiration for anti-colonial movements throughout the world.

14. Choice (C) is the correct answer. After defeating the Umayyads at the Battle of the Zab River in 750 C.E., the Abbasids moved the caliphate from Damascus to Baghdad. The Umayyad caliphs had held power of the Islamic world at Damascus since 661 C.E. The Abbasids were more open to relationships with non-Arab peoples, and were helped by Persian converts to Islam in their defeat of the Umayyads.

15. Choice (A) is the correct answer. A megalithic structure is a structure made of large rocks that may be free-standing or may be connected without the use of cement or mortar. Stonehenge is the most famous megalithic structure. Located near Amesbury, England, Stonehenge is a circular arrangement of stone monuments that was constructed between 3100 B.C.E. and 2000 B.C.E.

16. Choice (C) is the correct answer. The Toltec were a Native American people who thrived in central Mexico between the tenth and twelfth century C.E. When the Aztec came to power in the fourteenth century, they claimed that they had descended from the Toltec, whom they regarded as the givers of civilization. The Aztec did, in fact, speak Nahuatl, the language of the Toltec, and the two peoples shared many customs and rituals.

17. Choice (B) is the correct answer. Indo-European and Bantu are both terms historians use to describe language groups. Indo-European refers to the large language group now found throughout much of Europe and Asia that includes many modern languages such as English, Persian (or Farsi), Russian, Spanish, and Hindi. The Bantu language family, which includes Zulu, Xhosa, Kongo, Swahili, and Sotho, is found throughout much of Sub-Saharan Africa.

18. Choice (A) is the correct answer. One historical theory proposes that the need for flood protection and irrigation in river valleys caused civilizations in these areas to develop large bureaucratic, impersonal, and often despotic governments. Agricultural-based civilizations relied on the irrigation of water and large-scale irrigation projects required a strong centralized government to be successful. These river-valley civilizations (called "hydraulic civilizations" by Karl Wittfogel) developed a complex social organization, usually with forced labor, a bureaucratic government, and a powerful emperor who was often identified with the gods.

19. Choice (B) is the correct answer. Working-class women in nineteenth-century England had limited social and employment opportunities. Many young working-class women were encouraged by their parents to take jobs as domestic servants in higher-class homes, not for future professional training (D) or with the hopes of marrying wealthier men (C), but primarily to make extra money for their families, while learning habits and skills they could apply later on as wives.

20. Choice (C) is the correct answer. Beginning in the Zhou dynasty, emperors of China used the concept of the Mandate of Heaven to justify their power. According to the Mandate of Heaven, as long as an emperor ruled wisely and justly, he enjoyed divine blessing. If he began to misuse his position, he would lose the Mandate. Throughout Chinese history, the Mandate of Heaven was used to justify the passing of power from one dynasty to the next. As one dynasty began to misuse its power, the next claimed the authority of the Mandate to avoid suffering any disasters or disturbances.

21. Choice (C) is the correct answer. It is commonly accepted that the term *Homo sapiens* classifies humans who can consciously think. In evolutionary theory, *Homo sapiens* (translated from Latin as "wise or thinking man") are distinguished from their closest ancestors or related species by the advanced form of conscious thinking that their large brain allows. Other related species, like *Homo erectus*, may have walked upright, but probably lacked the level of conscious thinking of *Homo sapiens*.

22. Choice (A) is the correct answer. Although some later branches of Buddhism include belief in a god, Buddhism, in its original form, is a religious system that focuses on humanity's correct path through life without making reference to any god or gods. Buddhism originated in the late sixth century B.C.E. in northeastern India as a belief system centered on the religious and philosophical teachings of the Buddha. The wider tradition of Hinduism includes belief in many different deities (C). Christianity (B), Islam (D), and Judaism (E) are all religions that are centered on the belief in one god.

23. Choice (B) is the correct answer. Social Darwinism applies Charles Darwin's theory of natural selection in plant and animal development to the development of human societies. According to Social Darwinism, social groups follow the same natural law of "survival of the fittest" as plants and animals. Social groups naturally compete for power and resources and the strongest, most fit societies will be the ones that survive. In the late nineteenth and early twentieth century C.E., the theory of Social Darwinism was used to justify the competition of laissez-faire capitalism and class stratification, arguing that it was in the best interest of human development for weaker societies and classes to be eliminated in favor of stronger, more fit humans.

24. Choice (D) is the correct answer. The Second World War officially started on September 3, 1939, when Great Britain and France declared war on Germany in response to the German invasion of Poland. Germany had invaded Poland on September 1. Six days earlier, on August 25, Great Britain had signed a treaty with Poland pledging assistance in the event of a German invasion.

25. Choice (B) is the correct answer. The pyramids of ancient Egypt were built primarily to be huge monumental tombs. The Pyramids of Giza, located on the west bank of the Nile River in northern Egypt, were built as tombs for three kings—Khufu, Khafre, and Menkaure—who reigned during the Fourth dynasty (circa 2575–2465 B.C.E.).

26. Choice (A) is the correct answer. The term "caste system," often used to describe Hindu society, is characterized as a rigid socially stratified society. While the term "caste" itself does not originate in Hinduism, Hindu society was traditionally divided into four levels. The Brahman enjoy the highest position in society and were originally the priests and teachers of the Hindu scriptures.

27. Choice (D) is the correct answer. From his ascent to the Macedonian throne in 336 B.C.E. until his death in 323 B.C.E., Alexander the Great led continuous successful military expeditions that expanded the Greek Empire beyond the Middle East and into Asia. In 333 B.C.E., he defeated the main Persian army, and eventually gained control over the Persian Empire throughout western Asia. As he took control of lands with different cultures, Alexander encouraged the intermingling of Greek and non-Greek peoples and customs. By the time of his death, he had spread Greek cultural forms from the Mediterranean to India, laying the foundation for the Hellenistic Age.

28. Choice (A) is the correct answer. The Celts are a group of ancient Indo-European peoples who inhabited the British Isles and western Europe from prehistory until their eventual absorption into the Roman Empire. In the first century B.C.E., Julius

Caesar led the Roman conquests over the Celts in Gaul. Britain was conquered by the Romans a century later, thus ending the history of Celtic political power in Europe.

29. Choice (E) is the correct answer. Greek civilization did not originate along a river valley, but around the Aegean Sea, a branch of the Mediterranean Sea. The other four civilizations all originated in river valleys: the Chinese (A), along the Huang He (Yellow) River; the Indian (B), along the Indus and Ganges rivers; the Egyptian (C), along the Nile River; and the Mesopotamian (D), between the Tigris and Euphrates rivers.

30. Choice (A) is the correct answer. Beginning in the 1400s C.E., European states underwent a commercial revolution in which the capitalistic trade of goods became more central to their economies. In the developing capitalistic economies, the European states competed for new trade routes, products, and partners. With the invention of larger and stronger ships capable of navigating the Atlantic Ocean, European explorers expanded the reach of these economies to the Americas and Africa, during what has come to be called the Age of Exploration.

31. Choice (A) is the correct answer. All of these English words are derivations of Arabic words and reflect the intermingling of Arab and European cultures.

32. Choice (D) is the correct answer. The term "Neolithic" refers to the period in human technological development characterized by the domestication of plants and animals. Originally associated with the end of the Old Stone Age in Europe, Asia, and Africa, "Neolithic" is now more commonly used to refer to the developmental period of any culture when plant and animal domestication occurs. Metallurgy, or the development of metal tools, marks the end of the Neolithic Age.

33. Choice (A) is the correct answer. The spread of sugar cultivation to the Americas was accompanied by a major shift in human population. Sugar cultivation was labor intensive, and the Europeans who established plantations on Caribbean islands and the mainland relied on enslaved Africans to do most of the work. Though exact numbers are unobtainable, millions of Africans were transported to the Americas during the sixteenth through nineteenth centuries. Probably more than three-quarters of them were sent to sugar plantations. Choice (B) is incorrect. Although the importation of opium into China caused major disruptions of Chinese society, cultivation of opium was not associated with large-scale population shifts. Choice (C) is incorrect. In the Americas, the number of slaves employed in the production of tobacco was much smaller than the number employed in sugar production. Choice (D) is incorrect. Although the cultivation of tea spread from China to South Asia and

other areas, it was not accompanied by population shifts of the size associated with the spread of sugar cultivation. Choice (E) is incorrect. In the Americas, the number of slaves employed in cotton production was smaller than the number employed in sugar production. Although cotton cultivation spread through the southern United States in the early nineteenth century, the numbers of slaves moved and the distances they traveled were still smaller than was the case for sugar cultivation.

34. Choice (A) is the correct answer. Domestic cultivation of maize, or corn, probably began to spread from the Oaxaca Valley of Mexico (part of Mesoamerica) around 3500 B.C.E. Maize spread widely during the pre-Columbian era, becoming a staple food in many pre-Columbian cultures throughout North and South America.

35. Choice (A) is the correct answer. The West African Muslim kingdoms of Ghana (eighth to thirteenth century C.E.) and Mali (fourteenth to sixteenth century C.E.) acquired vast amounts of wealth through the trans-Saharan trade routes to the North African cities along the Mediterranean Sea. The West African kingdoms desired the salt of the Mediterranean regions and, in return, provided gold and slaves.

36. Choice (C) is the correct answer. This map shows the routes of Zheng He's seafaring voyages from China across the Indian Ocean to Africa, Arabia, India, Ceylon, and Southeast Asia. Zheng He, a Chinese Muslim, commanded massive expeditions of up to 30,000 men on more than 300 ships for the Ming emperors during the fifteenth century C.E.

37. Choice (A) is the correct answer. Mogadishu, Kilwa, Mombasa, and Sofala were all Swahili city-states along the coast of East Africa. Starting around 1000 C.E., numerous Swahili city-states developed along Africa's eastern coast through successful trading with one another and with landlocked African regions like Zimbabwe. Although it interacted with the Swahili city-states, Zimbabwe was an interior empire, not a Swahili city-state.

38. Choice (D) is the correct answer. Between the tenth and thirteenth centuries C.E., mound-building cultures thrived in North America. These cultures built large earthen mounds that were most likely used as sites for religious ceremonies and burials. The largest of these mounds was built in the 1000s C.E. in the Native American city of Cahokia, in present-day Illinois.

39. Choice (A) is the correct answer. During the First World War, many women in Europe and the United States filled industrial jobs left vacant by the men who were

fighting. By including women, who were previously excluded, in the workforce, industrial nations were able to maintain and increase productivity during the war. When the men returned at the end of the war, many women were asked to leave their jobs to make room for the unemployed veterans.

40. Choice (B) is the correct answer. Islam is the dominant religion in Indonesia. Arab merchants brought Islam to Indonesia beginning around the twelfth century C.E. Indonesia is now the most populous Muslim nation in the world.

41. Choice (C) is the correct answer. The shaded areas on the map together comprise the extent of the Mongol Khanates. The Mongol Empire, began by Genghis Khan, spread throughout Europe and Asia during the thirteenth and fourteenth centuries. At its height, it was the largest empire in world history, stretching, as the map indicates, from the Pacific Ocean to the Middle East. After the reign of Kublai Khan, the empire was divided into four Khanates as shown.

42. Choice (D) is the correct answer. The Maya civilization, which originated in Mesoamerica around 1500 B.C.E., was characterized by large cities that were politically independent of one another. In contrast, the Aztecs, a Mesoamerican civilization during the fourteenth to sixteenth centuries C.E., were governed by powerful emperors who ruled from the capital city of Tenochtitlán.

43. Choice (B) is the correct answer. In the period before 1500 C.E., the Indian Ocean was used primarily by Indian and Arab merchants. After 1500 C.E., Europeans, including many successful Portuguese merchants, began to use the Indian Ocean for trade. Chinese admiral Zheng He had sailed throughout the Indian Ocean before 1500 C.E., but he was primarily interested in diplomacy and exploration rather than trade.

44. Choice (D) is the correct answer. On September 16, 1810, Father Miguel Hidalgo began Mexico's long war with Spain to gain independence. A parish priest from the town of Dolores, Hidalgo roused his parishioners to arms with the famous Grito de Dolores (Cry of Dolores). Hidalgo's armed group was able to capture some towns, but failed to take Mexico City. It was not until 1821, in part under the leadership of Antonio López de Santa Anna (B), that Mexico gained its independence from Spain. José de San Martín (E) was an Argentine revolutionary leader; Bernardo O'Higgins (C) was a Chilean revolutionary leader; and Simón Bolívar (A) was a South American revolutionary hero.

45. Choice (B) is the correct answer. The feudal periods in both Japan and western Europe were characterized by frequent warfare. In feudal Japan (eleventh to nineteenth centuries C.E.), feudal families were led by daimyo (warlords) who fought both among each other as well as with outside invaders like the Mongols. The feudal period in western Europe (fifth to sixteenth centuries C.E.) was also characterized by warfare among small feudal principalities. In both Japan and Europe, the frequent warfare hindered the development of a money economy and a centralized monarchy.

46. Choice (A) is the correct answer. In 1000 C.E., Constantinople, now the Turkish city of Istanbul, was the capital of the Eastern Roman, or Byzantine, Empire and the largest city in Europe. At that time, London, Paris, Rome, and Toledo, although important cities in their own right, were all smaller than Constantinople.

47. Choice (D) is the correct answer. In early Islamic society, Jews and Christians were allowed to practice their own religions but were subject to some restrictions within society. Jews and Christians were allowed to hold some public offices, but could not be rulers (A). They were exempt from the Muslim *zakat* tax, but were required to pay the poll tax, *jizya,* which was often higher (B). They were exempt from serving in the army (C) and were tolerated, but they were considered second-class citizens (E).

48. Choice (A) is the correct answer. This Biblical passage (Matthew 16:19) was used in the early Catholic Church to argue for the authority of the pope. As Bishop of Rome, the pope traces his authority back to Peter the Apostle, who was martyred and buried in Rome. According to the doctrine of "the apostolic primacy of Peter," the Bishops of Rome had authority over the other bishops who traced their authority to other apostles of Jesus. This passage, in which Jesus states that he will build his church on Peter, was used as the Biblical basis for that doctrine.

49. Choice (A) is the correct answer. The period of Mongol rule over Russia during the thirteenth century reinforced Russia's isolation from western Europe. Under Mongol rule, large sections of Russia were unified, but because the Mongol Empire did not extend into western Europe, the political and cultural lines dividing Russia and western Europe became more defined. The Mongols did not force most Russians to adopt Mongol culture or Islam. As a result, when Mongol rule ended, Eastern Christian Orthodoxy was still thriving.

50. Choice (D) is the correct answer. The Inca road system was a series of foot trails traversing the high Andes Mountains in Peru and linking the towns of the Inca Empire. Unfit for wheeled vehicles, the roads were used by travelers on foot to carry messages and goods between distant Incan towns.

51. Choice (E) is the correct answer. British merchants were able to continue importing harmful opium into China. After losing the first Anglo-Chinese War (also known as the First Opium War) to the United Kingdom, the Chinese signed the Treaty of Nanking in 1842. This treaty, along with settlements after other defeats, ceded Hong Kong to the British (B), opened numerous ports to foreign traders (C), allowed Western missionaries in China (A), and granted Westerners the privilege of extraterritoriality (D). Additionally, China lost the power to ban the import of opium into China.

52. Choice (A) is the correct answer. Unlike Europe, China was a unified empire in 750 C.E. At this time, China was unified under the Tang dynasty, which is often considered to be a high point in China's cultural history. In contrast, in 750 C.E., Europe was undergoing a period of political division. After the fall of the Western Roman Empire in the fifth century C.E., Europe was subject to continual invasion from various peoples such as the Goths and the Huns.

53. Choice (E) is the correct answer. This quotation reflects a key tenet of the Chinese philosophy of Confucianism. Confucianism, developed from the teachings of Chinese philosopher Confucius (551–479 B.C.E.), draws a connection between the private lives of individuals and wider political stability. Much of Confucius' teachings centered on cultivating a personal life in line with principles of righteousness. Confucianism holds that wider political order rests on the order achieved by individuals in their own families.

54. Choice (C) is the correct answer. Many early Roman religious rituals and beliefs were influenced by the religious practices of the Etruscans. The Etruscans, who inhabited ancient Italy before the rise of Roman civilization, believed that there were many gods who interacted intimately with humans. Religious rituals were used to persuade the gods to act favorably toward humans. The Romans adopted the same system, appeasing and consulting the gods in all important affairs through religious rituals.

55. Choice (E) is the correct answer. The Mongol and Turkish people who made up the armies of the Mongol Khans who invaded central and south Asia later converted to Islam. Securing control over these territories, the Mongols and Turks helped define and defend the Islamic world against European Christian crusaders.

56. Choice (B) is the correct answer. During the seventeenth century, the Dutch dominated European maritime trade. In 1602, the Dutch East India Company, promoting Dutch colonization and trade throughout Asia, was established. The company gained European monopolies, often violently, on the trade of many spices throughout modern-day Indonesia. The Dutch West India Company, which was

granted a charter in 1621, established colonies and trade in North America and in the Caribbean. The success of these Dutch trading companies broke the dominance of European trade that Spain had enjoyed throughout the sixteenth century.

57. Choice (C) is the correct answer. The Irish Potato Famine, which occurred from 1845 to 1849, spurred mass emigration of starving Irish families to Great Britain, the United States, Canada, and Australia. The famine resulted from the failure of the potato crop, a staple food for many Irish families. After a devastating potato fungus destroyed the potato crop, oppressive economic policies and incompetent farming methods created widespread hunger throughout Ireland. Hundreds of thousands of Irish died or emigrated as a direct result of the famine.

58. Choice (D) is the correct answer. Corn and potatoes originated in South America and spread throughout the world as a result of European colonization. Potatoes, first grown in the Andes Mountains, were brought to Spain in the sixteenth century and eventually became a major European staple. Likewise, corn, also called maize, originated in ancient Mesoamerica and was brought to the Old World by Europeans.

59. Choice (B) is the correct answer. In 1856, Tsar Alexander II of Russia signed the Treaty of Paris with the United Kingdom, France, and the Ottoman Empire to end the Crimean War. Following the war, Alexander II emancipated the serfs and instituted radical government reforms that reflected the progressive ideas of the educated classes. He hoped these measures would help to restore Russian power.

60. Choice (D) is the correct answer. After gaining independence from the United Kingdom in 1947, India pursued a foreign policy of nonalignment. Prime Minister Jawaharlal Nehru first outlined the principles of nonalignment in 1954 as a guide to India's relationship with China. The principles were: respect for territorial integrity; mutual nonaggression; mutual noninterference in domestic affairs; equality and mutual benefit; and peaceful coexistence. These principles eventually became the foundation for the international organization, Nonaligned Movement, established in 1961.

61. Choice (A) is the correct answer. In 1776, Scottish economist Adam Smith published his economic theory in *The Wealth of Nations*. The basic idea of his theory is that when producers compete to sell their goods to consumers in an unrestricted market, consumers will benefit by paying the cheapest sustainable prices. Consequently, governments should regulate trade and manufacturing as little as possible, allowing

the natural forces of competition among producers to regulate the prices of products. This is known as laissez-faire economics.

62. Choice (E) is the correct answer. Venezuela, Nigeria, and Iraq are all members of OPEC. Founded in 1960 by Iran, Iraq, Kuwait, Saudi Arabia, and Venezuela, OPEC is an international association created to protect the interests of oil-producing countries. The organization was founded in response to price cuts of crude oil forced on these countries by European and U.S. oil companies. Since then, OPEC has worked to regulate and increase the profits of oil-producing countries. OPEC now has 13 members: Iran, Iraq, Kuwait, Saudi Arabia, Venezuela, Algeria, Indonesia, Libya, Qatar, United Arab Emirates, Nigeria, Ecuador, and Angola.

63. Choice (E) is the correct answer. Eighteenth-century British navigator James Cook charted the seas around Australia and New Zealand during his Pacific expeditions. A superior navigator and cartographer, Cook was the first European to discover the east coast of Australia and the Hawaiian Islands and to circumnavigate New Zealand.

64. Choice (A) is the correct answer. In the seventeenth century, the Tokugawa shogunate became increasingly hostile to the influence of Western culture on Japanese society. As a result of trade with European nations, Western cultural practices like Christianity were gaining ground in Japan. The Tokugawa enacted a number of anti-Western policies and eventually closed its trading seaports to all foreigners except China and the Dutch East India Company.

65. Choice (C) is the correct answer. During the 1500s, the Spanish colonies in the Americas, especially in Peru, opened large silver mines. The abundance of silver taken to European and world markets from these mines contributed to a huge price inflation in the European economy. As a result of the abundant mines and the increase in Spain's power, Spain strengthened its control over its colonies in the Americas. During this period, Spain was able to rebuff European attacks (E), suppress Native American culture (B), and quell political uprisings (D).

66. Choice (A) is the correct answer. The Aztec society relied primarily on agriculture for its subsistence. Most of their diet consisted of maize and beans. They did domesticate turkeys and dogs, but maintaining large animals as livestock was not a significant part of their society. The domestication of livestock was a significant part of Chinese (B), Persian (C), Tartar (D), and Roman (E) societies.

67. Choice (D) is the correct answer. In the nineteenth century, the Ottoman Empire was called "the Sick Man of Europe" by Nicholas I of Russia. The Ottoman Empire had been a major European power since the fifteenth century. By the nineteenth century, however, it had lost much of its territory in the Balkans and was economically dominated by other European nations. Following the end of the First World War, the Ottoman Empire finally collapsed in 1922.

68. Choice (B) is the correct answer. The eighteenth-century philosophy of Deism, which based theology on rationality rather than church authority, was strongly denounced by the Roman Catholic Church. Enlightenment thinkers like Voltaire and Thomas Paine proposed Deism as a rational approach to religion, arguing that God set the universe on its course governed by natural laws and then ceased to intervene in its affairs. Religious ideas like miracles, divine intervention, and petitionary prayer were seen as irrational and false. The Catholic Church denounced Deism as heretical.

69. Choice (C) is the correct answer. The 1400s and 1500s saw the decline of power for European feudal families and the rise of strong central monarchies, sometimes called the "new monarchs." The development of gunpowder gave a significant advantage to armies who used firearms. The high costs of equipping troops with firearms were more easily met by a larger centralized government, ruled by a monarch who had access to large tax revenues. Thus, monarchs were successful in gaining and maintaining power at the expense of feudal lords.

70. Choice (D) is the correct answer. In the early 1800s, many of Spain's colonies in the Americas successfully revolted and declared independence. The success of these revolts was, in large part, due to the fact that Spain was unable to dedicate enough troops and resources to maintain control over the colonies. Spain had drained its resources battling Napoleon's forces. In 1807, Napoleon had invaded Spain, triggering a long and draining war. By 1813, Napoleon's forces had been driven out of Spain. These efforts, however, had seriously weakened Spanish power.

71. Choice (C) is the correct answer. During the sixteenth and seventeenth centuries, European powers colonized the East Indies (Southeast Asia) to obtain spices for trading. In 1513, the Portuguese were the first Europeans to establish trade in modern-day Indonesia, obtaining cloves from Ternate, one of the Spice Islands. The United Kingdom, France, and Spain also established spice trade in the East Indies, but it was the Netherlands, through the Dutch East India Company, that eventually gained the greatest economic and political power in the region.

72. Choice (D) is the correct answer. Enlightenment thought was characterized by reliance on reason, rather than religious or traditional authority, in the pursuit of truth. During the period of time historians call the Enlightenment, or the Age of Reason (seventeenth and eighteenth centuries), philosophers such as René Descartes, Jean-Jacques Rousseau, Voltaire, and John Locke applied reason and the scientific method to the study of many aspects of human life. By shifting the study of philosophy, education, law, and politics away from tradition and religion and toward the use of rational methods of observation and argumentation, Enlightenment philosophers were profoundly influential.

73. Choice (B) is the correct answer. Giuseppe Mazzini, Count Camillo Benso di Cavour, and Giuseppe Garibaldi were all major contributors to the Italian unification (Il Risorgimento), the process of unifying the various countries on the Italian peninsula into one Italian state during the nineteenth century. All three men worked, in different capacities, for the modernization and unification of Italy.

74. Choice (C) is the correct answer. According to tradition, around 530 B.C.E., at age 29, Siddhartha Gautama (later called "the Buddha" or "the Enlightened One") left his life as a prince to travel as a monk in search of a way to relieve human suffering. After six years of extreme self-deprivation, Siddhartha achieved "enlightenment" and discovered "The Middle Way" between indulgence and deprivation to escape suffering. Siddhartha began to teach his idea that through correct thought and action, one could get rid of one's cravings, the source of human suffering. His teachings eventually developed into the major world religion known as Buddhism.

75. Choice (C) is the correct answer. The ancient Egyptian civilization flourished for years along the banks of the Nile River in northern Africa. The yearly flooding of the Nile watered and refertilized Egypt, allowing the land to sustain a large population. Without the yearly flooding, the region would remain too dry to grow large amounts of crops. Because it was so essential to the survival of the civilization, the yearly flooding of the Nile was prominent in Egyptian legend and society.

76. Choice (E) is the correct answer. In the eighteenth century, technological advances (particularly in agriculture and transportation) and industrialization began to change the lives of people in England. One benefit of the technological advances was a drop in death rates, which in turn led to population growth. Industrialization solidified gender roles and strengthened, not destroyed, the traditional nuclear family (A). Although unhealthy conditions in overcrowded cities contributed to a rising infant mortality rate (D), technological advances kept the death rate down (B), allowing the population to increase (C).

77. Choice (B) is the correct answer. President Gamal Abdel Nasser, second president of Egypt from 1956 to 1970, was extremely powerful and influential in stabilizing and modernizing Egypt. Nasser sought to influence as much of Egyptian society as possible. His attempts to raise the standard of living of Egyptians, however, were partially thwarted by a high birth rate in the lower classes. This cartoon depicts Nasser showing Egyptians that lowering the birth rate would increase the available resources for Egyptian economic development.

78. Choice (B) is the correct answer. All of these Southeast Asian countries are correctly matched with the dominating colonial power except Burma. Burma, also known as Myanmar, was colonized by Great Britain, not Germany. Under British control for most of the nineteenth century, Burma gained its independence from Great Britain in 1948.

79. Choice (D) is the correct answer. The Boxer Rebellion was a revolt of the Chinese against Western imperialists in northern China from 1899 to 1901. The term "Boxers" referred to the "Righteous Uprising Society," a group of Chinese who rebelled against the economic and political exploitation of German, British, French, Belgian, Japanese, Russian, Dutch, and U.S. forces. Although the Boxers were eventually supported by the Chinese Imperial army, the Western powers were able to suppress the uprising.

80. Choice (E) is the correct answer. This picture of Christ crowning a twelfth-century king of Sicily reflects the Byzantine influence on Sicilian culture. Sicily had been part of the Byzantine Empire from 552 to 965 C.E. After a period under a religiously tolerant Arab rule, it was governed by the Normans during the eleventh and twelfth centuries. Byzantine Christianity was still prevalent in Sicilian culture at this time, as seen in this traditional Byzantine iconic depiction of Christ crowning the monarch.

81. Choice (D) is the correct answer. The site of Great Zimbabwe in southern Africa was a major center of African civilization, reaching its peak in the fifteenth century. The powerful civilization traded extensively with Arabs and the Swahili city-states (A); mined and smelted gold (B), copper, and bronze (E); and expanded its population into much of the Zimbabwean Plateau (C); but it did not record its history in a written epic.

82. Choice (D) is the correct answer. Jazz originated in United States in the late 1800s. It combined African rhythms, European harmonies, and U.S. instruments, and emphasized the improvisational interplay of the musicians. Impressionism (A) is a school of painting that originated in France during the late 1800s. Surrealist poetry (B) is a movement in literature founded in Paris, France, in the 1920s. Social realism (C) is an artistic and literary movement that flourished in several countries in the

years between World Wars I and II. Atonal music (E) developed in Germany in the early 1900s.

83. Choice (E) is the correct answer. The Russian Provisional Government was created in 1917 when the Russian Empire finally collapsed and Tsar Nicholas II abdicated the throne. The Provisional Government continued Russia's involvement in the First World War. The Russian people, weary of fighting, rapidly became disillusioned with the government. The people's discontent and the Provisional Government's weakness eventually led to the Bolshevik Revolution (or October Revolution) and the rise to power of Vladimir Lenin.

84. Choice (A) is the correct answer. Founded in 1885 to advance the political aspirations of educated Indians, the Indian National Congress (INC) was the first Indian organization to challenge British rule. During India's struggle for independence in the 1940s, the INC grew to include a diverse representation of India's population, including both Hindus and Muslims. Although never an official member, Mahatma Gandhi was supported by and associated with the INC during his efforts to free India of British rule.

85. Choice (E) is the correct answer. Francisco Franco took control of the Spanish Nationalist Army in 1936, and later took control of all of Spain at the end of the Spanish Civil War in 1939. He ruled Spain for 36 years until his death in 1975. Hitler ruled Germany for 12 years, from 1933 to 1945 (A). Stalin ruled the Soviet Union for 29 years, from 1924 to 1953 (B). Mussolini ruled Italy for 21 years, from 1922 to 1943 (C). Pilsudski ruled Poland for 4 years, from 1918 to 1922 (D).

86. Choice (B) is the correct answer. The Byzantine Empire, also called the Eastern Roman Empire, began in the fourth century C.E. and flourished for over a thousand years until its final collapse in the fifteenth century. Reaching its peak from the ninth to the eleventh centuries, the empire's success came from a sound economic base fueled by high levels of production and trade. The Byzantine Empire was ruled by a centralized nonconstitutional monarchy—choices (A) and (C)—whose succession of power was not often clear (E). The Byzantine Empire also saw the separation of its Eastern Orthodox Christian church from the Roman Catholic Church (D).

87. Choice (A) is the correct answer. In 1919, the League of Nations was established at the Paris Peace Conference as a means of settling international disputes. The League received its first major test when Japan invaded the Chinese territory of Manchuria in 1931. The League of Nations eventually determined that Japan had acted unfairly and called for Japan to relinquish control of Manchuria. Japan withdrew their

membership from the League and ignored the decree. Unable to garner military or diplomatic support from its members or the United States, the League of Nations failed in rebuffing the Japanese aggression.

88. Choice (B) is the correct answer. During the 1980s, Islamic fundamentalism flourished in the Islamic Republic of Iran. In 1979, Ayatollah Ruhollah Khomeini successfully led the Iranian Revolution, overthrowing the constitutional monarchy and establishing an Islamic theocratic republic under his control. During his rule, which lasted until his death in 1989, Khomeini enforced the Sharia law that governed Iranians' entire lives according to Islamic fundamentalist ideas.

89. Choice (D) is the correct answer. In the 1920s, Mao Zedong revolutionized Chinese Marxist thought by claiming that the Chinese peasantry needed to be mobilized for a communist revolution to succeed in China. Traditional Marxist doctrine focused on the exploitation of the urban working class and their eventual overthrow of their oppressors. Mao Zedong argued that because China was predominantly an agrarian society, the massive support needed for a revolution had to be found in the rural peasantry. Eventually, in 1949, the Chinese communist revolution succeeded and the People's Republic of China was established under the leadership of Mao Zedong.

90. Choice (A) is the correct answer. During much of the third quarter of the twentieth century, the economies of China, North Korea, and North Vietnam were isolated from the world economy because of their adherence to Marxist economic policies. In these economies, economic decisions regarding production and trade are all centrally planned and governed by the state. Fully governed by their states, these economies were isolated from the competition among private companies in the international markets.

91. Choice (A) is the correct answer. The division of Korea into North and South Korea was primarily the result of the political rivalry between the United States and the Soviet Union. Japan ruled Korea from 1910 until the end of the Second World War. At the close of the war, the United States and the Soviet Union agreed that Japanese soldiers north of the 38th parallel would surrender to the Soviets, and those south of the line would surrender to the United States. The two powers then proceeded to establish and back governments aligned with their political perspectives. North Korea developed a communist government, while South Korea eventually developed into a democracy.

92. Choice (B) is the correct answer. During the U.S. occupation of Japan following the Second World War from 1945 to 1952, U.S. and Japanese authorities were supported by Japanese business leaders. The U.S. occupiers had the task of maintaining control while reconstructing Japan's infrastructure and economy. Many Japanese business leaders benefited from the production and trade policies established by the U.S. occupiers and, as a result, they were generally supportive.

93. Choice (E) is the correct answer. Many historians use the peace settlement reached by the major European powers at the Congress of Vienna in 1815 to mark the end of the French Revolutionary era. The settlement redefined European boundaries after the Napoleonic Wars and reestablished prerevolution monarchies. The Congress coincided with the final defeat of French Revolutionary leader Napoleon Bonaparte at Waterloo.

94. Choice (C) is the correct answer. The signing of the Helsinki Accords in 1975 by the United States, Canada, the Soviet Union, and most European countries concluded the Conference on Security and Cooperation in Europe held in Helsinki, Finland. The Conference and the Helsinki Accords largely focused on establishing mutual cooperation and respect for the basic freedoms and rights of all humans, including racial minorities.

95. Choice (B) is the correct answer. Toward the end of the twentieth century, politicians and engineers began questioning the value of building big dams to produce hydroelectricity because of their effect on the people who live along the dammed rivers. Although the huge dams produce electricity and create jobs, they also alter the flow of the river, flooding land and displacing many families from their homes. Many political activists have protested on behalf of the communities most affected, arguing that the detrimental effects of the projects outweigh their benefits.

World History – Practice Test 2

Practice Helps

The test that follows is an actual, previously administered SAT Subject Test in World History. To get an idea of what it's like to take this test, practice under conditions that are much like those of an actual test administration.

- Set aside an hour when you can take the test uninterrupted.
- Sit at a desk or table with no other books or papers. Dictionaries, other books, or notes are not allowed in the test room.
- Tear out an answer sheet from the back of this book and fill it in just as you would on the day of the test. One answer sheet can be used for up to three Subject Tests.
- Read the instructions that precede the practice test. During the actual administration, you will be asked to read them before answering test questions.
- Use a clock or kitchen timer to time yourself.
- After you finish the practice test, read the sections "How to Score the SAT Subject Test in World History" and "How Did You Do on the Subject Test in World History?"
- The appearance of the answer sheet in this book may differ from the answer sheet you see on test day.

WORLD HISTORY TEST

The top portion of the page of the answer sheet that you will use to take the World History Test must be filled in exactly as illustration below. When your supervisor tells you to fill in the circle next to the name of the test you are about to take, mark your answer sheet as shown.

○ Literature	○ Mathematics Level 1	○ German	○ Chinese Listening	○ Japanese Listening
○ Biology E	○ Mathematics Level 2	○ Italian	○ French Listening	○ Korean Listening
○ Biology M	○ U.S. History	○ Latin	○ German Listening	○ Spanish Listening
○ Chemistry	● World History	○ Modern Hebrew		
○ Physics	○ French	○ Spanish	**Background Questions:** ① ② ③ ④ ⑤ ⑥ ⑦ ⑧ ⑨	

After filling in the circle next to the name of the test you are taking, locate the Background Questions box on your answer sheet (as shown above). This is where you will answer the following Background Questions on your answer sheet.

BACKGROUND QUESTIONS

Please answer the two questions below by filling in the appropriate circle in the Background Questions box on your answer sheet. The information you provide is for statistical purposes only and will not affect your test score.

Question I

How many semesters of world history, world cultures, or European history have you taken from grade 9 to the present? (If you are taking a course this semester, count it as a full semester.) Fill in only one circle of circles 1- 4.

- One semester or less —Fill in circle 1.
- Two semesters —Fill in circle 2.
- Three semesters —Fill in circle 3.
- Four or more semesters —Fill in circle 4.

Question II

For the courses in world history, world cultures, or European history you have taken, which of the following geographical areas did you study? Fill in all of the circles that apply.

- Africa —Fill in circle 5.
- Asia —Fill in circle 6.
- Europe —Fill in circle 7.
- Latin America —Fill in circle 8.
- Middle East —Fill in circle 9.

When the supervisor gives the signal, turn the page and begin the World History Test. There are 100 numbered circles on the answer sheet and 95 questions in the World History Test. Therefore, use only circles 1 to 95 for recording your answers.

WORLD HISTORY TEST

Directions: Each of the questions or incomplete statements below is followed by five suggested answers or completions. Select the one that is best in each case and then fill in the corresponding circle on the answer sheet.

Note: The World History Test uses the chronological designations B.C.E. (before common era) and C.E. (common era). These labels correspond to B.C. (before Christ) and A.D. (anno Domini), which are used in some world history textbooks.

1. Current knowledge about the Paleolithic Age comes mainly from which of the following sources?

(A) Building foundations
(B) Inscriptions
(C) Woven textiles
(D) Stone tools
(E) Ruined forts and abandoned mines

2. Which of the following was the primary basis for the Roman persecution of Christians in the second and third centuries?

(A) Christianity was seen as a sect of Judaism.
(B) Christian slaves often refused to serve their masters.
(C) All sectarian religious movements were illegal under Roman law.
(D) Christians refused to serve in the Roman army.
(E) Christians refused to worship the Roman emperors.

3. Rome's most far-reaching contribution to the development of Western society was in the area of

(A) philosophy
(B) religion
(C) literature
(D) law
(E) art

4. The result of the Edict of Toleration issued by Emperor Constantine was to

(A) make Christianity the official religion of the Roman Empire
(B) make the cult of Mithra the official religion of the Roman Empire
(C) celebrate Constantine's initiation into the ancient mysteries of Eleusis
(D) legalize the practice of Christianity within the Roman Empire
(E) establish the supremacy of Rome over all other Christian bishoprics

5. Egyptian and Chinese civilizations before 1000 C.E. may both be used to support the argument that

(A) very little social stratification existed in classical civilizations
(B) civilizations thrive only when they are expanding through military conquest
(C) agricultural economies based on maize and potato cultivation cannot sustain rapid population growth
(D) large-scale irrigation is associated with the formation of centralized states
(E) agricultural economies cannot generate sufficient surplus to fund large building projects

GO ON TO THE NEXT PAGE

6. The Great Wall of China was built to

   (A) keep the Chinese people from having contact with foreigners
   (B) defend China's northern borders
   (C) bring peace among rival factions seeking to dominate China
   (D) stimulate China's stagnant economy
   (E) provide a barrier between China and Korea

7. At its peak, Mayan culture was characterized by all of the following EXCEPT

   (A) a sophisticated mathematical knowledge
   (B) a dual calendar system
   (C) cities dominated by colossal pyramidal tombs
   (D) priest-kings who presided over sacrifices
   (E) the belief in a single supreme god

8. When historians use the term "the Byzantine Empire," they are referring to the

   (A) Roman Empire between the reigns of Diocletian and Odoacer
   (B) empire of Charlemagne
   (C) Sassanid dynasty of Persia
   (D) western portions of the Muslim world
   (E) eastern Roman Empire after the fifth century C.E.

9. At its height, the Ottoman Empire bureaucracy was able to maintain internal peace primarily by

   (A) allowing France and Russia to protect Christians in the Empire
   (B) banning intermarriage between members of different religions
   (C) giving Muslim clerics control of education
   (D) encouraging separatist movements by Jews, Christians, and Muslims
   (E) giving considerable freedom and autonomy to all religious communities

10. "A ruler, therefore, must not mind incurring the charge of cruelty for the purpose of keeping his subjects united and faithful; . . . he will be more merciful than those who, from excess of tenderness, allow disorders to arise . . . for these [disorders] as a rule injure the whole community, while the executions carried out by the ruler injure only individuals."

    The passage above was written by

    (A) Pico della Mirandola
    (B) Niccolò Machiavelli
    (C) Martin Luther
    (D) Oliver Cromwell
    (E) John Calvin

11. Completion of the Suez Canal in 1869 was important for which of the following reasons?

    (A) It stabilized the control of the Egyptian government.
    (B) It shortened the sea route between Europe and Africa.
    (C) It shortened the sea route between Europe and Asia.
    (D) It alleviated competition among European powers.
    (E) It improved the economic status of the majority of Middle Eastern residents.

12. The country that acted to limit Germany's acquisition of African colonies in the late nineteenth century was

    (A) Belgium
    (B) Great Britain
    (C) Italy
    (D) Portugal
    (E) Spain

GO ON TO THE NEXT PAGE

13. "India can never become a great manufacturing country, but by cultivating her connection with England she may become one of the greatest agricultural countries in the world."

This observation made in Great Britain in 1937 reflects which of the following generalizations about the relationship between colonial powers and colonized nations?

(A) Colonial powers directly subsidized the economies of the colonies.
(B) Colonial powers allowed tariff-free exports from their colonies.
(C) Colonies lacked the population required to become industrial centers.
(D) Colonies could potentially attain the same status as the colonial powers.
(E) Colonial powers used their colonies chiefly as sources of raw materials.

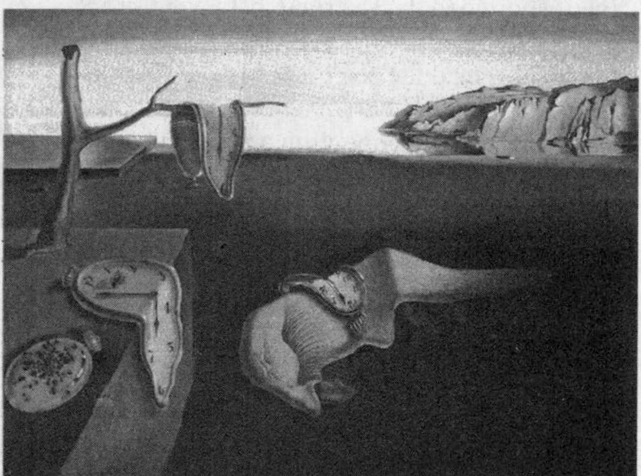

Collection, The Museum of Modern Art, New York. Given anonymously.

14. The painting above by Salvador Dalí is representative of which of the following artistic movements?

(A) Romanticism
(B) Art Nouveau
(C) Impressionism
(D) Bauhaus
(E) Surrealism

15. A devout Muslim is expected to do all of the following EXCEPT

(A) pray five times a day
(B) give alms to the poor
(C) fast from dawn to sundown during one month of the year
(D) devote two years to missionary service
(E) make a pilgrimage to Mecca once in a lifetime

16. Which of the following best describes matrilineal succession, as it was practiced in some African societies before 1500 ?

(A) Women passed their wealth only to their daughters.
(B) Women were responsible for controlling local governments.
(C) Women were trained as warriors and had primary responsibility for defense.
(D) Men were banned from owning property.
(E) Inheritance was passed to the oldest male through the mother's side of the family.

17. A candidate for the Chinese imperial civil service had to pass competitive examinations testing knowledge of

(A) foreign languages
(B) Manchu etiquette
(C) Confucian classics
(D) agricultural technology
(E) military tactics

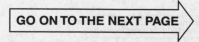

GO ON TO THE NEXT PAGE

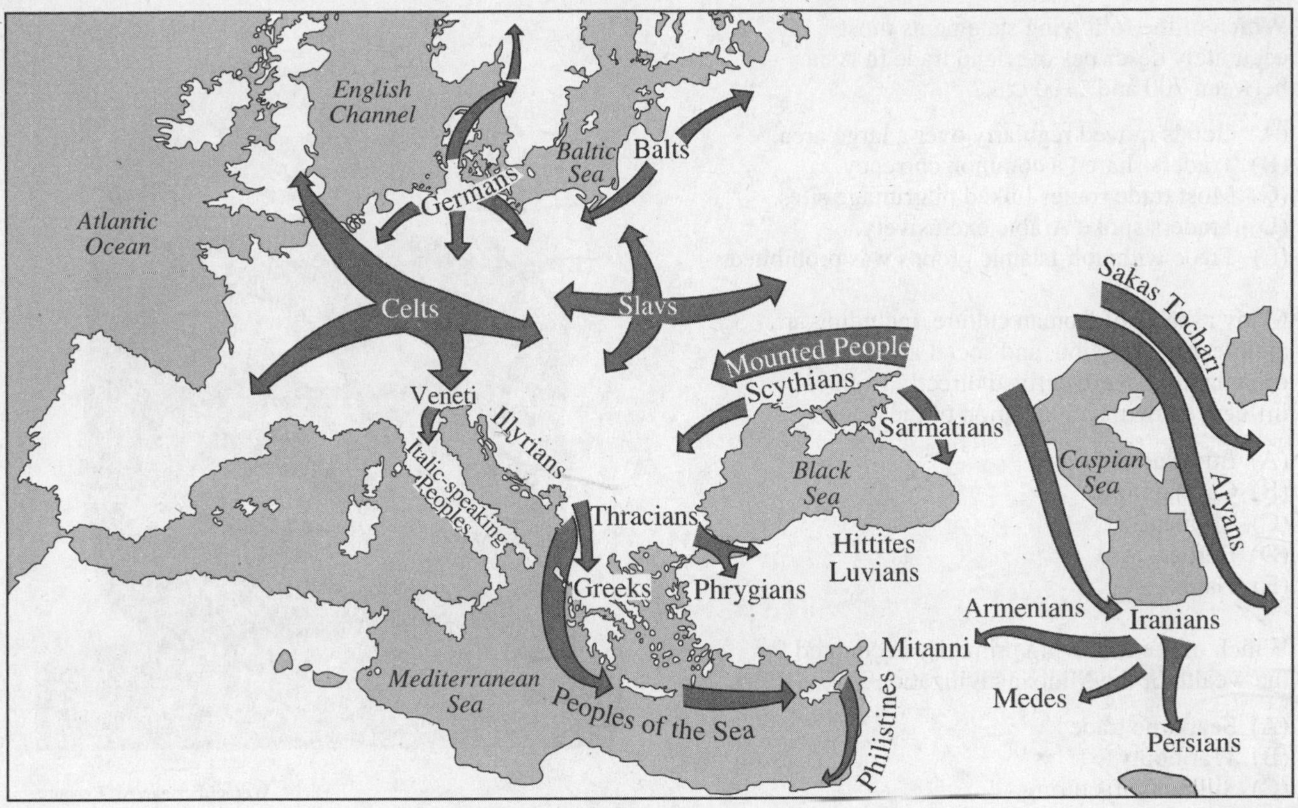

18. The map above illustrates

(A) invasions by Mongols
(B) the expansions of Indo-European peoples
(C) major central European trade routes
(D) invasions by Huns and Vandals
(E) the spread of the Black Death

GO ON TO THE NEXT PAGE

19. Which of the following statements most accurately describes overland trade in Asia between 700 and 1100 C.E.?

    (A) Goods moved regularly over a large area.
    (B) Traders shared a common currency.
    (C) Most trade routes linked pilgrimage sites.
    (D) Traders spoke Arabic exclusively.
    (E) Trade with non-Islamic groups was prohibited.

20. Many aspects of Roman culture, including art, architecture, religion, and social and military organization, were derived directly from or influenced by the civilization of the

    (A) Etruscans
    (B) Carthaginians
    (C) Minoans
    (D) Berbers
    (E) Gauls

21. Which of the following primarily accounted for the wealth of the Minoan civilization?

    (A) Seaborne trade
    (B) War booty
    (C) Silk manufacturing
    (D) Coal mining
    (E) Fishing

22. Toussaint L'Ouverture led a successful rebellion against French colonists that resulted in the establishment of which of the following nations?

    (A) Morocco
    (B) Liberia
    (C) Argentina
    (D) Cuba
    (E) Haiti

23. Renaissance humanism is most closely associated with which of the following?

    (A) Religious crusades
    (B) Monasticism
    (C) Scholarly study of classical texts
    (D) Rejection of Platonic philosophy
    (E) Translation of the Bible into the vernacular

Werner Forman/Art Resource

24. The large stone sculpture shown above is characteristic of artwork in which of the following civilizations?

    (A) Nubian
    (B) Assyrian
    (C) Olmec
    (D) Harappan
    (E) Shang

25. Germany was divided after the Second World War primarily because

    (A) the German people could not reach consensus on the kind of government they wanted
    (B) ethnic and religious divisions within Germany deepened after the war
    (C) the Allies were competing for economic and political control of central Europe
    (D) the Allies believed that the economic cost of uniting Germany was prohibitive
    (E) some parts of Germany had suffered more damage than others

GO ON TO THE NEXT PAGE

26. "The Proletarians have nothing to lose but their chains. They have a world to win. Workers of the world, unite!"

    The quotation above is taken from which of the following?

    (A) *Reason in History*, Georg Wilhelm Friedrich Hegel
    (B) *The Protestant Ethic and the Spirit of Capitalism*, Max Weber
    (C) *The Communist Manifesto*, Karl Marx and Friedrich Engels
    (D) *Utopia*, Thomas More
    (E) *The Wealth of Nations*, Adam Smith

27. Following the First World War, which of the following countries formerly in the Ottoman Empire modernized and nationalized most closely along the Western model?

    (A) Egypt
    (B) Syria
    (C) Turkey
    (D) Iran
    (E) Iraq

28. "The Great Royal Road was constructed to speed soldiers, supplies, and goods from one part of the empire to another. It was more than 1,500 miles long, extending from Susa, one of the capitals of the empire, to Sardis in Asia Minor. More than 100 way stations supplied travelers with lodging and state messengers with fresh horses."

    The paragraph above refers to the ancient kingdom of

    (A) Egypt
    (B) Macedonia
    (C) Persia
    (D) Sumeria
    (E) Judea

29. The British established informal rule over Egypt in the late nineteenth century primarily to

    (A) supply much of the raw cotton for the Lancashire cotton industry
    (B) compete with Germany in establishing a foothold in North Africa
    (C) exploit the oil resources of Egypt
    (D) establish a monopoly over Egyptian antiquities
    (E) exercise control over the Suez Canal

30. The population of which of the following Middle Eastern countries currently includes a sizeable Kurdish minority?

    (A) Iraq
    (B) Egypt
    (C) Lebanon
    (D) Saudi Arabia
    (E) Kuwait

31. The cultural and political development of Vietnam was most heavily influenced by which of the following countries?

    (A) Korea
    (B) Japan
    (C) China
    (D) Indonesia
    (E) Mongolia

32. From earliest to latest, what is the order in which the following religions came into existence?

    (A) Confucianism, Judaism, Christianity, Islam
    (B) Islam, Confucianism, Judaism, Christianity
    (C) Judaism, Confucianism, Christianity, Islam
    (D) Judaism, Christianity, Islam, Confucianism
    (E) Judaism, Confucianism, Islam, Christianity

33. The Sandinista Front for National Liberation dominated national politics in

    (A) Guatemala during the 1950's
    (B) Cuba during the 1960's
    (C) Puerto Rico during the 1970's
    (D) Nicaragua during the 1980's
    (E) El Salvador during the 1980's

34. One of the main aims of the groups who financed the European voyages of exploration in the fifteenth and sixteenth centuries was to

    (A) supply wealthy European households with non-European slaves
    (B) demonstrate European naval superiority over Africa and Asia
    (C) circumvent the Middle East to gain direct access to Asian goods
    (D) seek new crops to boost the European food supply
    (E) chart the extent of the Arab world

GO ON TO THE NEXT PAGE

35. Medieval Muslim merchants traveled more frequently to India than to Italy because

(A) travel to India was easier and safer
(B) papal bulls forbade Muslims from entering Christian harbors
(C) Christian crusades effectively closed off the Mediterranean Sea to Muslims
(D) there was a shortage of timber for shipbuilding along the southern Mediterranean coast
(E) Indian spices yielded greater profits than did Italian products

36. In the fifteenth century, overseas expeditions involving dozens of ships and thousands of men were mounted by the

(A) British
(B) French
(C) Maya
(D) Japanese
(E) Chinese

37. Saint Paul is known as the "second founder of Christianity" primarily because he

(A) gathered the materials for the New Testament
(B) became the leader of the apostles after Jesus' death
(C) was a great missionary and theologian
(D) founded the Vatican in Rome
(E) began the great monastic movement

38. Which of the following colonies in the Americas imported the largest number of slaves between 1500 and 1800 ?

(A) Argentina
(B) Cuba
(C) Mexico
(D) Jamaica
(E) Brazil

39. At the battle of Isandhlwana in 1879, the Zulu defeated armies from which of the following?

(A) Belgium
(B) Great Britain
(C) Germany
(D) France
(E) Italy

40. During the eighteenth century, the partitioning of Poland among Austria, Prussia, and Russia resulted mainly from

(A) Poland's lack of cultural unity
(B) Poland's small land area and population
(C) instability in the area as a result of constant civil wars
(D) the oppressive policies of the Polish kings
(E) Poland's weak central government

41. Persia became the focus of European imperialists in the late nineteenth century for all the following reasons EXCEPT:

(A) Persia was adjacent to India.
(B) Persia was the source of Islamic fundamentalism.
(C) Persia shared a border with Russia.
(D) Persia provided strategic access to the Arabian Sea.
(E) Persia's ruling dynasty was too weak to resist foreign advances.

42. All of the following technologies had widespread and important effects on nineteenth-century life EXCEPT

(A) railroads
(B) automobiles
(C) the telegraph
(D) the power loom
(E) the open-hearth furnace

43. Women gained the right to vote in most of western Europe and in the United States immediately after which of the following?

(A) The French Revolution
(B) The Seneca Falls Conference
(C) The American Civil War
(D) The First World War
(E) The Second World War

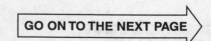

GO ON TO THE NEXT PAGE

44. The Indian caste system evolved because of the
    (A) clashes between patriarchal and matriarchal social orders
    (B) conquest of northern India by Alexander the Great
    (C) popular uprisings in the Indus Valley civilization
    (D) desire by Aryan invaders to distinguish themselves from non-Aryan groups
    (E) attempts by central Asian invaders to convert the people to Islam

45. Which of the following statements best characterizes the feudal system of medieval western Europe?
    (A) The social structure was nonhierarchical.
    (B) Peasants were not allowed to own land.
    (C) Lords and vassals were bound together by family ties.
    (D) The power structure was decentralized.
    (E) Only men were allowed to own land.

46. Which of the following statements regarding women's lives in Western Europe in the early medieval period is accurate?
    (A) Law and custom restricted women to working only in the home.
    (B) Changes in church law in the thirteenth century allowed women greater religious authority.
    (C) Aristocratic women enjoyed greater power and prominence in periods of military activity when men were away fighting.
    (D) Women could serve as feudal lords, but not as feudal vassals.
    (E) Among men and women of humbler status, the division of labor between the sexes was very strict.

47. Between 1638 and the mid-nineteenth century, Japan prohibited contact with all Western traders EXCEPT those from
    (A) Spain
    (B) Portugal
    (C) the Netherlands
    (D) France
    (E) England

48. Which of the following religions became firmly consolidated in Persia under the Safavid dynasty (1502-1736) ?
    (A) Shi'ite Islam
    (B) Sunni Islam
    (C) Sikhism
    (D) Nestorian Christianity
    (E) Jainism

49. Robert Owen sought to show through his textiles factory in New Lanark, Scotland, that
    (A) Great Britain could compete effectively in world trade
    (B) a profitable industry could be run without using the latest technology
    (C) increased profits and improved conditions could go hand in hand
    (D) manufactured goods could be equal in quality to handmade goods
    (E) the most effective way to increase productivity was through a combination of discipline and a longer working day

50. Which of the following was a legacy of the Napoleonic expedition to Egypt, 1798-1799 ?
    (A) Revival of the Coptic Church in Egypt
    (B) Plans for building the Suez Canal and the Aswan Dam
    (C) Interest in Egyptian archaeology and discovery of the Rosetta Stone
    (D) Heightened interest by Europeans in exploring the interior of Africa
    (E) Restoration of Mamluk rule in all of Egypt

GO ON TO THE NEXT PAGE

51. The February Revolution in Russia in 1917 was sparked primarily by which of the following events?

    (A) The death of Grigory Rasputin
    (B) The Allied invasion of Russia at Vladivostock
    (C) A Cossack rebellion
    (D) Strikes and food riots in Petrograd
    (E) The killing of the tsar and his family

52. Following 1910, political leaders in Mexico promoted the image of the mestizo as the "true Mexican" as a means of

    (A) fostering national unity
    (B) increasing the economic power of the mestizo after the revolution
    (C) recognizing the increased power of the mestizo in the military
    (D) countering the growing influence of the Roman Catholic Church
    (E) acknowledging European economic influence

53. One of Lenin's most important original contributions to Marxist ideology was his argument that

    (A) parliamentary elections would soon lead to a Communist party victory
    (B) a socialist revolution would first occur in a highly industrialized state
    (C) a centralized party had to organize and lead a socialist revolution
    (D) the dictatorship of the proletariat was not a necessary step in achieving a communist society
    (E) a mass coalition of socialist and democratic parties would rule after the revolution

54. Which of the following sentences best captures the essence of Jean-Jacques Rousseau's *The Social Contract* ?

    (A) Government should be based on the general will of the society.
    (B) Divine-right monarchy is the best form of government.
    (C) Industrialization will eliminate social and economic inequalities.
    (D) Most of Europe's social ills can be traced to a lack of land for agricultural expansion.
    (E) National economic prosperity can be maintained through constant involvement in war.

55. The Greek thinker Galen's study of anatomy in the second century C.E. was not significantly improved on in Europe until the sixteenth-century publication of the work of

    (A) Leonardo da Vinci
    (B) Tycho Brahe
    (C) Isaac Newton
    (D) Anton van Leeuwenhoek
    (E) Andreas Vesalius

56. From the thirteenth through the fourteenth centuries, the African empire of Mali did which of the following?

    (A) Rejected Islamic teaching
    (B) Resisted Christian missionaries
    (C) Exported large amounts of sorghum
    (D) Encouraged inhabitants to migrate eastward
    (E) Established a center of learning in Timbuktu

GO ON TO THE NEXT PAGE

57. Which of the following ancient written languages is still used by some priests in religious studies and ceremonies?

(A) Sumerian
(B) Sanskrit
(C) Etruscan
(D) Hittite
(E) Phoenician

58. In the 1960's the United States sent a large number of troops to support South Vietnam in its conflict with North Vietnam primarily because

(A) the Soviet Union was sending troops to North Vietnam
(B) such action would allow the United States to regain respect in Southeast Asia after losing the Korean War
(C) the United Nations Security Council encouraged all nations to send troops to defend South Vietnam against a North Vietnamese invasion
(D) the population of North Vietnam far exceeded that of South Vietnam and the United States sought to nullify this advantage
(E) United States policymakers believed the fall of South Vietnam to communism would endanger other countries in Southeast Asia

59. Which of the following best describes the twelfth and thirteenth centuries in Europe?

(A) A time of population expansion and urban growth
(B) A time of recovery from plague and famine
(C) A period of transition from an agricultural to an industrial society
(D) A period of political turmoil resulting in economic stagnation
(E) An era of prosperity due to an influx of silver and gold

60. In the tenth century, the Spanish cities of Córdoba and Seville were most renowned as centers of

(A) popular support for the Crusades
(B) Islamic architecture and scholarship
(C) the study of plant hybridization
(D) textile production
(E) gold and silver production

61. The first Russian state developed around which of the following cities?

(A) Kiev
(B) Novosibirsk
(C) Saint Petersburg
(D) Moscow
(E) Murmansk

62. A primary reason for the rapid drop in the economic growth rates of Venezuela and Mexico in the 1980's was

(A) low birthrates and a shrinking labor pool
(B) insurgencies that disrupted the democratic process
(C) the curtailment of aid from the Soviet Union
(D) the abrupt decline of world oil prices
(E) a decline in literacy rates

GO ON TO THE NEXT PAGE

63. When Hernando de Soto traveled from the region now called Florida to the region west of the Mississippi River, he observed which of the following?

(A) Domesticated horses
(B) Iron hoes
(C) Domesticated sheep and pigs
(D) Populated areas linked by trade
(E) Indians worshiping gold and silver objects

64. A common factor in the emergence of totalitarianism in Italy and Germany was

(A) the strife of civil wars
(B) rapid industrialization
(C) a decline in nationalism
(D) severe economic depression
(E) the violent overthrow of existing governments

65. Friedrich Nietzsche and Sigmund Freud would most likely have agreed that

(A) human nature is essentially good
(B) civic virtue holds society together in difficult times
(C) the nonrational is key to understanding the human condition
(D) there are natural laws that govern human relationships
(E) human reason is best used as a tool for social reform

66. Socialist political parties, once allied in a single international organization, split into socialist and communist wings immediately following the

(A) publication of the *Communist Manifesto* in 1848
(B) outbreak of the Franco-Prussian War in 1870
(C) outbreak of the Bolshevik Revolution in 1917
(D) signing of the Nazi-Soviet Pact in 1939
(E) outbreak of the Chinese Revolution in 1949

67. Which of the following Southeast Asian countries was the first to achieve political independence after the Second World War?

(A) Indonesia
(B) Malaysia
(C) Myanmar (Burma)
(D) The Philippines
(E) Vietnam

68. John Maynard Keynes believed that increased government intervention in the economy during a depression would lead to which of the following?

(A) Dangerous dependence on government subsidies
(B) Rapid and successful industrialization
(C) Stronger labor unions
(D) Increased employment and economic growth
(E) Disruption of the natural forces regulating a healthy economy

GO ON TO THE NEXT PAGE

69. Which of the following events occurred most recently in the history of Poland?

(A) The division of Poland among Russia, Prussia, and Austria
(B) The creation of the Grand Duchy of Warsaw
(C) The formation of the Solidarity Union
(D) The occupation of Poland by Soviet forces
(E) The defeat by Prussia and Russia of Polish forces under Tadeusz Kościuszko

70. Russia's eastward expansion, which began in the sixteenth century, was mainly possible because of its

(A) navigable rivers
(B) protected mountain ranges
(C) abundance of warm-water ports
(D) great uninterrupted plains
(E) moderate fluctuations in seasonal temperatures

71. British support for a Jewish national homeland in Palestine, with the provision that the rights of existing non-Jewish communities in Palestine be safeguarded, was stated in the

(A) Balfour Declaration
(B) Beveridge Report
(C) Camp David Accords
(D) Locarno Pact
(E) Atlantic Charter

72. The French *Encyclopédie*, a project to collect all human knowledge, was first published in 1751 under the editorship of

(A) Diderot and d'Alembert
(B) Montesquieu and Fénelon
(C) Lavoisier and Rousseau
(D) Condorcet and Turgot
(E) d'Holbach and Condillac

73. Which of the following technological innovations contributed to the Hyksos' success in overthrowing the ruling Egyptian dynasty?

(A) The horse-drawn chariot
(B) Gunpowder and cannons
(C) The lateen sail
(D) The crossbow
(E) Stirrups

74. Which of the following statements about European labor unions as they developed in the nineteenth and twentieth centuries is true?

(A) They descended with relatively few modifications from the medieval guild system.
(B) They developed mainly as the workers' response to industrialization.
(C) They were applauded by the Roman Catholic church and by the Protestant clergy.
(D) They were not supported by socialists.
(E) They were designed principally to nominate candidates for public office.

75. The First World War had which of the following effects on the continent of Africa?

(A) A number of former colonies gained their independence.
(B) The British and the French acquired territory formerly controlled by Germany.
(C) Russia received African colonies as part of the Paris Peace Conference.
(D) The United States became a new mandate power in Africa.
(E) China and Japan began to supply Africa with manufactured goods.

GO ON TO THE NEXT PAGE

"My wife is a woman of mind."

76. The purpose of the late nineteenth-century British cartoon above was to

(A) invite men to help their working wives with child care
(B) condemn intellectual women as unfit wives and mothers
(C) encourage women to use their education even though they had children
(D) criticize fathers who left the children's discipline to their wives
(E) suggest that fathers were just as good at looking after children as mothers were

GO ON TO THE NEXT PAGE

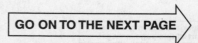

77. Which of the following was true of the European colonial penetration of Africa in the nineteenth century?

(A) The preexisting patterns of regional political organization determined colonial boundaries.
(B) Only the Bantu kingdoms south and west of Lake Tanganyika remained unconquered.
(C) The German and Austrian governments were the first to make military conquests.
(D) African social, economic, and religious organ-ations were left intact.
(E) Private ventures by Europeans were later recognized and supported by home governments.

78. In most areas of Europe during the medieval period, women were prohibited from

(A) reading and writing
(B) performing agricultural labor
(C) inheriting land and goods
(D) participating in business and trade
(E) administering sacraments in church

79. "I believe in the doctrine of nonviolence as a weapon of the weak. I believe in the doctrine of nonviolence as a weapon of the strongest. I believe that a man is the strongest soldier for daring to die unarmed."

The political philosophy stated above was espoused by many

(A) Nationalist Chinese in their attempt to wrest control from the Communists
(B) Indians in their attempt to gain independence from British rule
(C) Jews in their attempt to gain a national homeland
(D) Black South Africans in their struggle to end apartheid
(E) Irish Republican Army members in their attempt to unify Ireland

80. The first Indian empire was founded by

(A) Kanishka
(B) Samudragupta
(C) Chandragupta Maurya
(D) Ashoka
(E) Akbar

81. Which of the following was a goal of both Peter the Great of Russia and Joseph Stalin of the Soviet Union?

(A) Achievement of economic equality for all citizens
(B) Final conquest of Siberia
(C) An isolationist foreign policy
(D) Increased use of Western technology
(E) Preservation of traditional village life

82. During the 1960's "neocolonialism" was the term used to describe

(A) continued military control of parts of Africa by European powers
(B) the influx of workers from developing countries into Western countries
(C) the spread of revolutionary socialist doctrines in Africa and Latin America
(D) continued economic domination by Western states of former colonial areas
(E) Soviet control of Central Asian Muslim societies

83. "From every sentence deep, original, and sublime thoughts arise, and the whole is pervaded by a high and holy and earnest spirit. Indian air surrounds us, and original thoughts of kindred spirits."

The statement above about an ancient Indian text is most representative of which of the following intellectual movements?

(A) Materialism
(B) Deism
(C) Positivism
(D) Romanticism
(E) Utilitarianism

GO ON TO THE NEXT PAGE

84. Charles de Gaulle returned to power in 1958 following a national crisis in France over

(A) French colonial rule in Algeria
(B) France's military role in the North Atlantic Treaty Organization (NATO)
(C) France's continued role in the occupation of Germany
(D) the replacement of the French franc with a common European currency
(E) an attempted coup led by the Communist party

85. In response to European challenges in the nineteenth century, rulers in Morocco, Tunisia, Egypt, Persia, and the Ottoman Empire did which of the following?

(A) Embarked on a program of land reform that favored small farmers
(B) Encouraged the reform of Islamic doctrine and law
(C) Sought to unify themselves under a revived caliphate
(D) Expelled all foreigners and closed themselves off from the West
(E) Reformed their bureaucracies and armies

86. "From Magna Carta to the Declaration of Rights, it has been the uniform policy of our constitution to claim and assert our liberties as an *entailed inheritance* derived to us from our forefathers, and to be transmitted to our posterity; as an estate specially belonging to the people of this kingdom, without any reference whatever to any other more general or prior right."

The statement above was most likely made by which of the following?

(A) A French radical urging the crowd to storm the Bastille
(B) An American revolutionary urging the people to support the new Constitution as the law of the land
(C) A German philosopher who believed that freedom exists only within the human will, regardless of the laws
(D) An Indian leader arguing for the freeing of India from colonial domination by the British
(E) A British conservative who believed that freedom and human rights were part of a cultural inheritance

87. In Latin America, the term *caudillismo* refers to

(A) electoral reform
(B) land development
(C) economic independence
(D) social equality
(E) military dictatorship

88. Beginning in 1929, the value of Chile's exports fell by 80 percent, and the value of exports of other Latin American countries fell by at least half.

The economic disaster in Latin America referred to above was the result of

(A) internal political instability
(B) government confiscation of the means of production
(C) crop failures and other natural disasters
(D) the worldwide economic depression
(E) labor unrest in the factories and mines

89. The French Utopian socialists of the late eighteenth and the nineteenth centuries believed that

(A) revolution is essential to the formation of a socialist state
(B) all history is the history of class struggle
(C) capitalists are the key to the creation of socialism
(D) economic planning should not be the responsibility of the state
(E) property should be communally owned

GO ON TO THE NEXT PAGE

90. Which of the following groups spearheaded new nationalist movements in Egypt and the Ottoman Empire in the late nineteenth century?

    (A) Junior army officers
    (B) Writers
    (C) Religious leaders
    (D) Women's rights activists
    (E) Industrialists

91. The Sino-Japanese and Russo-Japanese wars were similar in that both

    (A) retarded Japan's economic growth
    (B) resulted in huge indemnities for Japan
    (C) began with disputes over Korea
    (D) were opposed by the bulk of Japan's citizens
    (E) were resolved with the help of the President of the United States

92. During the seventh and eighth centuries, the Arabs conquered all of the following EXCEPT

    (A) Spain
    (B) Persia
    (C) Constantinople
    (D) Jerusalem
    (E) Damascus

93. The Indian subcontinent was partitioned into India and Pakistan in order to

    (A) reflect linguistic and ethnic differences
    (B) reestablish the political boundaries of the ancient Indian kingdoms
    (C) provide for Indian Muslims who had been dispossessed under British rule
    (D) make a concession to the rajahs, who sought autonomy in Pakistan
    (E) satisfy the Muslim League's demand for an independent Muslim state

94. During the Middle Ages, Northern European agriculture differed from Mediterranean agriculture because Northern Europe

    (A) was more mountainous
    (B) was wetter and colder for most of the year
    (C) was dryer and colder for most of the year
    (D) produced more grapes and wine
    (E) did not have both hunting and agricultural economies

95. Which of the following African countries is a member of the Organization of Petroleum Exporting Countries (OPEC) and a major supplier of oil on the world market?

    (A) Liberia
    (B) Nigeria
    (C) Mali
    (D) Ivory Coast
    (E) Senegal

STOP

If you finish before time is called, you may check your work on this test only.
Do not turn to any other section in the test.

How to Score the SAT Subject Test in World History

When you take an actual SAT Subject Test in World History, your answer sheet will be "read" by a scanning machine that will record your responses to each question. Then a computer will compare your answers with the correct answers and produce your raw score. You get one point for each correct answer. For each wrong answer, you lose one-quarter of a point. Questions you omit (and any for which you mark more than one answer) are not counted. This raw score is converted to a scaled score that is reported to you and to the colleges you specify.

Worksheet 1. Finding Your Raw Test Score

STEP 1: Table A on the following page lists the correct answers for all the questions on the Subject Test in World History that is reproduced in this book. It also serves as a worksheet for you to calculate your raw score.

- Compare your answers with those given in the table.
- Put a check in the column marked "Right" if your answer is correct.
- Put a check in the column marked "Wrong" if your answer is incorrect.
- Leave both columns blank if you omitted the question.

STEP 2: Count the number of right answers.

Enter the total here: 82

STEP 3: Count the number of wrong answers.

Enter the total here: 13

STEP 4: Multiply the number of wrong answers by .250.

Enter the product here: ____________

STEP 5: Subtract the result obtained in Step 4 from the total you obtained in Step 2.

Enter the result here: ____________

STEP 6: Round the number obtained in Step 5 to the nearest whole number.

Enter the result here: ____________

The number you obtained in Step 6 is your raw score.

TABLE A

Answers to the SAT Subject Test in World History – Practice Test 2 and Percentage of Students Answering Each Question Correctly

Question Number	Correct Answer	Right	Wrong	Percentage of Students Answering the Question Correctly*	Question Number	Correct Answer	Right	Wrong	Percentage of Students Answering the Question Correctly*
1	D			74	33	D			23
2	E			63	34	C			74
3	D			57	35	E			44
4	D			71	36	E			22
5	D			63	37	C			26
6	B			85	38	E			36
7	E			79	39	B			38
8	E			68	40	E			61
9	E			74	41	B			55
10	B			68	42	B			51
11	C			61	43	D			53
12	B			79	44	D			44
13	E			59	45	D			39
14	E			74	46	C			32
15	D			87	47	C			37
16	E			55	48	A			35
17	C			63	49	C			41
18	B			72	50	C			37
19	A			54	51	D			50
20	A			40	52	A			57
21	A			47	53	C			51
22	E			60	54	A			76
23	C			59	55	E			21
24	C			46	56	E			38
25	C			58	57	B			52
26	C			78	58	E			83
27	C			63	59	A			20
28	C			48	60	B			41
29	E			72	61	A			37
30	A			29	62	D			20
31	C			59	63	D			29
32	C			33	64	D			65

Table A continued on next page

Table A continued from previous page

Question Number	Correct Answer	Right	Wrong	Percentage of Students Answering the Question Correctly*	Question Number	Correct Answer	Right	Wrong	Percentage of Students Answering the Question Correctly*
65	C			37	81	D			62
66	C			47	82	D			49
67	D			33	83	D			27
68	D			31	84	A			31
69	C			46	85	E			33
70	D			48	86	E			49
71	A			56	87	E			26
72	A			44	88	D			70
73	A			36	89	E			45
74	B			76	90	A			16
75	B			62	91	C			31
76	B			73	92	C			31
77	E			33	93	E			55
78	E			30	94	B			48
79	B			68	95	B			39
80	C			30					

* These percentages are based on an analysis of the answer sheets of a representative sample of 12,958 students who took the original administration of this test and whose mean score was 579. They may be used as an indication of the relative difficulty of a particular question.

Finding Your Scaled Score

When you take SAT Subject Tests, the scores sent to the colleges you specify are reported on the College Board scale, which ranges from 200 to 800. You can convert your practice test raw score to a scaled score by using Table B. To find your scaled score, locate your raw score in the left-hand column of Table B; the corresponding score in the right-hand column is your scaled score. For example, a raw score of 39 on this particular edition of the SAT Subject Test in World History corresponds to a scaled score of 580.

Raw scores are converted to scaled scores to ensure that a score earned on any one edition of a particular Subject Test is comparable to the same scaled score earned on any other edition of the same Subject Test. Because some editions of the tests may be slightly easier or more difficult than others, College Board scaled scores are adjusted so that they indicate the same level of performance regardless of the edition of the test taken and the ability of the group that takes it. Thus, for example, a score of 400 on one edition of a test taken at a particular administration indicates the same level of achievement as a score of 400 on a different edition of the test taken at a different administration.

When you take the SAT Subject Tests during a national administration, your scores are likely to differ somewhat from the scores you obtain on the tests in this book. People perform at different levels at different times for reasons unrelated to the tests themselves. The precision of any test is also limited because it represents only a sample of all the possible questions that could be asked.

Table B

Scaled Score Conversion Table Subject Test in World History Test – Practice Test 2					
Raw Score	Scaled Score	Raw Score	Scaled Score	Raw Score	Scaled Score
95	800	55	680	15	440
94	800	54	670	14	430
93	800	53	670	13	430
92	800	52	660	12	420
91	800	51	660	11	420
90	800	50	650	10	410
89	800	49	640	9	400
88	800	48	640	8	400
87	800	47	630	7	390
86	800	46	630	6	390
85	800	45	620	5	380
84	800	44	610	4	370
83	800	43	610	3	370
82	800	42	600	2	360
81	800	41	600	1	360
80	800	40	590	0	350
79	800	39	580	-1	340
78	800	38	580	-2	340
77	800	37	570	-3	330
76	800	36	570	-4	330
75	800	35	560	-5	320
74	790	34	550	-6	320
73	790	33	550	-7	310
72	780	32	540	-8	300
71	770	31	540	-9	300
70	770	30	530	-10	290
69	760	29	520	-11	290
68	760	28	520	-12	280
67	750	27	510	-13	270
66	740	26	510	-14	270
65	740	25	500	-15	260
64	730	24	490	-16	260
63	730	23	490	-17	250
62	720	22	480	-18	240
61	720	21	480	-19	240
60	710	20	470	-20	230
59	700	19	460	-21	230
58	700	18	460	-22	220
57	690	17	450	-23	210
56	690	16	450	-24	210

How Did You Do on the Subject Test in World History?

After you score your test and analyze your performance, think about the following questions:

Did you run out of time before reaching the end of the test?

If so, you may need to pace yourself better. For example, maybe you spent too much time on one or two hard questions. A better approach might be to skip the ones you can't answer right away and try answering all the remaining questions on the test. Then if there's time, go back to the questions you skipped.

Did you take a long time reading the directions?

You will save time when you take the test by learning the directions to the Subject Test in World History ahead of time. Each minute you spend reading directions during the test is a minute that you could use to answer questions.

How did you handle questions you were unsure of?

If you were able to eliminate one or more of the answer choices as wrong and guess from the remaining ones, your approach probably worked to your advantage. On the other hand, making haphazard guesses or omitting questions without trying to eliminate choices could cost you valuable points.

How difficult were the questions for you compared with other students who took the test?

Table A shows you how difficult the multiple-choice questions were for the group of students who took this test during its national administration. The right-hand column gives the percentage of students that answered each question correctly.

A question answered correctly by almost everyone in the group is obviously an easier question. For example, 85 percent of the students answered question 6 correctly. However, only 16 percent answered question 90 correctly.

Keep in mind that these percentages are based on just one group of students. They would probably be different with another group of students taking the test.

If you missed several easier questions, go back and try to find out why: Did the questions cover material you haven't yet reviewed? Did you misunderstand the directions?

Answer Explanations for World History – Practice Test 2

1. Choice (D) is the correct answer. Few artifacts have survived from the Paleolithic Age, which lasted from about 2.5 million years ago to about 10,000 years ago. Most of what we know about the Paleolithic Age comes primarily from the study of stone tools. Building foundations (A), inscriptions (B), woven textiles (C), and ruined forts and abandoned mines (E) would also be evidence of a human presence, but few of these types of remains dating from the Paleolithic Age have been found.

2. Choice (E) is the correct answer. Christians refused to worship the Roman emperors. Christianity within the Roman Empire was a predominantly urban religion that accepted and benefited from many facets of the Roman civil order, but Christians drew the line at accepting the divinity of the Roman emperor, which was required of all Roman citizens, because this practice conflicted with Christians' monotheistic belief. Many early Christians were persecuted and martyred over this issue by the Roman authorities. Choice (A) is incorrect because the Roman authorities had no particular interest in the fact that Christianity had sprung from Judaism. Choice (B) is incorrect because slave–master relationships were not a major point of contention between Christians and the Roman authorities. Christians accepted the institution of slavery in this period and did not encourage slaves to revolt or disobey. Choice (C) is incorrect; a wide variety of religions was tolerated by the Roman authorities, especially if their practice did not conflict with Roman law. Choice (D) is incorrect because Christians did serve in the Roman army throughout the Empire.

3. Choice (D) is the correct answer. Historians are in agreement that the most important and enduring Roman contribution to future generations was Roman law. Roman law and legal practice became the basis of law in all of western Europe, with the exception of England, and through colonial and commercial contacts it has spread worldwide. Roman civilization had achievements in the fields of philosophy (A), religion (B), literature (C), and art (E), but none of these have affected the daily lives of more people, worldwide, than has Roman law.

4. Choice (D) is the correct answer. Emperor Constantine's sudden decision in 313 C.E., at a conference held at Milan, to extend complete freedom of worship to Christians and to order the return of their confiscated property ended Christian persecution

by the Roman authorities. Christians acquired a privileged juridical status that they would retain, in many Western lands, until the eighteenth and nineteenth centuries. Choice (A) is incorrect; this did not occur until 392 C.E., when the Roman Emperor, Theodosius the Great, forbade the practice of all religions except the form of Christianity recognized by the government. Choice (B) is incorrect; Mithra was originally a Persian god that was popular with members of the Roman army. Choice (C) is incorrect; the mysteries of Eleusis refer to ancient religious rites celebrated at Eleusis, near ancient Athens, in honor of Demeter. Choice (E) is incorrect; the position of the bishoprics of Rome in the Church was not dealt with in the Edict of Toleration.

5. Choice (D) is the correct answer. One theory of why states first formed holds that in the late Neolithic period, the need to coordinate large-scale irrigation efforts in river valleys necessitated the creation of more centralized forms of government. Before 1000 C.E., both Egypt and China were early centralized states whose formation was associated with the beginning of large-scale irrigation. Choice (A) is incorrect; there was considerable social stratification in classical Egypt and classical China. Choice (B) is incorrect; expansion of ancient civilizations usually occurred during periods of peace, not during periods of conflict. Choice (C) is incorrect; rapid population expansion can be and has been sustained in civilizations based on cultivation of maize and potatoes, New World staple products. Choice (E) is incorrect; the economies of ancient Egypt and China were primarily agricultural and both generated food surpluses sufficient to support massive building projects.

6. Choice (B) is the correct answer. The Great Wall of China was built primarily to defend China's northern borders against raids and incursions by nomadic peoples living in the steppe regions north of the Great Wall. Choice (A) is incorrect; the Chinese continued to have extensive trade contact with peoples beyond the Great Wall after its construction. Choice (C) is incorrect; the Great Wall was not built as a means of bringing peace among internal Chinese factions. Choice (D) is incorrect; the Great Wall was not built to stimulate the Chinese economy. Choice (E) is incorrect; the Great Wall did not form a barrier between China and Korea.

7. Choice (E) is the correct answer. Mayan religion was not monotheistic; the Maya believed in many gods and goddesses. Choices (A), (B), (C), and (D) are all correct and cite important aspects of Mayan civilization.

8. Choice (E) is the correct answer. The Byzantine Empire is the name used by modern historians to describe the primarily Greek-speaking eastern portion of the Roman Empire that survived after the Western Roman Empire collapsed in the fifth century. The Byzantine Empire was centered in Constantinople (formerly called Byzantium) and it lasted until the fall of that city to the Ottoman Turks in 1453. Choice (A) is

incorrect; the Roman Empire is the designation generally used for the entire (eastern and western) Empire prior to the deposition of the last emperor in the west in 476 C.E. Choice (B) is incorrect; from 778 to 814 C.E., Charlemagne ruled over the Frankish Empire, which became the Holy Roman Empire in the year 800 C.E. Choice (C) is incorrect; the Sassanid dynasty ruled from 224 to 651 C.E. in ancient Iran. Choice (D) is incorrect; the official religion of the Byzantine Empire was Eastern Orthodox Christianity; it was later overwhelmed by the forces of Islam.

9. Choice (E) is the correct answer. The Ottoman Empire, at its peak, allowed considerable autonomy to the various religious communities within the Empire, though Islam was the favored religion. Choice (A) is incorrect; it was only late in Ottoman history, in the nineteenth and early twentieth centuries, when the Ottoman government was considerably weakened, that it allowed European powers to act as protectors of Christian minorities in the Ottoman Empire. Choice (B) is incorrect; banning of marriages between Muslims and non-Muslims was not used by the Ottoman government as a means of maintaining internal peace. Choice (C) is incorrect; control of education by the Muslim clerics was not a method used by the Ottoman rulers to maintain internal peace. Choice (D) is incorrect; separatist movements were not tolerated by the Ottoman Empire at its height.

10. Choice (B) is the correct answer. In his political essay, *The Prince* (written circa 1505), Machiavelli set down rules for princes or leaders of states to follow. This passage epitomizes Machiavelli's belief that a strong, ruthless ruler was often best for a state. Choice (A) is incorrect; Pico della Mirandola was primarily a Neoplatonist and a Renaissance humanist, not a political philosopher. Choice (C) is incorrect; Martin Luther was a theologian concerned primarily with questions of individual salvation and would not have written this passage. Choice (D) is incorrect; Oliver Cromwell was a seventeenth-century English soldier and revolutionary; he did not write this passage. Choice (E) is incorrect; John Calvin was a Swiss reform theologian and did not share this philosophy of government.

11. Choice (C) is the correct answer. The Suez Canal shortened the sea route between Europe and Asia. The canal linked the Mediterranean Sea and the Red Sea (and ultimately the Indian Ocean) and reduced the need for west–east shipping to go around the African continent. It changed military and commercial shipping patterns and made the Isthmus of Suez a major global strategic location. Choice (A) is incorrect because after the opening of the Suez Canal, the British gradually assumed financial and administrative control of the canal from the Egyptians. Choice (B) is incorrect; sea routes from Europe to some eastern African ports were shortened, but the primary importance of the canal was the shortening of commercial and military routes between Europe and South and East Asia. Choice (D) is incorrect; after 1869, military and colonial competition among the European powers intensified. Choice

(E) is incorrect; the opening of the Suez Canal had very little, if any immediate, impact on the economic status of the majority of Middle Eastern people.

12. Choice (B) is the correct answer. Great Britain tried to block some of Germany's attempts to establish a colonial empire in Africa. The other four countries, Belgium (A), Italy (C), Portugal (D), and Spain (E), all had colonies in Africa, but were not significant impediments to German colonial expansion in that area.

13. Choice (E) is the correct answer. Colonial powers used their colonies chiefly as sources of raw materials. The quotation refers to the mercantilist vision Britain had for its colonies, such as India. According to the mercantilist scheme, the colonies would provide raw materials that would be processed into finished industrial goods in Great Britain. These goods would later be distributed and sold worldwide with most of the economic gain going to Great Britain. Choice (A) is incorrect; Great Britain and other colonial powers expected the colonial economies to pay for the costs of their own administration and provide a revenue stream for the mother country. Choice (B) is incorrect; nothing is said in the passage concerning tariffs. Choice (C) is incorrect; the passage does not cite lack of population as an impediment to a colony's industrial development. Choice (D) is incorrect; it directly contradicts the main point of the passage.

14. Choice (E) is the correct answer. Salvador Dalí was a major member of the Surrealist school of painting, and the painting shown, *The Persistence of Memory*, is typical of the Surrealist style. Choices (A), (B), (C), and (D) are incorrect because this painting is not representative of any of these artistic movements.

15. Choice (D) is the correct answer. Muslims are not required to devote two years to missionary service. Choices (A), (B), (C), and (E) all describe obligations of devout Muslims as described in the Qur'an and are, in fact, statements of four of the "Five Pillars" of Islamic faith.

16. Choice (E) is the correct answer. Matrilineal succession, as it was practiced in some African societies prior to 1500, involved the passage of property and certain privileges and honors through the female line of descent, rather than through the male line. It is not to be confused with matriarchy, a form of government in which women wield the most political power. Choice (A) is incorrect; women did not pass their wealth only to their daughters. Choice (B) is incorrect; women did not control local governments. Choice (C) is incorrect; women did not have primary responsibility for defense. Choice (D) is incorrect; men were not banned from owning property in matrilineal African societies.

17. Choice (C) is the correct answer. Chinese imperial civil service examinations required extensive knowledge of the Confucian classics, which dealt with issues of social and political order. Questions on foreign languages (A), Manchu etiquette (B), agricultural technology (D), and military tactics (E) were not generally found on these examinations.

18. Choice (B) is the correct answer. The map shows the expansions of Indo-European peoples. The labels next to the arrows provide the names of the major groups speaking Indo-European languages and what is known of their expansion in the second and first millennia B.C.E. Choices (A), (C), (D), and (E) are incorrect.

19. Choice (A) is the correct answer. During the period from 700 to 1100 C.E., goods moved regularly overland over defined Asian caravan routes. Choice (B) is incorrect; the traders did not have a common currency. Choice (C) is incorrect; pilgrimage sites were associated with stops along some, but not a majority, of the trade routes. Choice (D) is incorrect; Arabic was not the exclusive language of the merchants on these routes. Choice (E) is incorrect; trade was not limited to Islamic groups.

20. Choice (A) is the correct answer. The Etruscans lived primarily in the area in the Italian peninsula between the Tiber and Arno rivers west and south of the Apennine Mountains (hence the modern name "Tuscany"). Their urban culture reached its height in the sixth century B.C.E. Many features of Etruscan culture were adopted by the Romans, their successors. Choices (B), (C), (D), and (E) are incorrect; these groups had little or no influence on Roman culture in its formative period.

21. Choice (A) is the correct answer. Minoan civilization, which flourished in the Aegean region in the second millennium B.C.E., was remarkable for its great cities and palaces and its extensive seaborne trade throughout the eastern Mediterranean basin and beyond. Choices (B), (C), (D), and (E) are incorrect; none of these were major factors accounting for the wealth of the Minoans.

22. Choice (E) is the correct answer. Toussaint L'Ouverture was responsible for the establishment of the independent country of Haiti. He had nothing to do with rebellions in Morocco (A), Liberia (B), Argentina (C), and Cuba (D).

23. Choice (C) is the correct answer. Renaissance humanists devoted their time to recovering, studying, and applying classical Greek and Roman texts. Renaissance humanism is not closely associated with religious crusades (A), monasticism (B), the rejection of Platonic philosophy (D), or the translation of the Bible into the vernacular (E).

24. Choice (C) is the correct answer. The stone sculpture depicted in the photograph is a famous example of Olmec artwork. The civilizations mentioned in choices (A), (B), (D), and (E) did not produce artwork in this style.

25. Choice (C) is the correct answer. Germany was a central point of contention in the Cold War rivalry between the Soviet Union and the United States that developed after the Second World War. Germany was originally divided into occupation zones by the victorious Allied powers, but the continued split between East and West Germany was an expression of the confrontation between liberal capitalism and communism. Germany remained divided until 1989; its reunification marked the end of the Cold War. Choices (A), (B), (D), and (E) were not reasons why Germany was divided.

26. Choice (C) is the correct answer. This is a quotation describing a central idea from *The Communist Manifesto.* The quotation is not from any of the works listed in choices (A), (B), (D), or (E).

27. Choice (C) is the correct answer. Under the post-First World War leadership of Mustafa Kemal Atatürk, Turkey (the ethnically Turkish core region of the defunct Ottoman Empire) undertook a radical modernization program, following a Western model, which included secularization of the state and the adoption of the Roman alphabet. Egypt (A), Syria (B), and Iraq (E) were new countries that also emerged from the breakup of the Ottoman Empire, but all of them were under European dominance in the post-First World War period and did not undertake modernization programs of the same scope as Turkey's. Iran (D) was not a state that emerged from the breakup of the Ottoman Empire, and it did not undertake a major modernization program at this time.

28. Choice (C) is the correct answer. The passage describes the course of the Persian Empire's Great Royal Road, which was constructed in the sixth century B.C.E. When completed, it stretched from the center of the Persian Empire across hundreds of miles of modern-day Iran, Iraq, Syria, and Turkey, terminating at Sardis, near the Aegean coast. The Great Royal Road was not located in Egypt (A), Macedonia (B), Sumeria (D), or Judea (E).

29. Choice (E) is the correct answer. It was in order to control the Suez Canal and to keep it open for vital commerce between Europe and Asia that Great Britain established a protectorate over Egypt in 1882. Great Britain maintained this informal rule until after the Second World War. Choice (A) is incorrect; Egypt was already supplying much of the cotton for the British textile industry before Great Britain took control. Choice (B) is incorrect; Germany was not seriously seeking holdings in North Africa.

Choice (C) is incorrect; no significant oil reserves had been discovered in Egypt by 1882. Choice (D) is incorrect; gaining access to antiquities was not sufficient motivation for Great Britain to take control of Egypt.

30. Choice (A) is the correct answer. A large Kurdish population dwells in northern Iraq. There are also significant Kurdish populations in Iran, Turkey, and Syria, but there are no significant Kurdish minorities in Egypt (B), Lebanon (C), Saudi Arabia (D), or Kuwait (E).

31. Choice (C) is the correct answer. For hundreds of years, Vietnamese culture and politics were heavily influenced by China and Chinese models. Korea (A), Japan (B), Indonesia (D), and Mongolia (E) did not serve as cultural or political models for Vietnam.

32. Choice (C) is the correct answer. Judaism emerged in the second millennium B.C.E. Confucius wrote his texts in the sixth and fifth centuries B.C.E. Christianity appeared in the first century C.E. Islam appeared in the seventh century C.E. The four religions are in the proper chronological sequence in choice (C); the other four choices are incorrect.

33. Choice (D) is the correct answer. The Sandinista Front for National Liberation played a key role in the overthrow of the Nicaraguan dictator, Anastasio Somoza, in 1979. The Front then ruled Nicaragua until its electoral defeat by an anti-Sandinista coalition in 1990. The Sandinista Front is not associated with Guatemala during the 1950s (A), Cuba during the 1960s (B), Puerto Rico during the 1970s (C), or El Salvador during the 1980s (E).

34. Choice (C) is the correct answer. Prior to the European voyages of exploration, the main route for spices and other luxury goods traveling from India, the East Indies, and China to Europe was through Muslim-held lands in the Middle East, with Muslim merchants acting as middlemen. European merchants and their backers sought to circumvent the Middle East to gain direct access to East and South Asian goods and thereby increase their profits. Choice (A) does not describe a major motive; though some slaves were taken in the course of early African exploration, this was much less important motivation than choice (C), and the slaves were generally not intended for noble households. Choice (B) is incorrect; Europeans came to dominate in the field of naval technology during this period, but there was no conscious effort to show the superiority of European ships over African and Asian vessels. Choice (D) is incorrect; it describes an unplanned gain from the voyages rather than a primary factor in persuading European investors to fund European voyages of exploration. Choice (E) is incorrect; this was not a major aim of the voyages.

35. Choice (E) is the correct answer. In their home markets, medieval Muslim merchants in the Levant (eastern Mediterranean coast) and Africa found a much larger and more lucrative market for Indian spices than for Italian luxury goods. Choice (A) is incorrect; travel to India was not easier or safer than travel to Italy. Choice (B) is incorrect; there was no papal restriction on Muslim traders entering Christian ports, though the pope did try to prevent Christian merchants from selling weapons to the Muslims. Choice (C) is incorrect; Christian crusaders were not able to close the Mediterranean Sea to Muslim vessels. Choice (D) is incorrect; this was not a factor in influencing whether Muslim merchants traveled to India rather than Italy to trade.

36. Choice (E) is the correct answer. During the fifteenth century, the Chinese admiral Zheng He built huge ocean-going vessels and led large treasure fleets to Malaya, Ceylon, India, Burma, the Philippines, the Persian Gulf, the southwest coast of Arabia, and the east coast of Africa with the aim of establishing the prestige of the Ming Empire and getting tribute. No voyages of this magnitude were undertaken during this period by the British (A), the French (B), the Maya (C), or the Japanese (D).

37. Choice (C) is the correct answer. Christianity was universalized and widely spread by Paul of Tarsus, a Jewish convert to Christianity who developed both an organization and a literature for the new Christian church. It was largely through Paul's efforts that Christianity spread beyond its initial community of Jewish converts. Choice (A) is incorrect; Paul did write some of the epistles, or letters, that were later compiled into the Christian New Testament, but he himself did not help put together the New Testament. Choice (B) is incorrect; Peter, not Paul, became the leader of the apostles after Jesus' death. Choice (D) is incorrect; Peter, not Paul, established Rome as the center of the Roman Catholic Church. Choice (E) is incorrect; Paul did not begin the monastic movement.

38. Choice (E) is the correct answer. Brazil imported by far the largest number of slaves of any nation in the Western Hemisphere. Choice (A) is incorrect; Argentina imported very few slaves. Choice (B) is incorrect; Cuba imported African slaves, but fewer than Brazil. Choice (C) is incorrect; Mexico also imported slaves during this period, but fewer than Brazil. Choice (D) is incorrect; Jamaica had a large plantation economy, but it imported fewer slaves than Brazil.

39. Choice (B) is the correct answer. During the 1870s, the British forces in South Africa engaged in a series of wars seeking domination of all the Zulu-controlled areas. They suffered a major defeat by the Zulu warriors at Isandhlwana, though they eventually defeated the Zulus. Armies of Belgium (A), Germany (C), France (D), and Italy (E) were not involved in this encounter.

40. Choice (E) is the correct answer. During this period, Poland's government was dominated by the landed aristocracy. The individual members of the assembly of nobles, which was Poland's legislature, each had an absolute veto over any government action, and they frequently used it to block attempts to strengthen the king and the central government. As a result, the more centralized states of Prussia, Russia, and Austria were eventually able to conquer and divide Poland. Choice (A) is incorrect; Poland had a strong linguistic and cultural identity. Choice (B) is incorrect; Poland covered a vast land area and had a large population. Choice (C) is incorrect; chronic civil war was not a problem in Poland during this period. Choice (D) is incorrect; because of the decentralization of authority, the Polish kings did not have the power to be oppressive.

41. Choice (B) is the correct answer. During the late nineteenth century, Islamic fundamentalism was not prevalent in Persia. Shi'ite (or Shi'a) fundamentalism became important there much later, in the 1960s and 1970s. Choices (A), (C), (D), and (E) all describe factors that contributed to Persia's becoming the object of intense European colonial power rivalries (particularly between Russia and Great Britain) during this period.

42. Choice (B) is the correct answer. The automobile had its major impact in the twentieth century, not the nineteenth century. The other four technologies—railroads (A), the telegraph (C), the power loom (D), and the open-hearth furnace (E)—were technologies that had important effects on the world economy in the nineteenth century.

43. Choice (D) is the correct answer. Suffrage was gained by women in the United States and much of western Europe after the First World War. The French Revolution (A) is too early, as are The Seneca Falls Conference (B), and the American Civil War (C). The Second World War (E) is too late; by this time, women in most countries of western Europe and in the United States had already won the vote.

44. Choice (D) is the correct answer. Many scholars believe that the Aryans, who are believed to have conquered the Harappan civilization of the Indus Valley around 1500 B.C.E., were very conscious of differences between themselves and the Harappans. Because of their strong sense of superiority, the Aryans tried to preserve social distinction between themselves and the Harappans. These efforts eventually evolved into a system of four hereditary castes. Choices (A), (B), and (C) are incorrect; the evolution of the caste system had nothing to do with patriarchal/matriarchal struggles (A), the appearance of Alexander the Great in northern India (B), or popular uprisings in the Indus Valley (C). Choice (E) is incorrect; the basic rules of caste were laid down between 1200 and 600 B.C.E., well over a thousand years before the advent of Islam.

45. Choice (D) is the correct answer. Feudalism was based on a decentralized system of hierarchical responsibilities. The primary linkage in feudal society was between lords and vassals; lords gave land to vassals in return for loyal service. Choice (A) is incorrect; the social structure was strongly hierarchical. Choice (B) is incorrect; peasants did sometimes own small plots of land. Choice (C) is incorrect; lords and vassals were at times related, but were not necessarily so. Choice (E) is incorrect; land ownership was not restricted to men.

46. Choice (C) is the correct answer. In feudal Europe, aristocratic women often assumed much more responsibility and power when their spouses and male relatives were away at war. Choice (A) is incorrect; women were not legally barred from working outside the home. Choice (B) is incorrect; no such changes occurred in thirteenth-century church law. Choice (D) is incorrect; women could be either lords or vassals. Choice (E) is incorrect; there were probably fewer gender divisions regarding work among those of humbler status; for example, women often worked beside men doing heavy farm work.

47. Choice (C) is the correct answer. Even when Japan was isolated from European trade and diplomacy under the Tokugawa Shoguns, one Dutch ship a year was allowed to come to Nagasaki and the Dutch were allowed to maintain a small trading post on an island in Nagasaki Harbor. Spain (A), Portugal (B), France (D), and England (E) had no regular contact with Japan during this period.

48. Choice (A) is the correct answer. The Safavids who ruled Persia during this period were Shi'ite (or Shi'a) Muslims, who had a dispute with the Sunni Muslims concerning who was the proper successor to Muhammad as the leader of Islam. Choice (B) is incorrect; Sunnis stood in opposition to the Shi'ites and accepted the legitimacy of the Umayyad caliphs as the successors to Muhammad. Sikhism (C) and Jainism (E) both originated in South Asia and had few adherents in Persia at this time. Nestorian Christians (D) were found mostly in central Asia and western China; there were few in Persia at this time.

49. Choice (C) is the correct answer. Owen believed that better-paid factory laborers working under humane conditions would be more productive than underpaid, exploited workers. Choice (A) is incorrect; Owen was comparing his mills to other mills in Great Britain, which was the world leader in industrialized textile production in the early nineteenth century. Choice (B) is incorrect; Owen was an advocate of utilizing the newest technology. Choice (D) is incorrect; Owen did not seek to show that manufactured goods equaled handmade goods in quality. Choice (E) is incorrect; Owen advocated more freedom for the workers and shorter working hours.

50. Choice (C) is the correct answer. French scientists accompanying Napoleon's military expedition brought back new information about ancient Egypt, including the Rosetta stone, which researchers used to decipher Egyptian hieroglyphics. Napoleon's expedition did not lead to a revival of the Coptic Church in Egypt (A), plans for building the Suez Canal and the Aswan Dam (B), or the restoration of Mamluk rule (E) (in fact, Napoleon destroyed Mamluk rule in Egypt). Choice (D) is incorrect; extensive European exploration of the African interior was not undertaken until much later and was not a direct consequence of Napoleon's expedition.

51. Choice (D) is the correct answer. Strikes and food riots in Petrograd were the primary cause for the February Revolution in Russia in 1917. Choice (A) is incorrect; the murder (in December 1916) of Rasputin, a self-proclaimed holy man and healer who wielded great influence over the tsar's family, actually removed a major source of discontent in Russia. Choice (C) is incorrect; no Cossack rebellion against the tsar's regime occurred. Choices (B) and (E) are incorrect; both events occurred after the February Revolution.

52. Choice (A) is the correct answer. The mestizos, people of mixed Spanish and Indian ancestry, formed the majority of the Mexican population, and the leaders of the Mexican Revolution needed their support to successfully govern the nation. There was no plan by the revolution's leaders to economically empower the mestizos as a class (B), or to increase the mestizo presence in the military (C). Choice (D) is incorrect; the Roman Catholic Church had been degraded and its property seized by the revolutionary government. Choice (E) is incorrect; there was no desire by the political leaders to acknowledge European economic influence in Mexico.

53. Choice (C) is the correct answer. Lenin asserted that in order for a socialist revolution to succeed, decision making must be concentrated within a small group of "professional revolutionaries." Choice (A) is incorrect; Lenin had no faith in parliamentary elections. Choice (B) is incorrect; this was a Marxist belief, which Lenin in effect set aside when he led a socialist revolution in Russia, a relatively undeveloped state. Choice (D) is incorrect; Lenin did believe, along with Marx, that the dictatorship of the proletariat was necessary to build a communist society; he differed with Marx as to the means by which the proletariat would gain power. Choice (E) is incorrect; Lenin did not believe in sharing power with nonsocialist groups.

54. Choice (A) is the correct answer. Government should be based on the general will of the society. Rousseau felt that each of us places his person and authority under the supreme direction of the general will of society through a "social contract." Governments that ignored the general will were in violation of this social contract. Choice (B) is incorrect; Rousseau grew up under divine-right monarchy and despised

it. Choice (C) is incorrect; Rousseau did not discuss the impact of industrialization in *The Social Contract.* Both choices (D) and (E) are incorrect; these ideas were not part of *The Social Contract.*

55. Choice (E) is the correct answer. Andreas Vesalius published his *On the Fabric of the Human Body* in 1543. It was the first major advance on Galen's work in Europe. Choice (A) is incorrect; da Vinci's work, though it includes some studies of anatomy, was not highly influential in this field. Choice (B) is incorrect; Brahe was an astronomer. Choice (C) is incorrect; Newton's main accomplishments were in mathematics and physics. Choice (D) is incorrect; van Leeuwenhoek was the inventor of the microscope, not an important anatomist.

56. Choice (E) is the correct answer. The Malian capital of Timbuktu included several colleges of Islamic scholars who taught theology, law, and other subjects. Choice (A) is incorrect; Mali's rulers were devout Muslims. Choice (B) is incorrect; there was no significant attempt by Christians to send missionaries to Mali during this period. Choice (C) is incorrect; although sorghum was an important crop in Mali, it was not exported in large quantities. Choice (D) is incorrect; Mali's rulers did not encourage emigration.

57. Choice (B) is the correct answer. The language spoken by the Aryan tribes that invaded the Indus Valley prior to 1200 B.C.E. was a form of Sanskrit, which became the language used by Hindu priests. Sumerian (A), Etruscan (C), Hittite (D), and Phoenician (E) are ancient languages that are no longer used for religious rites.

58. Choice (E) is the correct answer. United States policymakers believed in the "Domino Theory," fearing that if South Vietnam became communist, other Southeast Asian countries would soon also become communist. Choice (A) is incorrect; although the Soviet Union sent arms, economic aid, and military advisers to North Vietnam, it never committed troops. Choice (B) is incorrect; the Korean War was not seen as a United States defeat. Choice (C) is incorrect; the U.N. Security Council did not urge U.N. members to support the South Vietnamese government. Choice (D) is incorrect; the North Vietnamese population was not significantly larger than the population of South Vietnam.

59. Choice (A) is the correct answer. Spurred initially by increased agricultural productivity, the population and the economy of Europe (particularly western Europe) expanded greatly during this period. Towns grew rapidly, fueled by local and long-distance trade. Romanesque and Gothic art and architecture developed, and many great works of Latin and vernacular literature were written. Choice (B) is

incorrect; this is a description of the fourteenth and fifteenth centuries. Choice (C) is incorrect; this is a description of the late-eighteenth and the nineteenth centuries. Choice (D) is incorrect; this is a description of the seventeenth century. Choice (E) is incorrect; in the twelfth and thirteenth centuries, Europe experienced a net outflow of gold and silver; (E) is a description of the sixteenth century.

60. Choice (B) is the correct answer. Beginning in the eighth century, Muslim forces conquered most of Spain and established flourishing urban centers of learning and artistic creativity, including Córdoba and Seville. During this period, Córdoba and Seville were not noted as centers of those things described in choices (A), (C), (D), and (E).

61. Choice (A) is the correct answer. From the ninth to the twelfth century, Kiev was a center for trade and Orthodox Christianity and was the capital of the state known as Kievan Rus or Kievan Russia. The other Russian cities—Novosibirsk (B), Saint Petersburg (C), Moscow (D), and Murmansk (E)—developed later.

62. Choice (D) is the correct answer. In the 1980s, both Venezuela and Mexico were highly dependent on revenue from petroleum exports and suffered because of the sharp decline in oil prices worldwide in the mid-1980s. Choices (A), (B), (C), and (E) are not primary reasons for the decline of these countries' economic growth rates.

63. Choice (D) is the correct answer. From 1539 to 1542, Hernando de Soto led the first European expedition through what is now the southeastern United States. At the time, the region had flourishing Native American cultures with population centers linked by regular trade routes. Choices (A), (B), and (C) are incorrect; the Native Americans acquired the use of horses, sheep, pigs, and iron from the Europeans after de Soto's expedition. Choice (E) is incorrect; it is not an accurate description of Native American religious practices.

64. Choice (D) is the correct answer. Totalitarian governments in Germany and Italy arose in large part because of discontent caused by the economic hardships and social upheavals of the postwar period. Choice (A) is incorrect; both the Nazis and the Fascists gained power through a combination of violence and electoral politics; neither Germany nor Italy was involved in full-scale civil wars. Choice (B) is incorrect; neither country experienced particularly rapid industrialization during this period. Choice (C) is incorrect; both Nazism and Fascism were aggressive nationalist movements. Choice (E) is incorrect; neither the Nazis nor the Fascists took over through exclusively violent means; both had considerable popular support and won large proportions of the popular vote in parliamentary elections.

65. Choice (C) is the correct answer. In contrast to the Enlightenment tradition that stressed man's rational nature, both Nietzsche and Freud stressed the importance of nonrational factors, such as instinctive drives and early childhood conditioning, in determining human behavior, both individually and in groups. Choice (A) is incorrect; it is not a statement that would have had much meaning for either thinker. Choice (B) is incorrect; both would probably have disagreed with the statement. Choice (D) is incorrect; although Freud might have agreed with this, Nietzsche tended to see human relationships as grounded in contingent historical circumstances. Choice (E) is incorrect; although Freud had some hope of improving people's lives through a better understanding of the unconscious influences on their behavior, Nietzsche was not interested in social reform.

66. Choice (C) is the correct answer. With the outbreak of the Bolshevik Revolution in 1917, Lenin split from the international democratic socialist movement and formed a totalitarian communist movement under the leadership of the Supreme Soviet in order to achieve his objective of socialist revolution in Russia. Socialism had a united international organization in both 1848 (A) and 1870 (B); the split had already occurred by 1939 (D) and 1949 (E).

67. Choice (D) is the correct answer. The Philippines was granted independence from the United States in 1946, immediately after the Second World War. Independence for Indonesia (A), Malaysia (B), Myanmar (Burma) (C), and Vietnam (E) came later.

68. Choice (D) is the correct answer. Keynes believed that in times of economic recession, governments could stimulate the economy by deficit spending on goods and services. Choice (A) is incorrect; it expresses a belief almost diametrically opposed to Keynes' ideas. Choice (B) is incorrect; Keynes was not concerned with the process of industrialization. Choice (C) is incorrect; he was not particularly interested in strengthening labor unions. Choice (E), like choice (A), expresses a belief almost diametrically opposed to Keynes' ideas.

69. Choice (C) is the correct answer. The Solidarity Union was formed in Poland in 1980 and ultimately helped bring down the communist government. The other events listed occurred earlier in Polish history. The partitions mentioned in choice (A) happened in the late 1700s. Choice (B) happened in 1807. Choice (D) happened in 1939 and again in 1944. Choice (E) happened in 1794.

70. Choice (D) is the correct answer. The flat terrain of European Russia and Siberia presented few natural barriers to the political expansion of the Russian state. Choice (A) is incorrect; Russia's navigable rivers tend to flow north and south and were not

particularly helpful for its eastward growth. Choice (B) is incorrect; there were few significant mountain barriers to Russia's eastward expansion. Choice (C) is incorrect; Russia had few warm-water ports. Choice (E) is incorrect; most of Russia does in fact experience extreme seasonal temperature fluctuations.

71. Choice (A) is the correct answer. In 1917, the British government, seeking Jewish support for the war effort against the Central Powers, issued the Balfour Declaration, which promised British support for a Jewish homeland in Palestine (at the time controlled by the Ottoman Empire, which was at war with Great Britain). The Declaration also stated that non-Jewish communities in Palestine should be protected. Choices (B), (C), (D), and (E) refer to diplomatic documents dealing with other issues.

72. Choice (A) is the correct answer. The *Encyclopédie* (complete English title: *Encyclopedia, or the Classified Dictionary of Sciences, Arts, and Trades*) was probably the greatest effort to systematically present Enlightenment thought and technical knowledge. Denis Diderot (1713–1784) and Jean le Rond d'Alembert (1717–1783) were the editors of the first series of volumes, which began to be published in 1751. Choices (B), (C), (D), and (E) name pairs of distinguished French writers and thinkers, but they were not the editors of the *Encyclopédie*.

73. Choice (A) is the correct answer. In the eighteenth century B.C.E., the Hyksos, possibly a Semitic people, settled in northern Egypt as subjects of the pharaohs. In about 1630 B.C.E., they rebelled and conquered much of Egypt with the aid of swift, horse-drawn chariots. Their rule lasted about 100 years. The Hyksos did not originate or make use of gunpowder and cannons (B), the lateen sail (C), the crossbow (D), or stirrups (E).

74. Choice (B) is the correct answer. Trade unions first developed mainly by workers in response to low pay, unsafe working conditions, and chronic job insecurity during the early period of industrialization. Choice (A) is incorrect; modern unions were quite different from medieval guilds, which tended to be local associations of skilled artisans or merchants. Choice (C) is incorrect; for much of this period, unions were regarded with suspicion and even hostility by most members of both the Catholic and Protestant clergy. Choice (D) is incorrect; socialists were major supporters of unions. Choice (E) is incorrect; unions were designed to improve pay and working conditions. Involvement in politics was a means to that end, not an end in itself.

75. Choice (B) is the correct answer. At the end of the war, the British and the French acquired African territories formally controlled by Germany and administered them under League of Nations mandates. Choice (A) is incorrect; no territories were

granted independence. Choice (C) is incorrect; Russia was not represented at the Paris Peace Conference and received no African territories. Choice (D) is incorrect; the United States was not a member of the League of Nations and was not involved in the mandate system. Choice (E) is incorrect; China and Japan did not begin to supply manufactured goods to Africa until after the Second World War, when these areas gained political independence.

76. Choice (B) is the correct answer. The purpose of this cartoon was to condemn intellectual women as unfit wives and mothers by showing a chaotic home in which the intellectual wife (seated at the desk to the left) neglects what was regarded by many people at the time as her "proper" duties of child care and household management. Choices (A), (C), (D), and (E) are not plausible readings of this late-nineteenth-century cartoon.

77. Choice (E) is the correct answer. Many of the colonization efforts in the interior of Africa began as private ventures by European businessmen, explorers, or missionaries who were later recognized and supported by home governments. Choice (A) is incorrect; European explorers and administrators frequently ignored existing political and ethnic divisions in Africa. Choice (B) is incorrect; all of the Bantu kingdoms were conquered by Europeans. Choice (C) is incorrect; Germany was a latecomer in the race for African territory and Austria made no efforts to acquire African territory. Choice (D) is incorrect; generally the process of European colonization was highly destructive of indigenous African social, economic, and religious organizations.

78. Choice (E) is the correct answer. Women in the medieval Roman Catholic Church were barred from administering sacraments. This continues to be true today. Choices (A), (B), (C), and (D) were all options open to women in medieval Europe.

79. Choice (B) is the correct answer. This is a direct and well-known quote from Mohandas Gandhi, the most important leader in the Indian independence movement. Gandhi and his followers practiced a form of nonviolent resistance to British rule in India that proved highly effective. None of the other groups listed in choices (A), (C), (D), or (E) were exclusively devoted to nonviolence in the furtherance of their cause.

80. Choice (C) is the correct answer. Chandragupta Maurya (ruled circa 321–297 B.C.E.), starting from the kingdom of Magadha in the Indus valley, conquered much of northern India and established India's first great empire, the Mauryan Empire. Kanishka (A), Samudragupta (B), Ashoka (D), and Akbar (E) are important Indian rulers but not founders of the first Indian empire.

81. Choice (D) is the correct answer. It is the only statement that is true of both men. Peter the Great (ruled 1689–1725) worked with missionary zeal to introduce into Russia many new ideas and technologies from the more technologically advanced countries of western Europe. Communist leader Joseph Stalin (ruled 1924–1953) also pressed for the introduction of new technology and industrial processes into what was then the Soviet Union. Choice (A) is incorrect; Peter the Great was not a proponent of economic equality. Stalin paid lip service to this ideal but, in practice, considerable economic disparities existed within the Soviet state. Choice (B) is incorrect; Peter the Great sponsored Russian expansion in Siberia, but the region had been long incorporated into Russia when Stalin came to power. Choice (C) is incorrect; Peter the Great welcomed contact with other countries, and Stalin was isolationist only during part of his rule. Choice (E) is incorrect; neither Peter the Great nor Stalin had much interest in the preservation of traditional village life; both were more interested in economic development. Stalin, in particular, undertook a brutal campaign to eliminate the class of wealthy peasants (kulaks) who dominated most Russian villages.

82. Choice (D) is the correct answer. Many of the newly politically independent African and Asian states continued to depend on their former colonizers as their main source of capital, high-tech goods, and markets for their exports of raw materials. Resentment over this continuation of essentially the same economic relationships that existed under colonization led to the creation of the term "neocolonialism." Choice (A) is incorrect; although European powers did intervene militarily in many African nations that had been granted independence, this was not generally described as "neocolonialism." Choice (B) is incorrect; when this occurred it too was not described as "neocolonialism." Choice (C) is incorrect; although this was happening in the 1960s, it was generally seen as the antidote to "neocolonialism" rather than an expression of it. Choice (E) is incorrect; the central Asian republics were not openly expressing neocolonial feelings toward the Russians in the 1960s.

83. Choice (D) is the correct answer. Romanticism was an artistic and intellectual movement that emerged in Europe in the late-eighteenth and early-nineteenth centuries in reaction to the rationalism of the Enlightenment. Romanticism as an artistic approach stressed the importance of intuition, imagination, and irrationalism, an exaltation of the exceptional and creative; and a fascination with the mysterious and inaccessible. This passage is highly typical of a European Romantic's approach to an ancient Indian text. The thoughts expressed in the passage are not representative of materialism (A), deism (B), positivism (C), or utilitarianism (E).

84. Choice (A) is the correct answer. The war to retain French control of Algeria against an Arab independence movement caused deep divisions in French society. Over a million Europeans lived in the French colony of Algeria and, by 1956, 400,000

French troops were fighting there. The war and its brutalities caused deep divisions in French society and, in 1958, Charles de Gaulle was called out of retirement to lead the country during this crisis. He granted Algeria independence in 1962. Choices (B), (C), (D), and (E) are not reasons why de Gaulle took power in 1958.

85. Choice (E) is the correct answer. Nineteenth-century leaders in Morocco, Tunisia, Egypt, Persia, and the Ottoman Empire responded to the threat of European colonial takeovers by undertaking extensive reforms of their bureaucracies and armies following European models. Choice (A) is incorrect; there was no land reform favoring small farmers during this period. Choice (B) is incorrect; Islamic doctrines and law remained unchanged. Choice (C) is incorrect; there was no attempt to revive the caliphate in this area. Choice (D) is incorrect; these countries did not have the option of imitating Japan by expelling foreigners and ending contact with the West.

86. Choice (E) is the correct answer. Both documents mentioned (the Magna Carta and the Declaration of Rights) in the quote are British and the statement reflects the philosophy expounded by Edmund Burke, a politically conservative British statesman. Choice (A) is incorrect; a French radical at the Bastille would not have cited the Magna Carta. Choice (B) is incorrect; an American revolutionary would have cited the Declaration of Independence, not the British Declaration of Rights. Choice (C) is incorrect; the author of the passage has a high respect for law and legal limits. Choice (D) is incorrect; an Indian independence leader would not have cited these British documents to make his case.

87. Choice (E) is the correct answer. The term *caudillo* refers to a military strongman, many of whom ruled Latin American nations after they gained their independence. *Caudillismo* is the general term for this type of rule. Choices (A), (B), (C), and (D) are incorrect.

88. Choice (D) is the correct answer. Chile and other countries that depended heavily on the export of raw materials to industrial markets overseas were devastated by the Great Depression that swept the world beginning in 1929. Choices (A), (B), (C), and (E) are incorrect because they do not describe the actual cause of the economic problems mentioned.

89. Choice (E) is the correct answer. French Utopian socialism was a reaction to the extremes of wealth and poverty created by private property and the Industrial Revolution and to the widespread misery of millions of industrial workers. Utopian socialists believed that the evils of industrialization could be eased by setting up communities in which all the workers communally owned their factories and other

major property. Choice (A) is incorrect; Utopian socialists sought to create their new egalitarian society by peaceful means, not revolution. Choice (B) is incorrect; Utopian socialists did not generally share this belief, which is more typical of Marxist communists. Choice (C) is incorrect; Utopian socialists felt that capitalists were the source of many of the problems of industrialization, not the solution. Choice (D) is incorrect; Utopian socialists believed the state and the communes should take responsibility for economic planning; they did not favor a laissez-faire approach to the economy.

90. Choice (A) is the correct answer. Junior army officers, many of whom had been either trained in western Europe or had been trained by officers who were familiar with nationalist European writers, led nationalist movements in Egypt and the Ottoman Empire. In the Ottoman Empire, one such group was the Young Turks, who tried to modernize the Ottoman military and stressed Turkish nationalism. In Egypt, the most important such leader was Ahmad Urabi, a junior officer who led a nationalist revolt against the Turkish elite that ruled Egypt at the time. Writers (B), religious leaders (C), women's rights activists (D), and industrialists (E) were aware of European nationalism, but none of them took the leadership positions assumed by the junior army officers in these countries.

91. Choice (C) is the correct answer. The Sino-Japanese War (1894–95) developed out of rivalry for control of Korea. In 1875, Japan forced Korea to assert independence from China, its longtime overlord, and to open itself to foreign trade. Subsequently, Japan and China came to blows over who had the right to intervene in a Korean civil war in 1894. Similarly, the Russo-Japanese War (1904–05) was partly caused by disputes over spheres of influence in Korea. As part of the 1905 peace settlement of the Russo-Japanese War, Russia was forced to recognize Japanese interests in Korea and this paved the way for Japan's annexation of Korea in 1910. Choice (A) is incorrect; both wars stimulated the Japanese economic expansion. Choice (B) is incorrect; there were no indemnities for Japan. Choice (D) is incorrect; Japanese public opinion favored both wars. Choice (E) is incorrect; only the Russo-Japanese War was resolved by United States President Theodore Roosevelt.

92. Choice (C) is the correct answer. Constantinople did not fall to Islamic Ottoman forces until 1453. Islamic armies in the seventh and eighth centuries conquered Spain (A), Persia (B), Jerusalem (D), and Damascus (E).

93. Choice (E) is the correct answer. In 1947, the Muslim League, fearful that Muslims would suffer as a minority in the newly independent India, demanded partition and the creation of a separate Muslim state. Choice (A) is incorrect; the divisions were not primarily ethnic or linguistic. Choice (B) is incorrect; the borders drawn did not

reflect ancient boundaries. Choice (C) is incorrect; Muslims had not generally been dispossessed under British rule. Choice (D) is incorrect; there were no rajahs who sought autonomy in Pakistan.

94. Choice (B) is the correct answer. In the Middle Ages (and today as well), northern Europe's climate was colder and wetter than the climate of the Mediterranean region. This climatic difference meant that different crops and different agricultural techniques were found in each region. Choice (A) is incorrect; northern Europe was not more mountainous than the Mediterranean region. Choice (C) is incorrect; northern Europe's climate was not dryer, it was wetter. Choice (D) is incorrect; northern Europe did not produce more grapes and wine; it was the Mediterranean region that produced most of the wine. Choice (E) is incorrect; northern Europe did have both hunting and agricultural economies.

95. Choice (B) is the correct answer. Nigeria is the largest oil-producing nation in sub-Saharan Africa and a member of the Organization of Petroleum Exporting Countries (OPEC). Nigeria supplies a significant proportion of world oil production. Liberia (A), Mali (C), Ivory Coast (D), and Senegal (E) are not members of OPEC and are not significant oil producers.

2010-11 SAT Subject Tests™

MARKS MUST BE COMPLETE

COMPLETE MARK ●   EXAMPLES OF INCOMPLETE MARKS 

You must use a No. 2 pencil. Do not use a mechanical pencil. It is very important that you fill in the entire circle darkly and completely. If you change your response, erase as completely as possible. Incomplete marks or erasures may affect your score. It is very important that you follow these instructions when filling out your answer sheet.

1 **Your Name:** (Print) ______ Last ______ First ______ M.I.

I agree to the conditions on the front and back of the SAT Subject Tests™ book. I also agree to use only a No. 2 pencil to complete my answer sheet.

Signature: ______ **Date:** __/__/__ MM DD YY

Home Address: (Print) ______ Number and Street ______ City ______ State ______ Zip Code

Home Phone: ( ) ______ **Test Center:** (Print) ______ City ______ State/Country

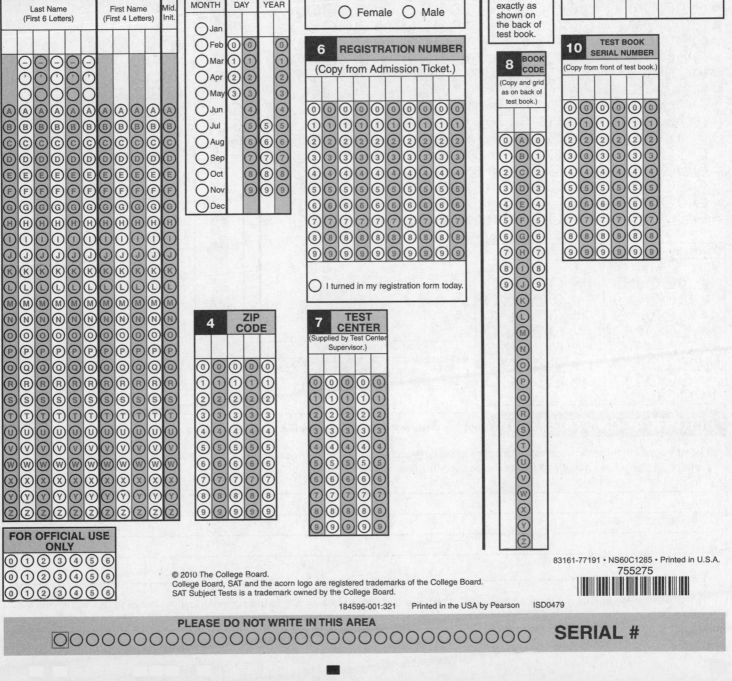

2 YOUR NAME

Last Name (First 6 Letters) | First Name (First 4 Letters) | Mid. Init.

– ' A B C D E F G H I J K L M N O P Q R S T U V W X Y Z

3 DATE OF BIRTH

MONTH: Jan Feb Mar Apr May Jun Jul Aug Sep Oct Nov Dec
DAY: 0 1 2 3 | 0 1 2 3 4 5 6 7 8 9
YEAR: 5 6 7 8 9 | 0 1 2 3 4 5 6 7 8 9

4 ZIP CODE

0 1 2 3 4 5 6 7 8 9

5 SEX

○ Female ○ Male

6 REGISTRATION NUMBER

(Copy from Admission Ticket.)

0 1 2 3 4 5 6 7 8 9

○ I turned in my registration form today.

7 TEST CENTER

(Supplied by Test Center Supervisor.)

0 1 2 3 4 5 6 7 8 9

Important: Fill in items 8 and 9 exactly as shown on the back of test book.

8 BOOK CODE

(Copy and grid as on back of test book.)

0 1 2 3 4 5 6 7 8 9 | A B C D E F G H I J K L M N O P Q R S T U V W X Y Z | 0 1 2 3 4 5 6 7 8 9

9 BOOK ID

(Copy from back of test book.)

10 TEST BOOK SERIAL NUMBER

(Copy from front of test book.)

0 1 2 3 4 5 6 7 8 9

FOR OFFICIAL USE ONLY

0 1 2 3 4 5 6
0 1 2 3 4 5 6
0 1 2 3 4 5 6

184596-001:321 Printed in the USA by Pearson ISD0479

83161-77191 • NS60C1285 • Printed in U.S.A.
755275

PLEASE DO NOT WRITE IN THIS AREA

SERIAL #

COMPLETE MARK ● **EXAMPLES OF INCOMPLETE MARKS**

You must use a No. 2 pencil and marks must be complete. Do not use a mechanical pencil. *It is very important that you fill in the entire circle darkly and completely. If you change your response, erase as completely as possible. Incomplete marks or erasures may affect your score.*

○ Literature ○ Biology E ○ Biology M ○ Chemistry ○ Physics
○ Mathematics Level 1 ○ Mathematics Level 2 ○ U.S. History ○ World History ○ French
○ German ○ Italian ○ Latin ○ Modern Hebrew ○ Spanish
○ Chinese Listening ○ French Listening ○ German Listening
○ Japanese Listening ○ Korean Listening ○ Spanish Listening

Background Questions: ① ② ③ ④ ⑤ ⑥ ⑦ ⑧ ⑨

1–100 Ⓐ Ⓑ Ⓒ Ⓓ Ⓔ

Important: Fill in items 8 and 9 exactly as shown on the back of test book.

8 BOOK CODE (Copy and grid as on back of test book.)

9 BOOK ID (Copy from back of test book.)

10 TEST BOOK SERIAL NUMBER (Copy from front of test book.)

Quality Assurance Mark

Chemistry *Fill in circle CE only if II is correct explanation of I.

	I	II	CE*		I	II	CE*
101	Ⓣ Ⓕ	Ⓣ Ⓕ	○	109	Ⓣ Ⓕ	Ⓣ Ⓕ	○
102	Ⓣ Ⓕ	Ⓣ Ⓕ	○	110	Ⓣ Ⓕ	Ⓣ Ⓕ	○
103	Ⓣ Ⓕ	Ⓣ Ⓕ	○	111	Ⓣ Ⓕ	Ⓣ Ⓕ	○
104	Ⓣ Ⓕ	Ⓣ Ⓕ	○	112	Ⓣ Ⓕ	Ⓣ Ⓕ	○
105	Ⓣ Ⓕ	Ⓣ Ⓕ	○	113	Ⓣ Ⓕ	Ⓣ Ⓕ	○
106	Ⓣ Ⓕ	Ⓣ Ⓕ	○	114	Ⓣ Ⓕ	Ⓣ Ⓕ	○
107	Ⓣ Ⓕ	Ⓣ Ⓕ	○	115	Ⓣ Ⓕ	Ⓣ Ⓕ	○
108	Ⓣ Ⓕ	Ⓣ Ⓕ	○				

FOR OFFICIAL USE ONLY

R/C	W/S1	FS/S2	CS/S3	WS

CERTIFICATION STATEMENT

Copy the statement below (do not print) and sign your name as you would an official document.

I hereby agree to the conditions set forth online at sat.collegeboard.com and in any paper registration materials given to me and certify that I am the person whose name and address appear on this answer sheet.

Signature ______________________ Date ______________

By registering, you agreed not to share any specific test question with anyone by any form of communication, including, but not limited to: email, text messages, or use of the Internet. Doing so can result in score cancellation and other possible sanctions.

COMPLETE MARK ● EXAMPLES OF INCOMPLETE MARKS

You must use a No. 2 pencil and marks must be complete. Do not use a mechanical pencil. *It is very important that you fill in the entire circle darkly and completely. If you change your response, erase as completely as possible. Incomplete marks or erasures may affect your score.*

○ Literature ○ Mathematics Level 1 ○ German
○ Biology E ○ Mathematics Level 2 ○ Italian
○ Biology M ○ U.S. History ○ Latin
○ Chemistry ○ World History ○ Modern Hebrew
○ Physics ○ French ○ Spanish

Background Questions: ① ② ③ ④ ⑤ ⑥ ⑦ ⑧ ⑨

1–100 Ⓐ Ⓑ Ⓒ Ⓓ Ⓔ

Quality Assurance Mark

Important: Fill in items 8 and 9 exactly as shown on the back of test book.

8 BOOK CODE (Copy and grid as on back of test book.)

9 BOOK ID (Copy from back of test book.)

10 TEST BOOK SERIAL NUMBER (Copy from front of test book.)

Chemistry *Fill in circle CE only if II is correct explanation of I.

	I	II	CE*		I	II	CE*
101	Ⓣ Ⓕ	Ⓣ Ⓕ	○	109	Ⓣ Ⓕ	Ⓣ Ⓕ	○
102	Ⓣ Ⓕ	Ⓣ Ⓕ	○	110	Ⓣ Ⓕ	Ⓣ Ⓕ	○
103	Ⓣ Ⓕ	Ⓣ Ⓕ	○	111	Ⓣ Ⓕ	Ⓣ Ⓕ	○
104	Ⓣ Ⓕ	Ⓣ Ⓕ	○	112	Ⓣ Ⓕ	Ⓣ Ⓕ	○
105	Ⓣ Ⓕ	Ⓣ Ⓕ	○	113	Ⓣ Ⓕ	Ⓣ Ⓕ	○
106	Ⓣ Ⓕ	Ⓣ Ⓕ	○	114	Ⓣ Ⓕ	Ⓣ Ⓕ	○
107	Ⓣ Ⓕ	Ⓣ Ⓕ	○	115	Ⓣ Ⓕ	Ⓣ Ⓕ	○
108	Ⓣ Ⓕ	Ⓣ Ⓕ	○				

FOR OFFICIAL USE ONLY

R/C	W/S1	FS/S2	CS/S3	WS

COMPLETE MARK ● EXAMPLES OF INCOMPLETE MARKS

You must use a No. 2 pencil and marks must be complete. Do not use a mechanical pencil. *It is very important that you fill in the entire circle darkly and completely. If you change your response, erase as completely as possible. Incomplete marks or erasures may affect your score.*

○ Literature	○ Mathematics Level 1	○ German
○ Biology E	○ Mathematics Level 2	○ Italian
○ Biology M	○ U.S. History	○ Latin
○ Chemistry	○ World History	○ Modern Hebrew
○ Physics	○ French	○ Spanish

Background Questions: ① ② ③ ④ ⑤ ⑥ ⑦ ⑧ ⑨

1 Ⓐ Ⓑ Ⓒ Ⓓ Ⓔ	26 Ⓐ Ⓑ Ⓒ Ⓓ Ⓔ	51 Ⓐ Ⓑ Ⓒ Ⓓ Ⓔ	76 Ⓐ Ⓑ Ⓒ Ⓓ Ⓔ
2 Ⓐ Ⓑ Ⓒ Ⓓ Ⓔ	27 Ⓐ Ⓑ Ⓒ Ⓓ Ⓔ	52 Ⓐ Ⓑ Ⓒ Ⓓ Ⓔ	77 Ⓐ Ⓑ Ⓒ Ⓓ Ⓔ
3 Ⓐ Ⓑ Ⓒ Ⓓ Ⓔ	28 Ⓐ Ⓑ Ⓒ Ⓓ Ⓔ	53 Ⓐ Ⓑ Ⓒ Ⓓ Ⓔ	78 Ⓐ Ⓑ Ⓒ Ⓓ Ⓔ
4 Ⓐ Ⓑ Ⓒ Ⓓ Ⓔ	29 Ⓐ Ⓑ Ⓒ Ⓓ Ⓔ	54 Ⓐ Ⓑ Ⓒ Ⓓ Ⓔ	79 Ⓐ Ⓑ Ⓒ Ⓓ Ⓔ
5 Ⓐ Ⓑ Ⓒ Ⓓ Ⓔ	30 Ⓐ Ⓑ Ⓒ Ⓓ Ⓔ	55 Ⓐ Ⓑ Ⓒ Ⓓ Ⓔ	80 Ⓐ Ⓑ Ⓒ Ⓓ Ⓔ
6 Ⓐ Ⓑ Ⓒ Ⓓ Ⓔ	31 Ⓐ Ⓑ Ⓒ Ⓓ Ⓔ	56 Ⓐ Ⓑ Ⓒ Ⓓ Ⓔ	81 Ⓐ Ⓑ Ⓒ Ⓓ Ⓔ
7 Ⓐ Ⓑ Ⓒ Ⓓ Ⓔ	32 Ⓐ Ⓑ Ⓒ Ⓓ Ⓔ	57 Ⓐ Ⓑ Ⓒ Ⓓ Ⓔ	82 Ⓐ Ⓑ Ⓒ Ⓓ Ⓔ
8 Ⓐ Ⓑ Ⓒ Ⓓ Ⓔ	33 Ⓐ Ⓑ Ⓒ Ⓓ Ⓔ	58 Ⓐ Ⓑ Ⓒ Ⓓ Ⓔ	83 Ⓐ Ⓑ Ⓒ Ⓓ Ⓔ
9 Ⓐ Ⓑ Ⓒ Ⓓ Ⓔ	34 Ⓐ Ⓑ Ⓒ Ⓓ Ⓔ	59 Ⓐ Ⓑ Ⓒ Ⓓ Ⓔ	84 Ⓐ Ⓑ Ⓒ Ⓓ Ⓔ
10 Ⓐ Ⓑ Ⓒ Ⓓ Ⓔ	35 Ⓐ Ⓑ Ⓒ Ⓓ Ⓔ	60 Ⓐ Ⓑ Ⓒ Ⓓ Ⓔ	85 Ⓐ Ⓑ Ⓒ Ⓓ Ⓔ
11 Ⓐ Ⓑ Ⓒ Ⓓ Ⓔ	36 Ⓐ Ⓑ Ⓒ Ⓓ Ⓔ	61 Ⓐ Ⓑ Ⓒ Ⓓ Ⓔ	86 Ⓐ Ⓑ Ⓒ Ⓓ Ⓔ
12 Ⓐ Ⓑ Ⓒ Ⓓ Ⓔ	37 Ⓐ Ⓑ Ⓒ Ⓓ Ⓔ	62 Ⓐ Ⓑ Ⓒ Ⓓ Ⓔ	87 Ⓐ Ⓑ Ⓒ Ⓓ Ⓔ
13 Ⓐ Ⓑ Ⓒ Ⓓ Ⓔ	38 Ⓐ Ⓑ Ⓒ Ⓓ Ⓔ	63 Ⓐ Ⓑ Ⓒ Ⓓ Ⓔ	88 Ⓐ Ⓑ Ⓒ Ⓓ Ⓔ
14 Ⓐ Ⓑ Ⓒ Ⓓ Ⓔ	39 Ⓐ Ⓑ Ⓒ Ⓓ Ⓔ	64 Ⓐ Ⓑ Ⓒ Ⓓ Ⓔ	89 Ⓐ Ⓑ Ⓒ Ⓓ Ⓔ
15 Ⓐ Ⓑ Ⓒ Ⓓ Ⓔ	40 Ⓐ Ⓑ Ⓒ Ⓓ Ⓔ	65 Ⓐ Ⓑ Ⓒ Ⓓ Ⓔ	90 Ⓐ Ⓑ Ⓒ Ⓓ Ⓔ
16 Ⓐ Ⓑ Ⓒ Ⓓ Ⓔ	41 Ⓐ Ⓑ Ⓒ Ⓓ Ⓔ	66 Ⓐ Ⓑ Ⓒ Ⓓ Ⓔ	91 Ⓐ Ⓑ Ⓒ Ⓓ Ⓔ
17 Ⓐ Ⓑ Ⓒ Ⓓ Ⓔ	42 Ⓐ Ⓑ Ⓒ Ⓓ Ⓔ	67 Ⓐ Ⓑ Ⓒ Ⓓ Ⓔ	92 Ⓐ Ⓑ Ⓒ Ⓓ Ⓔ
18 Ⓐ Ⓑ Ⓒ Ⓓ Ⓔ	43 Ⓐ Ⓑ Ⓒ Ⓓ Ⓔ	68 Ⓐ Ⓑ Ⓒ Ⓓ Ⓔ	93 Ⓐ Ⓑ Ⓒ Ⓓ Ⓔ
19 Ⓐ Ⓑ Ⓒ Ⓓ Ⓔ	44 Ⓐ Ⓑ Ⓒ Ⓓ Ⓔ	69 Ⓐ Ⓑ Ⓒ Ⓓ Ⓔ	94 Ⓐ Ⓑ Ⓒ Ⓓ Ⓔ
20 Ⓐ Ⓑ Ⓒ Ⓓ Ⓔ	45 Ⓐ Ⓑ Ⓒ Ⓓ Ⓔ	70 Ⓐ Ⓑ Ⓒ Ⓓ Ⓔ	95 Ⓐ Ⓑ Ⓒ Ⓓ Ⓔ
21 Ⓐ Ⓑ Ⓒ Ⓓ Ⓔ	46 Ⓐ Ⓑ Ⓒ Ⓓ Ⓔ	71 Ⓐ Ⓑ Ⓒ Ⓓ Ⓔ	96 Ⓐ Ⓑ Ⓒ Ⓓ Ⓔ
22 Ⓐ Ⓑ Ⓒ Ⓓ Ⓔ	47 Ⓐ Ⓑ Ⓒ Ⓓ Ⓔ	72 Ⓐ Ⓑ Ⓒ Ⓓ Ⓔ	97 Ⓐ Ⓑ Ⓒ Ⓓ Ⓔ
23 Ⓐ Ⓑ Ⓒ Ⓓ Ⓔ	48 Ⓐ Ⓑ Ⓒ Ⓓ Ⓔ	73 Ⓐ Ⓑ Ⓒ Ⓓ Ⓔ	98 Ⓐ Ⓑ Ⓒ Ⓓ Ⓔ
24 Ⓐ Ⓑ Ⓒ Ⓓ Ⓔ	49 Ⓐ Ⓑ Ⓒ Ⓓ Ⓔ	74 Ⓐ Ⓑ Ⓒ Ⓓ Ⓔ	99 Ⓐ Ⓑ Ⓒ Ⓓ Ⓔ
25 Ⓐ Ⓑ Ⓒ Ⓓ Ⓔ	50 Ⓐ Ⓑ Ⓒ Ⓓ Ⓔ	75 Ⓐ Ⓑ Ⓒ Ⓓ Ⓔ	100 Ⓐ Ⓑ Ⓒ Ⓓ Ⓔ

Chemistry *Fill in circle CE only if II is correct explanation of I.

	I	II	CE*		I	II	CE*
101	Ⓣ Ⓕ	Ⓣ Ⓕ	○	109	Ⓣ Ⓕ	Ⓣ Ⓕ	○
102	Ⓣ Ⓕ	Ⓣ Ⓕ	○	110	Ⓣ Ⓕ	Ⓣ Ⓕ	○
103	Ⓣ Ⓕ	Ⓣ Ⓕ	○	111	Ⓣ Ⓕ	Ⓣ Ⓕ	○
104	Ⓣ Ⓕ	Ⓣ Ⓕ	○	112	Ⓣ Ⓕ	Ⓣ Ⓕ	○
105	Ⓣ Ⓕ	Ⓣ Ⓕ	○	113	Ⓣ Ⓕ	Ⓣ Ⓕ	○
106	Ⓣ Ⓕ	Ⓣ Ⓕ	○	114	Ⓣ Ⓕ	Ⓣ Ⓕ	○
107	Ⓣ Ⓕ	Ⓣ Ⓕ	○	115	Ⓣ Ⓕ	Ⓣ Ⓕ	○
108	Ⓣ Ⓕ	Ⓣ Ⓕ	○				

FOR OFFICIAL USE ONLY

R/C	W/S1	FS/S2	CS/S3	WS

Important: Fill in items 8 and 9 exactly as shown on the back of test book.

8 BOOK CODE (Copy and grid as on back of test book.)

0–9 | A–Z | 0–9

9 BOOK ID (Copy from back of test book.)

10 TEST BOOK SERIAL NUMBER (Copy from front of test book.)

0–9 (six columns)

Quality Assurance Mark

PLEASE DO NOT WRITE IN THIS AREA

SERIAL #

2010-11 SAT Subject Tests™

MARKS MUST BE COMPLETE

COMPLETE MARK ● EXAMPLES OF INCOMPLETE MARKS 

You must use a No. 2 pencil. Do not use a mechanical pencil. It is very important that you fill in the entire circle darkly and completely. If you change your response, erase as completely as possible. Incomplete marks or erasures may affect your score. It is very important that you follow these instructions when filling out your answer sheet.

1 **Your Name:** (Print) Last First M.I.

I agree to the conditions on the front and back of the SAT Subject Tests™ book. I also agree to use only a No. 2 pencil to complete my answer sheet.

Signature: **Date:** MM / DD / YY

Home Address: (Print) Number and Street City State Zip Code

Home Phone: ( ) **Test Center:** (Print) City State/Country

2 YOUR NAME

Last Name (First 6 Letters) | First Name (First 4 Letters) | Mid. Init.

– ' A B C D E F G H I J K L M N O P Q R S T U V W X Y Z

3 DATE OF BIRTH

MONTH: Jan Feb Mar Apr May Jun Jul Aug Sep Oct Nov Dec

DAY | YEAR

0 1 2 3 4 5 6 7 8 9

4 ZIP CODE

0 1 2 3 4 5 6 7 8 9

5 SEX

○ Female ○ Male

6 REGISTRATION NUMBER

(Copy from Admission Ticket.)

0 1 2 3 4 5 6 7 8 9

○ I turned in my registration form today.

7 TEST CENTER

(Supplied by Test Center Supervisor.)

0 1 2 3 4 5 6 7 8 9

Important: Fill in items 8 and 9 exactly as shown on the back of test book.

8 BOOK CODE

(Copy and grid as on back of test book.)

0 1 2 3 4 5 6 7 8 9

A B C D E F G H I J K L M N O P Q R S T U V W X Y Z

9 BOOK ID

(Copy from back of test book.)

10 TEST BOOK SERIAL NUMBER

(Copy from front of test book.)

0 1 2 3 4 5 6 7 8 9

FOR OFFICIAL USE ONLY

0 1 2 3 4 5 6

0 1 2 3 4 5 6

0 1 2 3 4 5 6

83161-77191 • NS60C1285 • Printed in U.S.A.
755275

184596-001:321 Printed in the USA by Pearson ISD0479

PLEASE DO NOT WRITE IN THIS AREA

SERIAL #

COMPLETE MARK ● EXAMPLES OF INCOMPLETE MARKS

You must use a No. 2 pencil and marks must be complete. Do not use a mechanical pencil. *It is very important that you fill in the entire circle darkly and completely. If you change your response, erase as completely as possible. Incomplete marks or erasures may affect your score.*

○ Literature ○ Biology E ○ Biology M ○ Chemistry ○ Physics ○ Mathematics Level 1 ○ Mathematics Level 2 ○ U.S. History ○ World History ○ French ○ German ○ Italian ○ Latin ○ Modern Hebrew ○ Spanish ○ Chinese Listening ○ French Listening ○ German Listening ○ Japanese Listening ○ Korean Listening ○ Spanish Listening

Background Questions: ① ② ③ ④ ⑤ ⑥ ⑦ ⑧ ⑨

1–100 Ⓐ Ⓑ Ⓒ Ⓓ Ⓔ

Important: Fill in items 8 and 9 exactly as shown on the back of test book.

8 BOOK CODE (Copy and grid as on back of test book.)

9 BOOK ID (Copy from back of test book.)

10 TEST BOOK SERIAL NUMBER (Copy from front of test book.)

Quality Assurance Mark

Chemistry *Fill in circle CE only if II is correct explanation of I.

	I	II	CE*		I	II	CE*
101	Ⓣ Ⓕ	Ⓣ Ⓕ	○	109	Ⓣ Ⓕ	Ⓣ Ⓕ	○
102	Ⓣ Ⓕ	Ⓣ Ⓕ	○	110	Ⓣ Ⓕ	Ⓣ Ⓕ	○
103	Ⓣ Ⓕ	Ⓣ Ⓕ	○	111	Ⓣ Ⓕ	Ⓣ Ⓕ	○
104	Ⓣ Ⓕ	Ⓣ Ⓕ	○	112	Ⓣ Ⓕ	Ⓣ Ⓕ	○
105	Ⓣ Ⓕ	Ⓣ Ⓕ	○	113	Ⓣ Ⓕ	Ⓣ Ⓕ	○
106	Ⓣ Ⓕ	Ⓣ Ⓕ	○	114	Ⓣ Ⓕ	Ⓣ Ⓕ	○
107	Ⓣ Ⓕ	Ⓣ Ⓕ	○	115	Ⓣ Ⓕ	Ⓣ Ⓕ	○
108	Ⓣ Ⓕ	Ⓣ Ⓕ	○				

FOR OFFICIAL USE ONLY

R/C	W/S1	FS/S2	CS/S3	WS

CERTIFICATION STATEMENT

Copy the statement below (do not print) and sign your name as you would an official document.

I hereby agree to the conditions set forth online at sat.collegeboard.com and in any paper registration materials given to me and certify that I am the person whose name and address appear on this answer sheet.

Signature ____________________ Date ____________________

By registering, you agreed not to share any specific test question with anyone by any form of communication, including, but not limited to: email, text messages, or use of the Internet. Doing so can result in score cancellation and other possible sanctions.

COMPLETE MARK ● EXAMPLES OF INCOMPLETE MARKS

You must use a No. 2 pencil and marks must be complete. Do not use a mechanical pencil. *It is very important that you fill in the entire circle darkly and completely. If you change your response, erase as completely as possible. Incomplete marks or erasures may affect your score.*

○ Literature
○ Biology E
○ Biology M
○ Chemistry
○ Physics
○ Mathematics Level 1
○ Mathematics Level 2
○ U.S. History
○ World History
○ French
○ German
○ Italian
○ Latin
○ Modern Hebrew
○ Spanish

Background Questions: ① ② ③ ④ ⑤ ⑥ ⑦ ⑧ ⑨

1 Ⓐ Ⓑ Ⓒ Ⓓ Ⓔ	26 Ⓐ Ⓑ Ⓒ Ⓓ Ⓔ	51 Ⓐ Ⓑ Ⓒ Ⓓ Ⓔ	76 Ⓐ Ⓑ Ⓒ Ⓓ Ⓔ
2 Ⓐ Ⓑ Ⓒ Ⓓ Ⓔ	27 Ⓐ Ⓑ Ⓒ Ⓓ Ⓔ	52 Ⓐ Ⓑ Ⓒ Ⓓ Ⓔ	77 Ⓐ Ⓑ Ⓒ Ⓓ Ⓔ
3 Ⓐ Ⓑ Ⓒ Ⓓ Ⓔ	28 Ⓐ Ⓑ Ⓒ Ⓓ Ⓔ	53 Ⓐ Ⓑ Ⓒ Ⓓ Ⓔ	78 Ⓐ Ⓑ Ⓒ Ⓓ Ⓔ
4 Ⓐ Ⓑ Ⓒ Ⓓ Ⓔ	29 Ⓐ Ⓑ Ⓒ Ⓓ Ⓔ	54 Ⓐ Ⓑ Ⓒ Ⓓ Ⓔ	79 Ⓐ Ⓑ Ⓒ Ⓓ Ⓔ
5 Ⓐ Ⓑ Ⓒ Ⓓ Ⓔ	30 Ⓐ Ⓑ Ⓒ Ⓓ Ⓔ	55 Ⓐ Ⓑ Ⓒ Ⓓ Ⓔ	80 Ⓐ Ⓑ Ⓒ Ⓓ Ⓔ
6 Ⓐ Ⓑ Ⓒ Ⓓ Ⓔ	31 Ⓐ Ⓑ Ⓒ Ⓓ Ⓔ	56 Ⓐ Ⓑ Ⓒ Ⓓ Ⓔ	81 Ⓐ Ⓑ Ⓒ Ⓓ Ⓔ
7 Ⓐ Ⓑ Ⓒ Ⓓ Ⓔ	32 Ⓐ Ⓑ Ⓒ Ⓓ Ⓔ	57 Ⓐ Ⓑ Ⓒ Ⓓ Ⓔ	82 Ⓐ Ⓑ Ⓒ Ⓓ Ⓔ
8 Ⓐ Ⓑ Ⓒ Ⓓ Ⓔ	33 Ⓐ Ⓑ Ⓒ Ⓓ Ⓔ	58 Ⓐ Ⓑ Ⓒ Ⓓ Ⓔ	83 Ⓐ Ⓑ Ⓒ Ⓓ Ⓔ
9 Ⓐ Ⓑ Ⓒ Ⓓ Ⓔ	34 Ⓐ Ⓑ Ⓒ Ⓓ Ⓔ	59 Ⓐ Ⓑ Ⓒ Ⓓ Ⓔ	84 Ⓐ Ⓑ Ⓒ Ⓓ Ⓔ
10 Ⓐ Ⓑ Ⓒ Ⓓ Ⓔ	35 Ⓐ Ⓑ Ⓒ Ⓓ Ⓔ	60 Ⓐ Ⓑ Ⓒ Ⓓ Ⓔ	85 Ⓐ Ⓑ Ⓒ Ⓓ Ⓔ
11 Ⓐ Ⓑ Ⓒ Ⓓ Ⓔ	36 Ⓐ Ⓑ Ⓒ Ⓓ Ⓔ	61 Ⓐ Ⓑ Ⓒ Ⓓ Ⓔ	86 Ⓐ Ⓑ Ⓒ Ⓓ Ⓔ
12 Ⓐ Ⓑ Ⓒ Ⓓ Ⓔ	37 Ⓐ Ⓑ Ⓒ Ⓓ Ⓔ	62 Ⓐ Ⓑ Ⓒ Ⓓ Ⓔ	87 Ⓐ Ⓑ Ⓒ Ⓓ Ⓔ
13 Ⓐ Ⓑ Ⓒ Ⓓ Ⓔ	38 Ⓐ Ⓑ Ⓒ Ⓓ Ⓔ	63 Ⓐ Ⓑ Ⓒ Ⓓ Ⓔ	88 Ⓐ Ⓑ Ⓒ Ⓓ Ⓔ
14 Ⓐ Ⓑ Ⓒ Ⓓ Ⓔ	39 Ⓐ Ⓑ Ⓒ Ⓓ Ⓔ	64 Ⓐ Ⓑ Ⓒ Ⓓ Ⓔ	89 Ⓐ Ⓑ Ⓒ Ⓓ Ⓔ
15 Ⓐ Ⓑ Ⓒ Ⓓ Ⓔ	40 Ⓐ Ⓑ Ⓒ Ⓓ Ⓔ	65 Ⓐ Ⓑ Ⓒ Ⓓ Ⓔ	90 Ⓐ Ⓑ Ⓒ Ⓓ Ⓔ
16 Ⓐ Ⓑ Ⓒ Ⓓ Ⓔ	41 Ⓐ Ⓑ Ⓒ Ⓓ Ⓔ	66 Ⓐ Ⓑ Ⓒ Ⓓ Ⓔ	91 Ⓐ Ⓑ Ⓒ Ⓓ Ⓔ
17 Ⓐ Ⓑ Ⓒ Ⓓ Ⓔ	42 Ⓐ Ⓑ Ⓒ Ⓓ Ⓔ	67 Ⓐ Ⓑ Ⓒ Ⓓ Ⓔ	92 Ⓐ Ⓑ Ⓒ Ⓓ Ⓔ
18 Ⓐ Ⓑ Ⓒ Ⓓ Ⓔ	43 Ⓐ Ⓑ Ⓒ Ⓓ Ⓔ	68 Ⓐ Ⓑ Ⓒ Ⓓ Ⓔ	93 Ⓐ Ⓑ Ⓒ Ⓓ Ⓔ
19 Ⓐ Ⓑ Ⓒ Ⓓ Ⓔ	44 Ⓐ Ⓑ Ⓒ Ⓓ Ⓔ	69 Ⓐ Ⓑ Ⓒ Ⓓ Ⓔ	94 Ⓐ Ⓑ Ⓒ Ⓓ Ⓔ
20 Ⓐ Ⓑ Ⓒ Ⓓ Ⓔ	45 Ⓐ Ⓑ Ⓒ Ⓓ Ⓔ	70 Ⓐ Ⓑ Ⓒ Ⓓ Ⓔ	95 Ⓐ Ⓑ Ⓒ Ⓓ Ⓔ
21 Ⓐ Ⓑ Ⓒ Ⓓ Ⓔ	46 Ⓐ Ⓑ Ⓒ Ⓓ Ⓔ	71 Ⓐ Ⓑ Ⓒ Ⓓ Ⓔ	96 Ⓐ Ⓑ Ⓒ Ⓓ Ⓔ
22 Ⓐ Ⓑ Ⓒ Ⓓ Ⓔ	47 Ⓐ Ⓑ Ⓒ Ⓓ Ⓔ	72 Ⓐ Ⓑ Ⓒ Ⓓ Ⓔ	97 Ⓐ Ⓑ Ⓒ Ⓓ Ⓔ
23 Ⓐ Ⓑ Ⓒ Ⓓ Ⓔ	48 Ⓐ Ⓑ Ⓒ Ⓓ Ⓔ	73 Ⓐ Ⓑ Ⓒ Ⓓ Ⓔ	98 Ⓐ Ⓑ Ⓒ Ⓓ Ⓔ
24 Ⓐ Ⓑ Ⓒ Ⓓ Ⓔ	49 Ⓐ Ⓑ Ⓒ Ⓓ Ⓔ	74 Ⓐ Ⓑ Ⓒ Ⓓ Ⓔ	99 Ⓐ Ⓑ Ⓒ Ⓓ Ⓔ
25 Ⓐ Ⓑ Ⓒ Ⓓ Ⓔ	50 Ⓐ Ⓑ Ⓒ Ⓓ Ⓔ	75 Ⓐ Ⓑ Ⓒ Ⓓ Ⓔ	100 Ⓐ Ⓑ Ⓒ Ⓓ Ⓔ

Quality ● Assurance Mark

Chemistry *Fill in circle CE only if II is correct explanation of I.

	I	II	CE*		I	II	CE*
101	Ⓣ Ⓕ	Ⓣ Ⓕ	○	109	Ⓣ Ⓕ	Ⓣ Ⓕ	○
102	Ⓣ Ⓕ	Ⓣ Ⓕ	○	110	Ⓣ Ⓕ	Ⓣ Ⓕ	○
103	Ⓣ Ⓕ	Ⓣ Ⓕ	○	111	Ⓣ Ⓕ	Ⓣ Ⓕ	○
104	Ⓣ Ⓕ	Ⓣ Ⓕ	○	112	Ⓣ Ⓕ	Ⓣ Ⓕ	○
105	Ⓣ Ⓕ	Ⓣ Ⓕ	○	113	Ⓣ Ⓕ	Ⓣ Ⓕ	○
106	Ⓣ Ⓕ	Ⓣ Ⓕ	○	114	Ⓣ Ⓕ	Ⓣ Ⓕ	○
107	Ⓣ Ⓕ	Ⓣ Ⓕ	○	115	Ⓣ Ⓕ	Ⓣ Ⓕ	○
108	Ⓣ Ⓕ	Ⓣ Ⓕ	○				

FOR OFFICIAL USE ONLY

R/C	W/S1	FS/S2	CS/S3	WS

Important: Fill in items 8 and 9 exactly as shown on the back of test book.

8 BOOK CODE (Copy and grid as on back of test book.)

0	A	0
1	B	1
2	C	2
3	D	3
4	E	4
5	F	5
6	G	6
7	H	7
8	I	8
9	J	9
	K	
	L	
	M	
	N	
	O	
	P	
	Q	
	R	
	S	
	T	
	U	
	V	
	W	
	X	
	Y	
	Z	

9 BOOK ID (Copy from back of test book.)

10 TEST BOOK SERIAL NUMBER (Copy from front of test book.)

0	0	0	0	0	0
1	1	1	1	1	1
2	2	2	2	2	2
3	3	3	3	3	3
4	4	4	4	4	4
5	5	5	5	5	5
6	6	6	6	6	6
7	7	7	7	7	7
8	8	8	8	8	8
9	9	9	9	9	9

COMPLETE MARK ● **EXAMPLES OF INCOMPLETE MARKS**

You must use a No. 2 pencil and marks must be complete. Do not use a mechanical pencil. *It is very important that you fill in the entire circle darkly and completely. If you change your response, erase as completely as possible. Incomplete marks or erasures may affect your score.*

○ Literature ○ Biology E ○ Biology M ○ Chemistry ○ Physics
○ Mathematics Level 1 ○ Mathematics Level 2 ○ U.S. History ○ World History ○ French
○ German ○ Italian ○ Latin ○ Modern Hebrew ○ Spanish

Background Questions: (1) (2) (3) (4) (5) (6) (7) (8) (9)

1 (A)(B)(C)(D)(E)	26 (A)(B)(C)(D)(E)	51 (A)(B)(C)(D)(E)	76 (A)(B)(C)(D)(E)
2 (A)(B)(C)(D)(E)	27 (A)(B)(C)(D)(E)	52 (A)(B)(C)(D)(E)	77 (A)(B)(C)(D)(E)
3 (A)(B)(C)(D)(E)	28 (A)(B)(C)(D)(E)	53 (A)(B)(C)(D)(E)	78 (A)(B)(C)(D)(E)
4 (A)(B)(C)(D)(E)	29 (A)(B)(C)(D)(E)	54 (A)(B)(C)(D)(E)	79 (A)(B)(C)(D)(E)
5 (A)(B)(C)(D)(E)	30 (A)(B)(C)(D)(E)	55 (A)(B)(C)(D)(E)	80 (A)(B)(C)(D)(E)
6 (A)(B)(C)(D)(E)	31 (A)(B)(C)(D)(E)	56 (A)(B)(C)(D)(E)	81 (A)(B)(C)(D)(E)
7 (A)(B)(C)(D)(E)	32 (A)(B)(C)(D)(E)	57 (A)(B)(C)(D)(E)	82 (A)(B)(C)(D)(E)
8 (A)(B)(C)(D)(E)	33 (A)(B)(C)(D)(E)	58 (A)(B)(C)(D)(E)	83 (A)(B)(C)(D)(E)
9 (A)(B)(C)(D)(E)	34 (A)(B)(C)(D)(E)	59 (A)(B)(C)(D)(E)	84 (A)(B)(C)(D)(E)
10 (A)(B)(C)(D)(E)	35 (A)(B)(C)(D)(E)	60 (A)(B)(C)(D)(E)	85 (A)(B)(C)(D)(E)
11 (A)(B)(C)(D)(E)	36 (A)(B)(C)(D)(E)	61 (A)(B)(C)(D)(E)	86 (A)(B)(C)(D)(E)
12 (A)(B)(C)(D)(E)	37 (A)(B)(C)(D)(E)	62 (A)(B)(C)(D)(E)	87 (A)(B)(C)(D)(E)
13 (A)(B)(C)(D)(E)	38 (A)(B)(C)(D)(E)	63 (A)(B)(C)(D)(E)	88 (A)(B)(C)(D)(E)
14 (A)(B)(C)(D)(E)	39 (A)(B)(C)(D)(E)	64 (A)(B)(C)(D)(E)	89 (A)(B)(C)(D)(E)
15 (A)(B)(C)(D)(E)	40 (A)(B)(C)(D)(E)	65 (A)(B)(C)(D)(E)	90 (A)(B)(C)(D)(E)
16 (A)(B)(C)(D)(E)	41 (A)(B)(C)(D)(E)	66 (A)(B)(C)(D)(E)	91 (A)(B)(C)(D)(E)
17 (A)(B)(C)(D)(E)	42 (A)(B)(C)(D)(E)	67 (A)(B)(C)(D)(E)	92 (A)(B)(C)(D)(E)
18 (A)(B)(C)(D)(E)	43 (A)(B)(C)(D)(E)	68 (A)(B)(C)(D)(E)	93 (A)(B)(C)(D)(E)
19 (A)(B)(C)(D)(E)	44 (A)(B)(C)(D)(E)	69 (A)(B)(C)(D)(E)	94 (A)(B)(C)(D)(E)
20 (A)(B)(C)(D)(E)	45 (A)(B)(C)(D)(E)	70 (A)(B)(C)(D)(E)	95 (A)(B)(C)(D)(E)
21 (A)(B)(C)(D)(E)	46 (A)(B)(C)(D)(E)	71 (A)(B)(C)(D)(E)	96 (A)(B)(C)(D)(E)
22 (A)(B)(C)(D)(E)	47 (A)(B)(C)(D)(E)	72 (A)(B)(C)(D)(E)	97 (A)(B)(C)(D)(E)
23 (A)(B)(C)(D)(E)	48 (A)(B)(C)(D)(E)	73 (A)(B)(C)(D)(E)	98 (A)(B)(C)(D)(E)
24 (A)(B)(C)(D)(E)	49 (A)(B)(C)(D)(E)	74 (A)(B)(C)(D)(E)	99 (A)(B)(C)(D)(E)
25 (A)(B)(C)(D)(E)	50 (A)(B)(C)(D)(E)	75 (A)(B)(C)(D)(E)	100 (A)(B)(C)(D)(E)

Chemistry *Fill in circle CE only if II is correct explanation of I.

	I	II	CE*		I	II	CE*
101	(T)(F)	(T)(F)	○	109	(T)(F)	(T)(F)	○
102	(T)(F)	(T)(F)	○	110	(T)(F)	(T)(F)	○
103	(T)(F)	(T)(F)	○	111	(T)(F)	(T)(F)	○
104	(T)(F)	(T)(F)	○	112	(T)(F)	(T)(F)	○
105	(T)(F)	(T)(F)	○	113	(T)(F)	(T)(F)	○
106	(T)(F)	(T)(F)	○	114	(T)(F)	(T)(F)	○
107	(T)(F)	(T)(F)	○	115	(T)(F)	(T)(F)	○
108	(T)(F)	(T)(F)	○				

FOR OFFICIAL USE ONLY

R/C	W/S1	FS/S2	CS/S3	WS

Important: Fill in items 8 and 9 exactly as shown on the back of test book.

8 BOOK CODE (Copy and grid as on back of test book.)

0–9 | A–Z | 0–9

9 BOOK ID (Copy from back of test book.)

10 TEST BOOK SERIAL NUMBER (Copy from front of test book.)

0–9 (six columns)

Quality Assurance Mark

Page 4

PLEASE DO NOT WRITE IN THIS AREA

SERIAL #

2010-11 SAT Subject Tests™

MARKS MUST BE COMPLETE

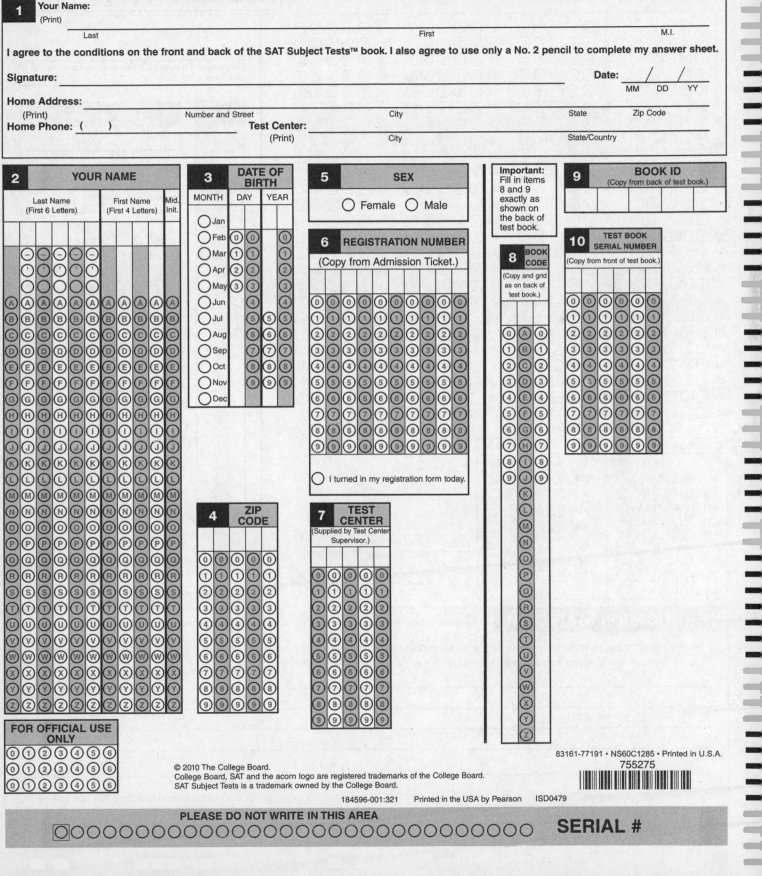

COMPLETE MARK ● EXAMPLES OF INCOMPLETE MARKS 

You must use a No. 2 pencil. Do not use a mechanical pencil. It is very important that you fill in the entire circle darkly and completely. If you change your response, erase as completely as possible. Incomplete marks or erasures may affect your score. It is very important that you follow these instructions when filling out your answer sheet.

1 **Your Name:** (Print) ______ Last ______ First ______ M.I.

I agree to the conditions on the front and back of the SAT Subject Tests™ book. I also agree to use only a No. 2 pencil to complete my answer sheet.

Signature: ______ **Date:** ___/___/___ MM DD YY

Home Address: (Print) ______ Number and Street ______ City ______ State ______ Zip Code

Home Phone: ( ) ______ **Test Center:** (Print) ______ City ______ State/Country

2 YOUR NAME

Last Name (First 6 Letters) | First Name (First 4 Letters) | Mid. Init.

– ' A B C D E F G H I J K L M N O P Q R S T U V W X Y Z

3 DATE OF BIRTH

MONTH: Jan Feb Mar Apr May Jun Jul Aug Sep Oct Nov Dec

DAY: 0 1 2 3 | 0 1 2 3 4 5 6 7 8 9

YEAR: 5 6 7 8 9 | 0 1 2 3 4 5 6 7 8 9

4 ZIP CODE

0 1 2 3 4 5 6 7 8 9

5 SEX

○ Female ○ Male

6 REGISTRATION NUMBER

(Copy from Admission Ticket.)

0 1 2 3 4 5 6 7 8 9

○ I turned in my registration form today.

7 TEST CENTER

(Supplied by Test Center Supervisor.)

0 1 2 3 4 5 6 7 8 9

Important: Fill in items 8 and 9 exactly as shown on the back of test book.

8 BOOK CODE

(Copy and grid as on back of test book.)

0 1 2 3 4 5 6 7 8 9 | A B C D E F G H I J K L M N O P Q R S T U V W X Y Z | 0 1 2 3 4 5 6 7 8 9

9 BOOK ID

(Copy from back of test book.)

10 TEST BOOK SERIAL NUMBER

(Copy from front of test book.)

0 1 2 3 4 5 6 7 8 9

FOR OFFICIAL USE ONLY

0 1 2 3 4 5 6

0 1 2 3 4 5 6

0 1 2 3 4 5 6

184596-001:321 Printed in the USA by Pearson ISD0479

83161-77191 • NS60C1285 • Printed in U.S.A.
755275

PLEASE DO NOT WRITE IN THIS AREA

SERIAL #

COMPLETE MARK ● **EXAMPLES OF INCOMPLETE MARKS**

You must use a No. 2 pencil and marks must be complete. Do not use a mechanical pencil. *It is very important that you fill in the entire circle darkly and completely. If you change your response, erase as completely as possible. Incomplete marks or erasures may affect your score.*

◯ Literature	◯ Mathematics Level 1	◯ German	◯ Chinese Listening	◯ Japanese Listening
◯ Biology E	◯ Mathematics Level 2	◯ Italian	◯ French Listening	◯ Korean Listening
◯ Biology M	◯ U.S. History	◯ Latin	◯ German Listening	◯ Spanish Listening
◯ Chemistry	◯ World History	◯ Modern Hebrew		
◯ Physics	◯ French	◯ Spanish		

Background Questions: ① ② ③ ④ ⑤ ⑥ ⑦ ⑧ ⑨

1 Ⓐ Ⓑ Ⓒ Ⓓ Ⓔ	26 Ⓐ Ⓑ Ⓒ Ⓓ Ⓔ	51 Ⓐ Ⓑ Ⓒ Ⓓ Ⓔ	76 Ⓐ Ⓑ Ⓒ Ⓓ Ⓔ
2 Ⓐ Ⓑ Ⓒ Ⓓ Ⓔ	27 Ⓐ Ⓑ Ⓒ Ⓓ Ⓔ	52 Ⓐ Ⓑ Ⓒ Ⓓ Ⓔ	77 Ⓐ Ⓑ Ⓒ Ⓓ Ⓔ
3 Ⓐ Ⓑ Ⓒ Ⓓ Ⓔ	28 Ⓐ Ⓑ Ⓒ Ⓓ Ⓔ	53 Ⓐ Ⓑ Ⓒ Ⓓ Ⓔ	78 Ⓐ Ⓑ Ⓒ Ⓓ Ⓔ
4 Ⓐ Ⓑ Ⓒ Ⓓ Ⓔ	29 Ⓐ Ⓑ Ⓒ Ⓓ Ⓔ	54 Ⓐ Ⓑ Ⓒ Ⓓ Ⓔ	79 Ⓐ Ⓑ Ⓒ Ⓓ Ⓔ
5 Ⓐ Ⓑ Ⓒ Ⓓ Ⓔ	30 Ⓐ Ⓑ Ⓒ Ⓓ Ⓔ	55 Ⓐ Ⓑ Ⓒ Ⓓ Ⓔ	80 Ⓐ Ⓑ Ⓒ Ⓓ Ⓔ
6 Ⓐ Ⓑ Ⓒ Ⓓ Ⓔ	31 Ⓐ Ⓑ Ⓒ Ⓓ Ⓔ	56 Ⓐ Ⓑ Ⓒ Ⓓ Ⓔ	81 Ⓐ Ⓑ Ⓒ Ⓓ Ⓔ
7 Ⓐ Ⓑ Ⓒ Ⓓ Ⓔ	32 Ⓐ Ⓑ Ⓒ Ⓓ Ⓔ	57 Ⓐ Ⓑ Ⓒ Ⓓ Ⓔ	82 Ⓐ Ⓑ Ⓒ Ⓓ Ⓔ
8 Ⓐ Ⓑ Ⓒ Ⓓ Ⓔ	33 Ⓐ Ⓑ Ⓒ Ⓓ Ⓔ	58 Ⓐ Ⓑ Ⓒ Ⓓ Ⓔ	83 Ⓐ Ⓑ Ⓒ Ⓓ Ⓔ
9 Ⓐ Ⓑ Ⓒ Ⓓ Ⓔ	34 Ⓐ Ⓑ Ⓒ Ⓓ Ⓔ	59 Ⓐ Ⓑ Ⓒ Ⓓ Ⓔ	84 Ⓐ Ⓑ Ⓒ Ⓓ Ⓔ
10 Ⓐ Ⓑ Ⓒ Ⓓ Ⓔ	35 Ⓐ Ⓑ Ⓒ Ⓓ Ⓔ	60 Ⓐ Ⓑ Ⓒ Ⓓ Ⓔ	85 Ⓐ Ⓑ Ⓒ Ⓓ Ⓔ
11 Ⓐ Ⓑ Ⓒ Ⓓ Ⓔ	36 Ⓐ Ⓑ Ⓒ Ⓓ Ⓔ	61 Ⓐ Ⓑ Ⓒ Ⓓ Ⓔ	86 Ⓐ Ⓑ Ⓒ Ⓓ Ⓔ
12 Ⓐ Ⓑ Ⓒ Ⓓ Ⓔ	37 Ⓐ Ⓑ Ⓒ Ⓓ Ⓔ	62 Ⓐ Ⓑ Ⓒ Ⓓ Ⓔ	87 Ⓐ Ⓑ Ⓒ Ⓓ Ⓔ
13 Ⓐ Ⓑ Ⓒ Ⓓ Ⓔ	38 Ⓐ Ⓑ Ⓒ Ⓓ Ⓔ	63 Ⓐ Ⓑ Ⓒ Ⓓ Ⓔ	88 Ⓐ Ⓑ Ⓒ Ⓓ Ⓔ
14 Ⓐ Ⓑ Ⓒ Ⓓ Ⓔ	39 Ⓐ Ⓑ Ⓒ Ⓓ Ⓔ	64 Ⓐ Ⓑ Ⓒ Ⓓ Ⓔ	89 Ⓐ Ⓑ Ⓒ Ⓓ Ⓔ
15 Ⓐ Ⓑ Ⓒ Ⓓ Ⓔ	40 Ⓐ Ⓑ Ⓒ Ⓓ Ⓔ	65 Ⓐ Ⓑ Ⓒ Ⓓ Ⓔ	90 Ⓐ Ⓑ Ⓒ Ⓓ Ⓔ
16 Ⓐ Ⓑ Ⓒ Ⓓ Ⓔ	41 Ⓐ Ⓑ Ⓒ Ⓓ Ⓔ	66 Ⓐ Ⓑ Ⓒ Ⓓ Ⓔ	91 Ⓐ Ⓑ Ⓒ Ⓓ Ⓔ
17 Ⓐ Ⓑ Ⓒ Ⓓ Ⓔ	42 Ⓐ Ⓑ Ⓒ Ⓓ Ⓔ	67 Ⓐ Ⓑ Ⓒ Ⓓ Ⓔ	92 Ⓐ Ⓑ Ⓒ Ⓓ Ⓔ
18 Ⓐ Ⓑ Ⓒ Ⓓ Ⓔ	43 Ⓐ Ⓑ Ⓒ Ⓓ Ⓔ	68 Ⓐ Ⓑ Ⓒ Ⓓ Ⓔ	93 Ⓐ Ⓑ Ⓒ Ⓓ Ⓔ
19 Ⓐ Ⓑ Ⓒ Ⓓ Ⓔ	44 Ⓐ Ⓑ Ⓒ Ⓓ Ⓔ	69 Ⓐ Ⓑ Ⓒ Ⓓ Ⓔ	94 Ⓐ Ⓑ Ⓒ Ⓓ Ⓔ
20 Ⓐ Ⓑ Ⓒ Ⓓ Ⓔ	45 Ⓐ Ⓑ Ⓒ Ⓓ Ⓔ	70 Ⓐ Ⓑ Ⓒ Ⓓ Ⓔ	95 Ⓐ Ⓑ Ⓒ Ⓓ Ⓔ
21 Ⓐ Ⓑ Ⓒ Ⓓ Ⓔ	46 Ⓐ Ⓑ Ⓒ Ⓓ Ⓔ	71 Ⓐ Ⓑ Ⓒ Ⓓ Ⓔ	96 Ⓐ Ⓑ Ⓒ Ⓓ Ⓔ
22 Ⓐ Ⓑ Ⓒ Ⓓ Ⓔ	47 Ⓐ Ⓑ Ⓒ Ⓓ Ⓔ	72 Ⓐ Ⓑ Ⓒ Ⓓ Ⓔ	97 Ⓐ Ⓑ Ⓒ Ⓓ Ⓔ
23 Ⓐ Ⓑ Ⓒ Ⓓ Ⓔ	48 Ⓐ Ⓑ Ⓒ Ⓓ Ⓔ	73 Ⓐ Ⓑ Ⓒ Ⓓ Ⓔ	98 Ⓐ Ⓑ Ⓒ Ⓓ Ⓔ
24 Ⓐ Ⓑ Ⓒ Ⓓ Ⓔ	49 Ⓐ Ⓑ Ⓒ Ⓓ Ⓔ	74 Ⓐ Ⓑ Ⓒ Ⓓ Ⓔ	99 Ⓐ Ⓑ Ⓒ Ⓓ Ⓔ
25 Ⓐ Ⓑ Ⓒ Ⓓ Ⓔ	50 Ⓐ Ⓑ Ⓒ Ⓓ Ⓔ	75 Ⓐ Ⓑ Ⓒ Ⓓ Ⓔ	100 Ⓐ Ⓑ Ⓒ Ⓓ Ⓔ

Important: Fill in items 8 and 9 exactly as shown on the back of test book.

8 BOOK CODE (Copy and grid as on back of test book.)

0	A	0
1	B	1
2	C	2
3	D	3
4	E	4
5	F	5
6	G	6
7	H	7
8	I	8
9	J	9
	K	
	L	
	M	
	N	
	O	
	P	
	Q	
	R	
	S	
	T	
	U	
	V	
	W	
	X	
	Y	
	Z	

9 BOOK ID (Copy from back of test book.)

10 TEST BOOK SERIAL NUMBER (Copy from front of test book.)

0	0	0	0	0	0
1	1	1	1	1	1
2	2	2	2	2	2
3	3	3	3	3	3
4	4	4	4	4	4
5	5	5	5	5	5
6	6	6	6	6	6
7	7	7	7	7	7
8	8	8	8	8	8
9	9	9	9	9	9

Quality Assurance Mark

Chemistry *Fill in circle CE only if II is correct explanation of I.

	I	II	CE*		I	II	CE*
101	Ⓣ Ⓕ	Ⓣ Ⓕ	◯	109	Ⓣ Ⓕ	Ⓣ Ⓕ	◯
102	Ⓣ Ⓕ	Ⓣ Ⓕ	◯	110	Ⓣ Ⓕ	Ⓣ Ⓕ	◯
103	Ⓣ Ⓕ	Ⓣ Ⓕ	◯	111	Ⓣ Ⓕ	Ⓣ Ⓕ	◯
104	Ⓣ Ⓕ	Ⓣ Ⓕ	◯	112	Ⓣ Ⓕ	Ⓣ Ⓕ	◯
105	Ⓣ Ⓕ	Ⓣ Ⓕ	◯	113	Ⓣ Ⓕ	Ⓣ Ⓕ	◯
106	Ⓣ Ⓕ	Ⓣ Ⓕ	◯	114	Ⓣ Ⓕ	Ⓣ Ⓕ	◯
107	Ⓣ Ⓕ	Ⓣ Ⓕ	◯	115	Ⓣ Ⓕ	Ⓣ Ⓕ	◯
108	Ⓣ Ⓕ	Ⓣ Ⓕ	◯				

FOR OFFICIAL USE ONLY

R/C	W/S1	FS/S2	CS/S3	WS

CERTIFICATION STATEMENT

Copy the statement below (do not print) and sign your name as you would an official document.

I hereby agree to the conditions set forth online at sat.collegeboard.com and in any paper registration materials given to me and certify that I am the person whose name and address appear on this answer sheet.

Signature ______________________ Date ______________

By registering, you agreed not to share any specific test question with anyone by any form of communication, including, but not limited to: email, text messages, or use of the Internet. Doing so can result in score cancellation and other possible sanctions.

COMPLETE MARK ● EXAMPLES OF INCOMPLETE MARKS

You must use a No. 2 pencil and marks must be complete. Do not use a mechanical pencil. *It is very important that you fill in the entire circle darkly and completely. If you change your response, erase as completely as possible. Incomplete marks or erasures may affect your score.*

○ Literature	○ Mathematics Level 1	○ German
○ Biology E	○ Mathematics Level 2	○ Italian
○ Biology M	○ U.S. History	○ Latin
○ Chemistry	○ World History	○ Modern Hebrew
○ Physics	○ French	○ Spanish

Background Questions: ① ② ③ ④ ⑤ ⑥ ⑦ ⑧ ⑨

1 Ⓐ Ⓑ Ⓒ Ⓓ Ⓔ	26 Ⓐ Ⓑ Ⓒ Ⓓ Ⓔ	51 Ⓐ Ⓑ Ⓒ Ⓓ Ⓔ	76 Ⓐ Ⓑ Ⓒ Ⓓ Ⓔ
2 Ⓐ Ⓑ Ⓒ Ⓓ Ⓔ	27 Ⓐ Ⓑ Ⓒ Ⓓ Ⓔ	52 Ⓐ Ⓑ Ⓒ Ⓓ Ⓔ	77 Ⓐ Ⓑ Ⓒ Ⓓ Ⓔ
3 Ⓐ Ⓑ Ⓒ Ⓓ Ⓔ	28 Ⓐ Ⓑ Ⓒ Ⓓ Ⓔ	53 Ⓐ Ⓑ Ⓒ Ⓓ Ⓔ	78 Ⓐ Ⓑ Ⓒ Ⓓ Ⓔ
4 Ⓐ Ⓑ Ⓒ Ⓓ Ⓔ	29 Ⓐ Ⓑ Ⓒ Ⓓ Ⓔ	54 Ⓐ Ⓑ Ⓒ Ⓓ Ⓔ	79 Ⓐ Ⓑ Ⓒ Ⓓ Ⓔ
5 Ⓐ Ⓑ Ⓒ Ⓓ Ⓔ	30 Ⓐ Ⓑ Ⓒ Ⓓ Ⓔ	55 Ⓐ Ⓑ Ⓒ Ⓓ Ⓔ	80 Ⓐ Ⓑ Ⓒ Ⓓ Ⓔ
6 Ⓐ Ⓑ Ⓒ Ⓓ Ⓔ	31 Ⓐ Ⓑ Ⓒ Ⓓ Ⓔ	56 Ⓐ Ⓑ Ⓒ Ⓓ Ⓔ	81 Ⓐ Ⓑ Ⓒ Ⓓ Ⓔ
7 Ⓐ Ⓑ Ⓒ Ⓓ Ⓔ	32 Ⓐ Ⓑ Ⓒ Ⓓ Ⓔ	57 Ⓐ Ⓑ Ⓒ Ⓓ Ⓔ	82 Ⓐ Ⓑ Ⓒ Ⓓ Ⓔ
8 Ⓐ Ⓑ Ⓒ Ⓓ Ⓔ	33 Ⓐ Ⓑ Ⓒ Ⓓ Ⓔ	58 Ⓐ Ⓑ Ⓒ Ⓓ Ⓔ	83 Ⓐ Ⓑ Ⓒ Ⓓ Ⓔ
9 Ⓐ Ⓑ Ⓒ Ⓓ Ⓔ	34 Ⓐ Ⓑ Ⓒ Ⓓ Ⓔ	59 Ⓐ Ⓑ Ⓒ Ⓓ Ⓔ	84 Ⓐ Ⓑ Ⓒ Ⓓ Ⓔ
10 Ⓐ Ⓑ Ⓒ Ⓓ Ⓔ	35 Ⓐ Ⓑ Ⓒ Ⓓ Ⓔ	60 Ⓐ Ⓑ Ⓒ Ⓓ Ⓔ	85 Ⓐ Ⓑ Ⓒ Ⓓ Ⓔ
11 Ⓐ Ⓑ Ⓒ Ⓓ Ⓔ	36 Ⓐ Ⓑ Ⓒ Ⓓ Ⓔ	61 Ⓐ Ⓑ Ⓒ Ⓓ Ⓔ	86 Ⓐ Ⓑ Ⓒ Ⓓ Ⓔ
12 Ⓐ Ⓑ Ⓒ Ⓓ Ⓔ	37 Ⓐ Ⓑ Ⓒ Ⓓ Ⓔ	62 Ⓐ Ⓑ Ⓒ Ⓓ Ⓔ	87 Ⓐ Ⓑ Ⓒ Ⓓ Ⓔ
13 Ⓐ Ⓑ Ⓒ Ⓓ Ⓔ	38 Ⓐ Ⓑ Ⓒ Ⓓ Ⓔ	63 Ⓐ Ⓑ Ⓒ Ⓓ Ⓔ	88 Ⓐ Ⓑ Ⓒ Ⓓ Ⓔ
14 Ⓐ Ⓑ Ⓒ Ⓓ Ⓔ	39 Ⓐ Ⓑ Ⓒ Ⓓ Ⓔ	64 Ⓐ Ⓑ Ⓒ Ⓓ Ⓔ	89 Ⓐ Ⓑ Ⓒ Ⓓ Ⓔ
15 Ⓐ Ⓑ Ⓒ Ⓓ Ⓔ	40 Ⓐ Ⓑ Ⓒ Ⓓ Ⓔ	65 Ⓐ Ⓑ Ⓒ Ⓓ Ⓔ	90 Ⓐ Ⓑ Ⓒ Ⓓ Ⓔ
16 Ⓐ Ⓑ Ⓒ Ⓓ Ⓔ	41 Ⓐ Ⓑ Ⓒ Ⓓ Ⓔ	66 Ⓐ Ⓑ Ⓒ Ⓓ Ⓔ	91 Ⓐ Ⓑ Ⓒ Ⓓ Ⓔ
17 Ⓐ Ⓑ Ⓒ Ⓓ Ⓔ	42 Ⓐ Ⓑ Ⓒ Ⓓ Ⓔ	67 Ⓐ Ⓑ Ⓒ Ⓓ Ⓔ	92 Ⓐ Ⓑ Ⓒ Ⓓ Ⓔ
18 Ⓐ Ⓑ Ⓒ Ⓓ Ⓔ	43 Ⓐ Ⓑ Ⓒ Ⓓ Ⓔ	68 Ⓐ Ⓑ Ⓒ Ⓓ Ⓔ	93 Ⓐ Ⓑ Ⓒ Ⓓ Ⓔ
19 Ⓐ Ⓑ Ⓒ Ⓓ Ⓔ	44 Ⓐ Ⓑ Ⓒ Ⓓ Ⓔ	69 Ⓐ Ⓑ Ⓒ Ⓓ Ⓔ	94 Ⓐ Ⓑ Ⓒ Ⓓ Ⓔ
20 Ⓐ Ⓑ Ⓒ Ⓓ Ⓔ	45 Ⓐ Ⓑ Ⓒ Ⓓ Ⓔ	70 Ⓐ Ⓑ Ⓒ Ⓓ Ⓔ	95 Ⓐ Ⓑ Ⓒ Ⓓ Ⓔ
21 Ⓐ Ⓑ Ⓒ Ⓓ Ⓔ	46 Ⓐ Ⓑ Ⓒ Ⓓ Ⓔ	71 Ⓐ Ⓑ Ⓒ Ⓓ Ⓔ	96 Ⓐ Ⓑ Ⓒ Ⓓ Ⓔ
22 Ⓐ Ⓑ Ⓒ Ⓓ Ⓔ	47 Ⓐ Ⓑ Ⓒ Ⓓ Ⓔ	72 Ⓐ Ⓑ Ⓒ Ⓓ Ⓔ	97 Ⓐ Ⓑ Ⓒ Ⓓ Ⓔ
23 Ⓐ Ⓑ Ⓒ Ⓓ Ⓔ	48 Ⓐ Ⓑ Ⓒ Ⓓ Ⓔ	73 Ⓐ Ⓑ Ⓒ Ⓓ Ⓔ	98 Ⓐ Ⓑ Ⓒ Ⓓ Ⓔ
24 Ⓐ Ⓑ Ⓒ Ⓓ Ⓔ	49 Ⓐ Ⓑ Ⓒ Ⓓ Ⓔ	74 Ⓐ Ⓑ Ⓒ Ⓓ Ⓔ	99 Ⓐ Ⓑ Ⓒ Ⓓ Ⓔ
25 Ⓐ Ⓑ Ⓒ Ⓓ Ⓔ	50 Ⓐ Ⓑ Ⓒ Ⓓ Ⓔ	75 Ⓐ Ⓑ Ⓒ Ⓓ Ⓔ	100 Ⓐ Ⓑ Ⓒ Ⓓ Ⓔ

Quality Assurance Mark

Chemistry *Fill in circle CE only if II is correct explanation of I.

	I	II	CE*		I	II	CE*
101	Ⓣ Ⓕ	Ⓣ Ⓕ	○	109	Ⓣ Ⓕ	Ⓣ Ⓕ	○
102	Ⓣ Ⓕ	Ⓣ Ⓕ	○	110	Ⓣ Ⓕ	Ⓣ Ⓕ	○
103	Ⓣ Ⓕ	Ⓣ Ⓕ	○	111	Ⓣ Ⓕ	Ⓣ Ⓕ	○
104	Ⓣ Ⓕ	Ⓣ Ⓕ	○	112	Ⓣ Ⓕ	Ⓣ Ⓕ	○
105	Ⓣ Ⓕ	Ⓣ Ⓕ	○	113	Ⓣ Ⓕ	Ⓣ Ⓕ	○
106	Ⓣ Ⓕ	Ⓣ Ⓕ	○	114	Ⓣ Ⓕ	Ⓣ Ⓕ	○
107	Ⓣ Ⓕ	Ⓣ Ⓕ	○	115	Ⓣ Ⓕ	Ⓣ Ⓕ	○
108	Ⓣ Ⓕ	Ⓣ Ⓕ	○				

FOR OFFICIAL USE ONLY

R/C	W/S1	FS/S2	CS/S3	WS

Important: Fill in items 8 and 9 exactly as shown on the back of test book.

8 BOOK CODE (Copy and grid as on back of test book.)

0	A	0
1	B	1
2	C	2
3	D	3
4	E	4
5	F	5
6	G	6
7	H	7
8	I	8
9	J	9
	K	
	L	
	M	
	N	
	O	
	P	
	Q	
	R	
	S	
	T	
	U	
	V	
	W	
	X	
	Y	
	Z	

9 BOOK ID (Copy from back of test book.)

10 TEST BOOK SERIAL NUMBER (Copy from front of test book.)

0	0	0	0	0	0
1	1	1	1	1	1
2	2	2	2	2	2
3	3	3	3	3	3
4	4	4	4	4	4
5	5	5	5	5	5
6	6	6	6	6	6
7	7	7	7	7	7
8	8	8	8	8	8
9	9	9	9	9	9

COMPLETE MARK ● EXAMPLES OF INCOMPLETE MARKS

You must use a No. 2 pencil and marks must be complete. Do not use a mechanical pencil. *It is very important that you fill in the entire circle darkly and completely. If you change your response, erase as completely as possible. Incomplete marks or erasures may affect your score.*

○ Literature ○ Biology E ○ Biology M ○ Chemistry ○ Physics
○ Mathematics Level 1 ○ Mathematics Level 2 ○ U.S. History ○ World History ○ French
○ German ○ Italian ○ Latin ○ Modern Hebrew ○ Spanish

Background Questions: ① ② ③ ④ ⑤ ⑥ ⑦ ⑧ ⑨

1 Ⓐ Ⓑ Ⓒ Ⓓ Ⓔ	26 Ⓐ Ⓑ Ⓒ Ⓓ Ⓔ	51 Ⓐ Ⓑ Ⓒ Ⓓ Ⓔ	76 Ⓐ Ⓑ Ⓒ Ⓓ Ⓔ
2 Ⓐ Ⓑ Ⓒ Ⓓ Ⓔ	27 Ⓐ Ⓑ Ⓒ Ⓓ Ⓔ	52 Ⓐ Ⓑ Ⓒ Ⓓ Ⓔ	77 Ⓐ Ⓑ Ⓒ Ⓓ Ⓔ
3 Ⓐ Ⓑ Ⓒ Ⓓ Ⓔ	28 Ⓐ Ⓑ Ⓒ Ⓓ Ⓔ	53 Ⓐ Ⓑ Ⓒ Ⓓ Ⓔ	78 Ⓐ Ⓑ Ⓒ Ⓓ Ⓔ
4 Ⓐ Ⓑ Ⓒ Ⓓ Ⓔ	29 Ⓐ Ⓑ Ⓒ Ⓓ Ⓔ	54 Ⓐ Ⓑ Ⓒ Ⓓ Ⓔ	79 Ⓐ Ⓑ Ⓒ Ⓓ Ⓔ
5 Ⓐ Ⓑ Ⓒ Ⓓ Ⓔ	30 Ⓐ Ⓑ Ⓒ Ⓓ Ⓔ	55 Ⓐ Ⓑ Ⓒ Ⓓ Ⓔ	80 Ⓐ Ⓑ Ⓒ Ⓓ Ⓔ
6 Ⓐ Ⓑ Ⓒ Ⓓ Ⓔ	31 Ⓐ Ⓑ Ⓒ Ⓓ Ⓔ	56 Ⓐ Ⓑ Ⓒ Ⓓ Ⓔ	81 Ⓐ Ⓑ Ⓒ Ⓓ Ⓔ
7 Ⓐ Ⓑ Ⓒ Ⓓ Ⓔ	32 Ⓐ Ⓑ Ⓒ Ⓓ Ⓔ	57 Ⓐ Ⓑ Ⓒ Ⓓ Ⓔ	82 Ⓐ Ⓑ Ⓒ Ⓓ Ⓔ
8 Ⓐ Ⓑ Ⓒ Ⓓ Ⓔ	33 Ⓐ Ⓑ Ⓒ Ⓓ Ⓔ	58 Ⓐ Ⓑ Ⓒ Ⓓ Ⓔ	83 Ⓐ Ⓑ Ⓒ Ⓓ Ⓔ
9 Ⓐ Ⓑ Ⓒ Ⓓ Ⓔ	34 Ⓐ Ⓑ Ⓒ Ⓓ Ⓔ	59 Ⓐ Ⓑ Ⓒ Ⓓ Ⓔ	84 Ⓐ Ⓑ Ⓒ Ⓓ Ⓔ
10 Ⓐ Ⓑ Ⓒ Ⓓ Ⓔ	35 Ⓐ Ⓑ Ⓒ Ⓓ Ⓔ	60 Ⓐ Ⓑ Ⓒ Ⓓ Ⓔ	85 Ⓐ Ⓑ Ⓒ Ⓓ Ⓔ
11 Ⓐ Ⓑ Ⓒ Ⓓ Ⓔ	36 Ⓐ Ⓑ Ⓒ Ⓓ Ⓔ	61 Ⓐ Ⓑ Ⓒ Ⓓ Ⓔ	86 Ⓐ Ⓑ Ⓒ Ⓓ Ⓔ
12 Ⓐ Ⓑ Ⓒ Ⓓ Ⓔ	37 Ⓐ Ⓑ Ⓒ Ⓓ Ⓔ	62 Ⓐ Ⓑ Ⓒ Ⓓ Ⓔ	87 Ⓐ Ⓑ Ⓒ Ⓓ Ⓔ
13 Ⓐ Ⓑ Ⓒ Ⓓ Ⓔ	38 Ⓐ Ⓑ Ⓒ Ⓓ Ⓔ	63 Ⓐ Ⓑ Ⓒ Ⓓ Ⓔ	88 Ⓐ Ⓑ Ⓒ Ⓓ Ⓔ
14 Ⓐ Ⓑ Ⓒ Ⓓ Ⓔ	39 Ⓐ Ⓑ Ⓒ Ⓓ Ⓔ	64 Ⓐ Ⓑ Ⓒ Ⓓ Ⓔ	89 Ⓐ Ⓑ Ⓒ Ⓓ Ⓔ
15 Ⓐ Ⓑ Ⓒ Ⓓ Ⓔ	40 Ⓐ Ⓑ Ⓒ Ⓓ Ⓔ	65 Ⓐ Ⓑ Ⓒ Ⓓ Ⓔ	90 Ⓐ Ⓑ Ⓒ Ⓓ Ⓔ
16 Ⓐ Ⓑ Ⓒ Ⓓ Ⓔ	41 Ⓐ Ⓑ Ⓒ Ⓓ Ⓔ	66 Ⓐ Ⓑ Ⓒ Ⓓ Ⓔ	91 Ⓐ Ⓑ Ⓒ Ⓓ Ⓔ
17 Ⓐ Ⓑ Ⓒ Ⓓ Ⓔ	42 Ⓐ Ⓑ Ⓒ Ⓓ Ⓔ	67 Ⓐ Ⓑ Ⓒ Ⓓ Ⓔ	92 Ⓐ Ⓑ Ⓒ Ⓓ Ⓔ
18 Ⓐ Ⓑ Ⓒ Ⓓ Ⓔ	43 Ⓐ Ⓑ Ⓒ Ⓓ Ⓔ	68 Ⓐ Ⓑ Ⓒ Ⓓ Ⓔ	93 Ⓐ Ⓑ Ⓒ Ⓓ Ⓔ
19 Ⓐ Ⓑ Ⓒ Ⓓ Ⓔ	44 Ⓐ Ⓑ Ⓒ Ⓓ Ⓔ	69 Ⓐ Ⓑ Ⓒ Ⓓ Ⓔ	94 Ⓐ Ⓑ Ⓒ Ⓓ Ⓔ
20 Ⓐ Ⓑ Ⓒ Ⓓ Ⓔ	45 Ⓐ Ⓑ Ⓒ Ⓓ Ⓔ	70 Ⓐ Ⓑ Ⓒ Ⓓ Ⓔ	95 Ⓐ Ⓑ Ⓒ Ⓓ Ⓔ
21 Ⓐ Ⓑ Ⓒ Ⓓ Ⓔ	46 Ⓐ Ⓑ Ⓒ Ⓓ Ⓔ	71 Ⓐ Ⓑ Ⓒ Ⓓ Ⓔ	96 Ⓐ Ⓑ Ⓒ Ⓓ Ⓔ
22 Ⓐ Ⓑ Ⓒ Ⓓ Ⓔ	47 Ⓐ Ⓑ Ⓒ Ⓓ Ⓔ	72 Ⓐ Ⓑ Ⓒ Ⓓ Ⓔ	97 Ⓐ Ⓑ Ⓒ Ⓓ Ⓔ
23 Ⓐ Ⓑ Ⓒ Ⓓ Ⓔ	48 Ⓐ Ⓑ Ⓒ Ⓓ Ⓔ	73 Ⓐ Ⓑ Ⓒ Ⓓ Ⓔ	98 Ⓐ Ⓑ Ⓒ Ⓓ Ⓔ
24 Ⓐ Ⓑ Ⓒ Ⓓ Ⓔ	49 Ⓐ Ⓑ Ⓒ Ⓓ Ⓔ	74 Ⓐ Ⓑ Ⓒ Ⓓ Ⓔ	99 Ⓐ Ⓑ Ⓒ Ⓓ Ⓔ
25 Ⓐ Ⓑ Ⓒ Ⓓ Ⓔ	50 Ⓐ Ⓑ Ⓒ Ⓓ Ⓔ	75 Ⓐ Ⓑ Ⓒ Ⓓ Ⓔ	100 Ⓐ Ⓑ Ⓒ Ⓓ Ⓔ

Chemistry *Fill in circle CE only if II is correct explanation of I.

	I	II	CE*		I	II	CE*
101	Ⓣ Ⓕ	Ⓣ Ⓕ	○	109	Ⓣ Ⓕ	Ⓣ Ⓕ	○
102	Ⓣ Ⓕ	Ⓣ Ⓕ	○	110	Ⓣ Ⓕ	Ⓣ Ⓕ	○
103	Ⓣ Ⓕ	Ⓣ Ⓕ	○	111	Ⓣ Ⓕ	Ⓣ Ⓕ	○
104	Ⓣ Ⓕ	Ⓣ Ⓕ	○	112	Ⓣ Ⓕ	Ⓣ Ⓕ	○
105	Ⓣ Ⓕ	Ⓣ Ⓕ	○	113	Ⓣ Ⓕ	Ⓣ Ⓕ	○
106	Ⓣ Ⓕ	Ⓣ Ⓕ	○	114	Ⓣ Ⓕ	Ⓣ Ⓕ	○
107	Ⓣ Ⓕ	Ⓣ Ⓕ	○	115	Ⓣ Ⓕ	Ⓣ Ⓕ	○
108	Ⓣ Ⓕ	Ⓣ Ⓕ	○				

FOR OFFICIAL USE ONLY

R/C	W/S1	FS/S2	CS/S3	WS

Important: Fill in items 8 and 9 exactly as shown on the back of test book.

8 BOOK CODE (Copy and grid as on back of test book.)

⓪	Ⓐ	⓪
①	Ⓑ	①
②	Ⓒ	②
③	Ⓓ	③
④	Ⓔ	④
⑤	Ⓕ	⑤
⑥	Ⓖ	⑥
⑦	Ⓗ	⑦
⑧	Ⓘ	⑧
⑨	Ⓙ	⑨
	Ⓚ	
	Ⓛ	
	Ⓜ	
	Ⓝ	
	Ⓞ	
	Ⓟ	
	Ⓠ	
	Ⓡ	
	Ⓢ	
	Ⓣ	
	Ⓤ	
	Ⓥ	
	Ⓦ	
	Ⓧ	
	Ⓨ	
	Ⓩ	

9 BOOK ID (Copy from back of test book.)

10 TEST BOOK SERIAL NUMBER (Copy from front of test book.)

⓪	⓪	⓪	⓪	⓪	⓪
①	①	①	①	①	①
②	②	②	②	②	②
③	③	③	③	③	③
④	④	④	④	④	④
⑤	⑤	⑤	⑤	⑤	⑤
⑥	⑥	⑥	⑥	⑥	⑥
⑦	⑦	⑦	⑦	⑦	⑦
⑧	⑧	⑧	⑧	⑧	⑧
⑨	⑨	⑨	⑨	⑨	⑨

Quality ● Assurance Mark

PLEASE DO NOT WRITE IN THIS AREA

SERIAL #

2010-11 SAT Subject Tests™

MARKS MUST BE COMPLETE

COMPLETE MARK ● EXAMPLES OF INCOMPLETE MARKS

You must use a No. 2 pencil. Do not use a mechanical pencil. *It is very important that you fill in the entire circle darkly and completely. If you change your response, erase as completely as possible. Incomplete marks or erasures may affect your score. It is very important that you follow these instructions when filling out your answer sheet.*

1 **Your Name:** (Print) Last First M.I.

I agree to the conditions on the front and back of the SAT Subject Tests™ book. I also agree to use only a No. 2 pencil to complete my answer sheet.

Signature: **Date:** MM / DD / YY

Home Address: (Print) Number and Street City State Zip Code

Home Phone: ( ) **Test Center:** (Print) City State/Country

2 YOUR NAME

Last Name (First 6 Letters) | First Name (First 4 Letters) | Mid. Init.

– ' A B C D E F G H I J K L M N O P Q R S T U V W X Y Z

3 DATE OF BIRTH

MONTH: Jan Feb Mar Apr May Jun Jul Aug Sep Oct Nov Dec

DAY: 0 1 2 3 / 0 1 2 3 4 5 6 7 8 9

YEAR: 5 6 7 8 9 / 0 1 2 3 4 5 6 7 8 9

4 ZIP CODE

0 1 2 3 4 5 6 7 8 9

5 SEX

○ Female ○ Male

6 REGISTRATION NUMBER

(Copy from Admission Ticket.)

0 1 2 3 4 5 6 7 8 9

○ I turned in my registration form today.

7 TEST CENTER

(Supplied by Test Center Supervisor.)

0 1 2 3 4 5 6 7 8 9

Important: Fill in items 8 and 9 exactly as shown on the back of test book.

8 BOOK CODE

(Copy and grid as on back of test book.)

0 1 2 3 4 5 6 7 8 9 / A B C D E F G H I J K L M N O P Q R S T U V W X Y Z / 0 1 2 3 4 5 6 7 8 9

9 BOOK ID

(Copy from back of test book.)

10 TEST BOOK SERIAL NUMBER

(Copy from front of test book.)

0 1 2 3 4 5 6 7 8 9

FOR OFFICIAL USE ONLY

0 1 2 3 4 5 6

0 1 2 3 4 5 6

0 1 2 3 4 5 6

83161-77191 • NS60C1285 • Printed in U.S.A.

755275

184596-001:321 Printed in the USA by Pearson ISD0479

PLEASE DO NOT WRITE IN THIS AREA

SERIAL #

COMPLETE MARK ● EXAMPLES OF INCOMPLETE MARKS

You must use a No. 2 pencil and marks must be complete. Do not use a mechanical pencil. *It is very important that you fill in the entire circle darkly and completely. If you change your response, erase as completely as possible. Incomplete marks or erasures may affect your score.*

○ Literature ○ Biology E ○ Biology M ○ Chemistry ○ Physics ○ Mathematics Level 1 ○ Mathematics Level 2 ○ U.S. History ○ World History ○ French ○ German ○ Italian ○ Latin ○ Modern Hebrew ○ Spanish ○ Chinese Listening ○ French Listening ○ German Listening ○ Japanese Listening ○ Korean Listening ○ Spanish Listening

Background Questions: ① ② ③ ④ ⑤ ⑥ ⑦ ⑧ ⑨

1–100 Ⓐ Ⓑ Ⓒ Ⓓ Ⓔ

Important: Fill in items 8 and 9 exactly as shown on the back of test book.

8 BOOK CODE (Copy and grid as on back of test book.)

9 BOOK ID (Copy from back of test book.)

10 TEST BOOK SERIAL NUMBER (Copy from front of test book.)

Quality Assurance Mark

Chemistry *Fill in circle CE only if II is correct explanation of I.

	I	II	CE*
101–115	Ⓣ Ⓕ	Ⓣ Ⓕ	○

FOR OFFICIAL USE ONLY

R/C	W/S1	FS/S2	CS/S3	WS

CERTIFICATION STATEMENT

Copy the statement below (do not print) and sign your name as you would an official document.

I hereby agree to the conditions set forth online at sat.collegeboard.com and in any paper registration materials given to me and certify that I am the person whose name and address appear on this answer sheet.

Signature ____________________ Date ____________________

By registering, you agreed not to share any specific test question with anyone by any form of communication, including, but not limited to: email, text messages, or use of the Internet. Doing so can result in score cancellation and other possible sanctions.

COMPLETE MARK ● EXAMPLES OF INCOMPLETE MARKS

You must use a No. 2 pencil and marks must be complete. Do not use a mechanical pencil. *It is very important that you fill in the entire circle darkly and completely. If you change your response, erase as completely as possible. Incomplete marks or erasures may affect your score.*

○ Literature ○ Mathematics Level 1 ○ German
○ Biology E ○ Mathematics Level 2 ○ Italian
○ Biology M ○ U.S. History ○ Latin
○ Chemistry ○ World History ○ Modern Hebrew
○ Physics ○ French ○ Spanish

Background Questions: ① ② ③ ④ ⑤ ⑥ ⑦ ⑧ ⑨

1 Ⓐ Ⓑ Ⓒ Ⓓ Ⓔ	26 Ⓐ Ⓑ Ⓒ Ⓓ Ⓔ	51 Ⓐ Ⓑ Ⓒ Ⓓ Ⓔ	76 Ⓐ Ⓑ Ⓒ Ⓓ Ⓔ
2 Ⓐ Ⓑ Ⓒ Ⓓ Ⓔ	27 Ⓐ Ⓑ Ⓒ Ⓓ Ⓔ	52 Ⓐ Ⓑ Ⓒ Ⓓ Ⓔ	77 Ⓐ Ⓑ Ⓒ Ⓓ Ⓔ
3 Ⓐ Ⓑ Ⓒ Ⓓ Ⓔ	28 Ⓐ Ⓑ Ⓒ Ⓓ Ⓔ	53 Ⓐ Ⓑ Ⓒ Ⓓ Ⓔ	78 Ⓐ Ⓑ Ⓒ Ⓓ Ⓔ
4 Ⓐ Ⓑ Ⓒ Ⓓ Ⓔ	29 Ⓐ Ⓑ Ⓒ Ⓓ Ⓔ	54 Ⓐ Ⓑ Ⓒ Ⓓ Ⓔ	79 Ⓐ Ⓑ Ⓒ Ⓓ Ⓔ
5 Ⓐ Ⓑ Ⓒ Ⓓ Ⓔ	30 Ⓐ Ⓑ Ⓒ Ⓓ Ⓔ	55 Ⓐ Ⓑ Ⓒ Ⓓ Ⓔ	80 Ⓐ Ⓑ Ⓒ Ⓓ Ⓔ
6 Ⓐ Ⓑ Ⓒ Ⓓ Ⓔ	31 Ⓐ Ⓑ Ⓒ Ⓓ Ⓔ	56 Ⓐ Ⓑ Ⓒ Ⓓ Ⓔ	81 Ⓐ Ⓑ Ⓒ Ⓓ Ⓔ
7 Ⓐ Ⓑ Ⓒ Ⓓ Ⓔ	32 Ⓐ Ⓑ Ⓒ Ⓓ Ⓔ	57 Ⓐ Ⓑ Ⓒ Ⓓ Ⓔ	82 Ⓐ Ⓑ Ⓒ Ⓓ Ⓔ
8 Ⓐ Ⓑ Ⓒ Ⓓ Ⓔ	33 Ⓐ Ⓑ Ⓒ Ⓓ Ⓔ	58 Ⓐ Ⓑ Ⓒ Ⓓ Ⓔ	83 Ⓐ Ⓑ Ⓒ Ⓓ Ⓔ
9 Ⓐ Ⓑ Ⓒ Ⓓ Ⓔ	34 Ⓐ Ⓑ Ⓒ Ⓓ Ⓔ	59 Ⓐ Ⓑ Ⓒ Ⓓ Ⓔ	84 Ⓐ Ⓑ Ⓒ Ⓓ Ⓔ
10 Ⓐ Ⓑ Ⓒ Ⓓ Ⓔ	35 Ⓐ Ⓑ Ⓒ Ⓓ Ⓔ	60 Ⓐ Ⓑ Ⓒ Ⓓ Ⓔ	85 Ⓐ Ⓑ Ⓒ Ⓓ Ⓔ
11 Ⓐ Ⓑ Ⓒ Ⓓ Ⓔ	36 Ⓐ Ⓑ Ⓒ Ⓓ Ⓔ	61 Ⓐ Ⓑ Ⓒ Ⓓ Ⓔ	86 Ⓐ Ⓑ Ⓒ Ⓓ Ⓔ
12 Ⓐ Ⓑ Ⓒ Ⓓ Ⓔ	37 Ⓐ Ⓑ Ⓒ Ⓓ Ⓔ	62 Ⓐ Ⓑ Ⓒ Ⓓ Ⓔ	87 Ⓐ Ⓑ Ⓒ Ⓓ Ⓔ
13 Ⓐ Ⓑ Ⓒ Ⓓ Ⓔ	38 Ⓐ Ⓑ Ⓒ Ⓓ Ⓔ	63 Ⓐ Ⓑ Ⓒ Ⓓ Ⓔ	88 Ⓐ Ⓑ Ⓒ Ⓓ Ⓔ
14 Ⓐ Ⓑ Ⓒ Ⓓ Ⓔ	39 Ⓐ Ⓑ Ⓒ Ⓓ Ⓔ	64 Ⓐ Ⓑ Ⓒ Ⓓ Ⓔ	89 Ⓐ Ⓑ Ⓒ Ⓓ Ⓔ
15 Ⓐ Ⓑ Ⓒ Ⓓ Ⓔ	40 Ⓐ Ⓑ Ⓒ Ⓓ Ⓔ	65 Ⓐ Ⓑ Ⓒ Ⓓ Ⓔ	90 Ⓐ Ⓑ Ⓒ Ⓓ Ⓔ
16 Ⓐ Ⓑ Ⓒ Ⓓ Ⓔ	41 Ⓐ Ⓑ Ⓒ Ⓓ Ⓔ	66 Ⓐ Ⓑ Ⓒ Ⓓ Ⓔ	91 Ⓐ Ⓑ Ⓒ Ⓓ Ⓔ
17 Ⓐ Ⓑ Ⓒ Ⓓ Ⓔ	42 Ⓐ Ⓑ Ⓒ Ⓓ Ⓔ	67 Ⓐ Ⓑ Ⓒ Ⓓ Ⓔ	92 Ⓐ Ⓑ Ⓒ Ⓓ Ⓔ
18 Ⓐ Ⓑ Ⓒ Ⓓ Ⓔ	43 Ⓐ Ⓑ Ⓒ Ⓓ Ⓔ	68 Ⓐ Ⓑ Ⓒ Ⓓ Ⓔ	93 Ⓐ Ⓑ Ⓒ Ⓓ Ⓔ
19 Ⓐ Ⓑ Ⓒ Ⓓ Ⓔ	44 Ⓐ Ⓑ Ⓒ Ⓓ Ⓔ	69 Ⓐ Ⓑ Ⓒ Ⓓ Ⓔ	94 Ⓐ Ⓑ Ⓒ Ⓓ Ⓔ
20 Ⓐ Ⓑ Ⓒ Ⓓ Ⓔ	45 Ⓐ Ⓑ Ⓒ Ⓓ Ⓔ	70 Ⓐ Ⓑ Ⓒ Ⓓ Ⓔ	95 Ⓐ Ⓑ Ⓒ Ⓓ Ⓔ
21 Ⓐ Ⓑ Ⓒ Ⓓ Ⓔ	46 Ⓐ Ⓑ Ⓒ Ⓓ Ⓔ	71 Ⓐ Ⓑ Ⓒ Ⓓ Ⓔ	96 Ⓐ Ⓑ Ⓒ Ⓓ Ⓔ
22 Ⓐ Ⓑ Ⓒ Ⓓ Ⓔ	47 Ⓐ Ⓑ Ⓒ Ⓓ Ⓔ	72 Ⓐ Ⓑ Ⓒ Ⓓ Ⓔ	97 Ⓐ Ⓑ Ⓒ Ⓓ Ⓔ
23 Ⓐ Ⓑ Ⓒ Ⓓ Ⓔ	48 Ⓐ Ⓑ Ⓒ Ⓓ Ⓔ	73 Ⓐ Ⓑ Ⓒ Ⓓ Ⓔ	98 Ⓐ Ⓑ Ⓒ Ⓓ Ⓔ
24 Ⓐ Ⓑ Ⓒ Ⓓ Ⓔ	49 Ⓐ Ⓑ Ⓒ Ⓓ Ⓔ	74 Ⓐ Ⓑ Ⓒ Ⓓ Ⓔ	99 Ⓐ Ⓑ Ⓒ Ⓓ Ⓔ
25 Ⓐ Ⓑ Ⓒ Ⓓ Ⓔ	50 Ⓐ Ⓑ Ⓒ Ⓓ Ⓔ	75 Ⓐ Ⓑ Ⓒ Ⓓ Ⓔ	100 Ⓐ Ⓑ Ⓒ Ⓓ Ⓔ

Quality ● Assurance Mark

Chemistry *Fill in circle CE only if II is correct explanation of I.

	I	II	CE*		I	II	CE*
101	Ⓣ Ⓕ	Ⓣ Ⓕ	○	109	Ⓣ Ⓕ	Ⓣ Ⓕ	○
102	Ⓣ Ⓕ	Ⓣ Ⓕ	○	110	Ⓣ Ⓕ	Ⓣ Ⓕ	○
103	Ⓣ Ⓕ	Ⓣ Ⓕ	○	111	Ⓣ Ⓕ	Ⓣ Ⓕ	○
104	Ⓣ Ⓕ	Ⓣ Ⓕ	○	112	Ⓣ Ⓕ	Ⓣ Ⓕ	○
105	Ⓣ Ⓕ	Ⓣ Ⓕ	○	113	Ⓣ Ⓕ	Ⓣ Ⓕ	○
106	Ⓣ Ⓕ	Ⓣ Ⓕ	○	114	Ⓣ Ⓕ	Ⓣ Ⓕ	○
107	Ⓣ Ⓕ	Ⓣ Ⓕ	○	115	Ⓣ Ⓕ	Ⓣ Ⓕ	○
108	Ⓣ Ⓕ	Ⓣ Ⓕ	○				

FOR OFFICIAL USE ONLY

R/C	W/S1	FS/S2	CS/S3	WS

Important: Fill in items 8 and 9 exactly as shown on the back of test book.

8 BOOK CODE (Copy and grid as on back of test book.)

⓪–⑨ | Ⓐ–Ⓩ | ⓪–⑨

9 BOOK ID (Copy from back of test book.)

10 TEST BOOK SERIAL NUMBER (Copy from front of test book.)

⓪ ① ② ③ ④ ⑤ ⑥ ⑦ ⑧ ⑨ (six columns)

COMPLETE MARK ● EXAMPLES OF INCOMPLETE MARKS

You must use a No. 2 pencil and marks must be complete. Do not use a mechanical pencil. *It is very important that you fill in the entire circle darkly and completely. If you change your response, erase as completely as possible. Incomplete marks or erasures may affect your score.*

○ Literature ○ Biology E ○ Biology M ○ Chemistry ○ Physics
○ Mathematics Level 1 ○ Mathematics Level 2 ○ U.S. History ○ World History ○ French
○ German ○ Italian ○ Latin ○ Modern Hebrew ○ Spanish

Background Questions: ① ② ③ ④ ⑤ ⑥ ⑦ ⑧ ⑨

1 Ⓐ Ⓑ Ⓒ Ⓓ Ⓔ	26 Ⓐ Ⓑ Ⓒ Ⓓ Ⓔ	51 Ⓐ Ⓑ Ⓒ Ⓓ Ⓔ	76 Ⓐ Ⓑ Ⓒ Ⓓ Ⓔ
2 Ⓐ Ⓑ Ⓒ Ⓓ Ⓔ	27 Ⓐ Ⓑ Ⓒ Ⓓ Ⓔ	52 Ⓐ Ⓑ Ⓒ Ⓓ Ⓔ	77 Ⓐ Ⓑ Ⓒ Ⓓ Ⓔ
3 Ⓐ Ⓑ Ⓒ Ⓓ Ⓔ	28 Ⓐ Ⓑ Ⓒ Ⓓ Ⓔ	53 Ⓐ Ⓑ Ⓒ Ⓓ Ⓔ	78 Ⓐ Ⓑ Ⓒ Ⓓ Ⓔ
4 Ⓐ Ⓑ Ⓒ Ⓓ Ⓔ	29 Ⓐ Ⓑ Ⓒ Ⓓ Ⓔ	54 Ⓐ Ⓑ Ⓒ Ⓓ Ⓔ	79 Ⓐ Ⓑ Ⓒ Ⓓ Ⓔ
5 Ⓐ Ⓑ Ⓒ Ⓓ Ⓔ	30 Ⓐ Ⓑ Ⓒ Ⓓ Ⓔ	55 Ⓐ Ⓑ Ⓒ Ⓓ Ⓔ	80 Ⓐ Ⓑ Ⓒ Ⓓ Ⓔ
6 Ⓐ Ⓑ Ⓒ Ⓓ Ⓔ	31 Ⓐ Ⓑ Ⓒ Ⓓ Ⓔ	56 Ⓐ Ⓑ Ⓒ Ⓓ Ⓔ	81 Ⓐ Ⓑ Ⓒ Ⓓ Ⓔ
7 Ⓐ Ⓑ Ⓒ Ⓓ Ⓔ	32 Ⓐ Ⓑ Ⓒ Ⓓ Ⓔ	57 Ⓐ Ⓑ Ⓒ Ⓓ Ⓔ	82 Ⓐ Ⓑ Ⓒ Ⓓ Ⓔ
8 Ⓐ Ⓑ Ⓒ Ⓓ Ⓔ	33 Ⓐ Ⓑ Ⓒ Ⓓ Ⓔ	58 Ⓐ Ⓑ Ⓒ Ⓓ Ⓔ	83 Ⓐ Ⓑ Ⓒ Ⓓ Ⓔ
9 Ⓐ Ⓑ Ⓒ Ⓓ Ⓔ	34 Ⓐ Ⓑ Ⓒ Ⓓ Ⓔ	59 Ⓐ Ⓑ Ⓒ Ⓓ Ⓔ	84 Ⓐ Ⓑ Ⓒ Ⓓ Ⓔ
10 Ⓐ Ⓑ Ⓒ Ⓓ Ⓔ	35 Ⓐ Ⓑ Ⓒ Ⓓ Ⓔ	60 Ⓐ Ⓑ Ⓒ Ⓓ Ⓔ	85 Ⓐ Ⓑ Ⓒ Ⓓ Ⓔ
11 Ⓐ Ⓑ Ⓒ Ⓓ Ⓔ	36 Ⓐ Ⓑ Ⓒ Ⓓ Ⓔ	61 Ⓐ Ⓑ Ⓒ Ⓓ Ⓔ	86 Ⓐ Ⓑ Ⓒ Ⓓ Ⓔ
12 Ⓐ Ⓑ Ⓒ Ⓓ Ⓔ	37 Ⓐ Ⓑ Ⓒ Ⓓ Ⓔ	62 Ⓐ Ⓑ Ⓒ Ⓓ Ⓔ	87 Ⓐ Ⓑ Ⓒ Ⓓ Ⓔ
13 Ⓐ Ⓑ Ⓒ Ⓓ Ⓔ	38 Ⓐ Ⓑ Ⓒ Ⓓ Ⓔ	63 Ⓐ Ⓑ Ⓒ Ⓓ Ⓔ	88 Ⓐ Ⓑ Ⓒ Ⓓ Ⓔ
14 Ⓐ Ⓑ Ⓒ Ⓓ Ⓔ	39 Ⓐ Ⓑ Ⓒ Ⓓ Ⓔ	64 Ⓐ Ⓑ Ⓒ Ⓓ Ⓔ	89 Ⓐ Ⓑ Ⓒ Ⓓ Ⓔ
15 Ⓐ Ⓑ Ⓒ Ⓓ Ⓔ	40 Ⓐ Ⓑ Ⓒ Ⓓ Ⓔ	65 Ⓐ Ⓑ Ⓒ Ⓓ Ⓔ	90 Ⓐ Ⓑ Ⓒ Ⓓ Ⓔ
16 Ⓐ Ⓑ Ⓒ Ⓓ Ⓔ	41 Ⓐ Ⓑ Ⓒ Ⓓ Ⓔ	66 Ⓐ Ⓑ Ⓒ Ⓓ Ⓔ	91 Ⓐ Ⓑ Ⓒ Ⓓ Ⓔ
17 Ⓐ Ⓑ Ⓒ Ⓓ Ⓔ	42 Ⓐ Ⓑ Ⓒ Ⓓ Ⓔ	67 Ⓐ Ⓑ Ⓒ Ⓓ Ⓔ	92 Ⓐ Ⓑ Ⓒ Ⓓ Ⓔ
18 Ⓐ Ⓑ Ⓒ Ⓓ Ⓔ	43 Ⓐ Ⓑ Ⓒ Ⓓ Ⓔ	68 Ⓐ Ⓑ Ⓒ Ⓓ Ⓔ	93 Ⓐ Ⓑ Ⓒ Ⓓ Ⓔ
19 Ⓐ Ⓑ Ⓒ Ⓓ Ⓔ	44 Ⓐ Ⓑ Ⓒ Ⓓ Ⓔ	69 Ⓐ Ⓑ Ⓒ Ⓓ Ⓔ	94 Ⓐ Ⓑ Ⓒ Ⓓ Ⓔ
20 Ⓐ Ⓑ Ⓒ Ⓓ Ⓔ	45 Ⓐ Ⓑ Ⓒ Ⓓ Ⓔ	70 Ⓐ Ⓑ Ⓒ Ⓓ Ⓔ	95 Ⓐ Ⓑ Ⓒ Ⓓ Ⓔ
21 Ⓐ Ⓑ Ⓒ Ⓓ Ⓔ	46 Ⓐ Ⓑ Ⓒ Ⓓ Ⓔ	71 Ⓐ Ⓑ Ⓒ Ⓓ Ⓔ	96 Ⓐ Ⓑ Ⓒ Ⓓ Ⓔ
22 Ⓐ Ⓑ Ⓒ Ⓓ Ⓔ	47 Ⓐ Ⓑ Ⓒ Ⓓ Ⓔ	72 Ⓐ Ⓑ Ⓒ Ⓓ Ⓔ	97 Ⓐ Ⓑ Ⓒ Ⓓ Ⓔ
23 Ⓐ Ⓑ Ⓒ Ⓓ Ⓔ	48 Ⓐ Ⓑ Ⓒ Ⓓ Ⓔ	73 Ⓐ Ⓑ Ⓒ Ⓓ Ⓔ	98 Ⓐ Ⓑ Ⓒ Ⓓ Ⓔ
24 Ⓐ Ⓑ Ⓒ Ⓓ Ⓔ	49 Ⓐ Ⓑ Ⓒ Ⓓ Ⓔ	74 Ⓐ Ⓑ Ⓒ Ⓓ Ⓔ	99 Ⓐ Ⓑ Ⓒ Ⓓ Ⓔ
25 Ⓐ Ⓑ Ⓒ Ⓓ Ⓔ	50 Ⓐ Ⓑ Ⓒ Ⓓ Ⓔ	75 Ⓐ Ⓑ Ⓒ Ⓓ Ⓔ	100 Ⓐ Ⓑ Ⓒ Ⓓ Ⓔ

Chemistry *Fill in circle CE only if II is correct explanation of I.

	I	II	CE*		I	II	CE*
101	Ⓣ Ⓕ	Ⓣ Ⓕ	○	109	Ⓣ Ⓕ	Ⓣ Ⓕ	○
102	Ⓣ Ⓕ	Ⓣ Ⓕ	○	110	Ⓣ Ⓕ	Ⓣ Ⓕ	○
103	Ⓣ Ⓕ	Ⓣ Ⓕ	○	111	Ⓣ Ⓕ	Ⓣ Ⓕ	○
104	Ⓣ Ⓕ	Ⓣ Ⓕ	○	112	Ⓣ Ⓕ	Ⓣ Ⓕ	○
105	Ⓣ Ⓕ	Ⓣ Ⓕ	○	113	Ⓣ Ⓕ	Ⓣ Ⓕ	○
106	Ⓣ Ⓕ	Ⓣ Ⓕ	○	114	Ⓣ Ⓕ	Ⓣ Ⓕ	○
107	Ⓣ Ⓕ	Ⓣ Ⓕ	○	115	Ⓣ Ⓕ	Ⓣ Ⓕ	○
108	Ⓣ Ⓕ	Ⓣ Ⓕ	○				

Important: Fill in items 8 and 9 exactly as shown on the back of test book.

8 BOOK CODE (Copy and grid as on back of test book.)

0	A	0
1	B	1
2	C	2
3	D	3
4	E	4
5	F	5
6	G	6
7	H	7
8	I	8
9	J	9
	K	
	L	
	M	
	N	
	O	
	P	
	Q	
	R	
	S	
	T	
	U	
	V	
	W	
	X	
	Y	
	Z	

9 BOOK ID (Copy from back of test book.)

10 TEST BOOK SERIAL NUMBER (Copy from front of test book.)

0	0	0	0	0	0
1	1	1	1	1	1
2	2	2	2	2	2
3	3	3	3	3	3
4	4	4	4	4	4
5	5	5	5	5	5
6	6	6	6	6	6
7	7	7	7	7	7
8	8	8	8	8	8
9	9	9	9	9	9

Quality Assurance Mark

FOR OFFICIAL USE ONLY

R/C	W/S1	FS/S2	CS/S3	WS

PLEASE DO NOT WRITE IN THIS AREA

SERIAL #

2010-11 SAT Subject Tests™

MARKS MUST BE COMPLETE

COMPLETE MARK ● **EXAMPLES OF INCOMPLETE MARKS**

You must use a No. 2 pencil. Do not use a mechanical pencil. It is very important that you fill in the entire circle darkly and completely. If you change your response, erase as completely as possible. Incomplete marks or erasures may affect your score. It is very important that you follow these instructions when filling out your answer sheet.

1 **Your Name:** (Print) ______ Last ______ First ______ M.I.

I agree to the conditions on the front and back of the SAT Subject Tests™ book. I also agree to use only a No. 2 pencil to complete my answer sheet.

Signature: ______ **Date:** __/__/__ MM DD YY

Home Address: (Print) ______ Number and Street ______ City ______ State ______ Zip Code

Home Phone: ( ) ______ **Test Center:** (Print) ______ City ______ State/Country

2 YOUR NAME

Last Name (First 6 Letters) | First Name (First 4 Letters) | Mid. Init.

– ' A B C D E F G H I J K L M N O P Q R S T U V W X Y Z

3 DATE OF BIRTH

MONTH: Jan Feb Mar Apr May Jun Jul Aug Sep Oct Nov Dec

DAY: 0 1 2 3 / 0 1 2 3 4 5 6 7 8 9

YEAR: 5 6 7 8 9 / 0 1 2 3 4 5 6 7 8 9

4 ZIP CODE

0 1 2 3 4 5 6 7 8 9

5 SEX

○ Female ○ Male

6 REGISTRATION NUMBER

(Copy from Admission Ticket.)

0 1 2 3 4 5 6 7 8 9

○ I turned in my registration form today.

7 TEST CENTER

(Supplied by Test Center Supervisor.)

0 1 2 3 4 5 6 7 8 9

Important: Fill in items 8 and 9 exactly as shown on the back of test book.

8 BOOK CODE

(Copy and grid as on back of test book.)

0 1 2 3 4 5 6 7 8 9 / A B C D E F G H I J K L M N O P Q R S T U V W X Y Z / 0 1 2 3 4 5 6 7 8 9

9 BOOK ID

(Copy from back of test book.)

10 TEST BOOK SERIAL NUMBER

(Copy from front of test book.)

0 1 2 3 4 5 6 7 8 9

FOR OFFICIAL USE ONLY

0 1 2 3 4 5 6
0 1 2 3 4 5 6
0 1 2 3 4 5 6

184596-001:321 Printed in the USA by Pearson ISD0479

83161-77191 • NS60C1285 • Printed in U.S.A.
755275

PLEASE DO NOT WRITE IN THIS AREA

SERIAL #

COMPLETE MARK ● EXAMPLES OF INCOMPLETE MARKS

You must use a No. 2 pencil and marks must be complete. Do not use a mechanical pencil. *It is very important that you fill in the entire circle darkly and completely. If you change your response, erase as completely as possible. Incomplete marks or erasures may affect your score.*

○ Literature	○ Mathematics Level 1	○ German	○ Chinese Listening	○ Japanese Listening
○ Biology E	○ Mathematics Level 2	○ Italian	○ French Listening	○ Korean Listening
○ Biology M	○ U.S. History	○ Latin	○ German Listening	○ Spanish Listening
○ Chemistry	○ World History	○ Modern Hebrew		
○ Physics	○ French	○ Spanish		

Background Questions: ① ② ③ ④ ⑤ ⑥ ⑦ ⑧ ⑨

1 Ⓐ Ⓑ Ⓒ Ⓓ Ⓔ	26 Ⓐ Ⓑ Ⓒ Ⓓ Ⓔ	51 Ⓐ Ⓑ Ⓒ Ⓓ Ⓔ	76 Ⓐ Ⓑ Ⓒ Ⓓ Ⓔ
2 Ⓐ Ⓑ Ⓒ Ⓓ Ⓔ	27 Ⓐ Ⓑ Ⓒ Ⓓ Ⓔ	52 Ⓐ Ⓑ Ⓒ Ⓓ Ⓔ	77 Ⓐ Ⓑ Ⓒ Ⓓ Ⓔ
3 Ⓐ Ⓑ Ⓒ Ⓓ Ⓔ	28 Ⓐ Ⓑ Ⓒ Ⓓ Ⓔ	53 Ⓐ Ⓑ Ⓒ Ⓓ Ⓔ	78 Ⓐ Ⓑ Ⓒ Ⓓ Ⓔ
4 Ⓐ Ⓑ Ⓒ Ⓓ Ⓔ	29 Ⓐ Ⓑ Ⓒ Ⓓ Ⓔ	54 Ⓐ Ⓑ Ⓒ Ⓓ Ⓔ	79 Ⓐ Ⓑ Ⓒ Ⓓ Ⓔ
5 Ⓐ Ⓑ Ⓒ Ⓓ Ⓔ	30 Ⓐ Ⓑ Ⓒ Ⓓ Ⓔ	55 Ⓐ Ⓑ Ⓒ Ⓓ Ⓔ	80 Ⓐ Ⓑ Ⓒ Ⓓ Ⓔ
6 Ⓐ Ⓑ Ⓒ Ⓓ Ⓔ	31 Ⓐ Ⓑ Ⓒ Ⓓ Ⓔ	56 Ⓐ Ⓑ Ⓒ Ⓓ Ⓔ	81 Ⓐ Ⓑ Ⓒ Ⓓ Ⓔ
7 Ⓐ Ⓑ Ⓒ Ⓓ Ⓔ	32 Ⓐ Ⓑ Ⓒ Ⓓ Ⓔ	57 Ⓐ Ⓑ Ⓒ Ⓓ Ⓔ	82 Ⓐ Ⓑ Ⓒ Ⓓ Ⓔ
8 Ⓐ Ⓑ Ⓒ Ⓓ Ⓔ	33 Ⓐ Ⓑ Ⓒ Ⓓ Ⓔ	58 Ⓐ Ⓑ Ⓒ Ⓓ Ⓔ	83 Ⓐ Ⓑ Ⓒ Ⓓ Ⓔ
9 Ⓐ Ⓑ Ⓒ Ⓓ Ⓔ	34 Ⓐ Ⓑ Ⓒ Ⓓ Ⓔ	59 Ⓐ Ⓑ Ⓒ Ⓓ Ⓔ	84 Ⓐ Ⓑ Ⓒ Ⓓ Ⓔ
10 Ⓐ Ⓑ Ⓒ Ⓓ Ⓔ	35 Ⓐ Ⓑ Ⓒ Ⓓ Ⓔ	60 Ⓐ Ⓑ Ⓒ Ⓓ Ⓔ	85 Ⓐ Ⓑ Ⓒ Ⓓ Ⓔ
11 Ⓐ Ⓑ Ⓒ Ⓓ Ⓔ	36 Ⓐ Ⓑ Ⓒ Ⓓ Ⓔ	61 Ⓐ Ⓑ Ⓒ Ⓓ Ⓔ	86 Ⓐ Ⓑ Ⓒ Ⓓ Ⓔ
12 Ⓐ Ⓑ Ⓒ Ⓓ Ⓔ	37 Ⓐ Ⓑ Ⓒ Ⓓ Ⓔ	62 Ⓐ Ⓑ Ⓒ Ⓓ Ⓔ	87 Ⓐ Ⓑ Ⓒ Ⓓ Ⓔ
13 Ⓐ Ⓑ Ⓒ Ⓓ Ⓔ	38 Ⓐ Ⓑ Ⓒ Ⓓ Ⓔ	63 Ⓐ Ⓑ Ⓒ Ⓓ Ⓔ	88 Ⓐ Ⓑ Ⓒ Ⓓ Ⓔ
14 Ⓐ Ⓑ Ⓒ Ⓓ Ⓔ	39 Ⓐ Ⓑ Ⓒ Ⓓ Ⓔ	64 Ⓐ Ⓑ Ⓒ Ⓓ Ⓔ	89 Ⓐ Ⓑ Ⓒ Ⓓ Ⓔ
15 Ⓐ Ⓑ Ⓒ Ⓓ Ⓔ	40 Ⓐ Ⓑ Ⓒ Ⓓ Ⓔ	65 Ⓐ Ⓑ Ⓒ Ⓓ Ⓔ	90 Ⓐ Ⓑ Ⓒ Ⓓ Ⓔ
16 Ⓐ Ⓑ Ⓒ Ⓓ Ⓔ	41 Ⓐ Ⓑ Ⓒ Ⓓ Ⓔ	66 Ⓐ Ⓑ Ⓒ Ⓓ Ⓔ	91 Ⓐ Ⓑ Ⓒ Ⓓ Ⓔ
17 Ⓐ Ⓑ Ⓒ Ⓓ Ⓔ	42 Ⓐ Ⓑ Ⓒ Ⓓ Ⓔ	67 Ⓐ Ⓑ Ⓒ Ⓓ Ⓔ	92 Ⓐ Ⓑ Ⓒ Ⓓ Ⓔ
18 Ⓐ Ⓑ Ⓒ Ⓓ Ⓔ	43 Ⓐ Ⓑ Ⓒ Ⓓ Ⓔ	68 Ⓐ Ⓑ Ⓒ Ⓓ Ⓔ	93 Ⓐ Ⓑ Ⓒ Ⓓ Ⓔ
19 Ⓐ Ⓑ Ⓒ Ⓓ Ⓔ	44 Ⓐ Ⓑ Ⓒ Ⓓ Ⓔ	69 Ⓐ Ⓑ Ⓒ Ⓓ Ⓔ	94 Ⓐ Ⓑ Ⓒ Ⓓ Ⓔ
20 Ⓐ Ⓑ Ⓒ Ⓓ Ⓔ	45 Ⓐ Ⓑ Ⓒ Ⓓ Ⓔ	70 Ⓐ Ⓑ Ⓒ Ⓓ Ⓔ	95 Ⓐ Ⓑ Ⓒ Ⓓ Ⓔ
21 Ⓐ Ⓑ Ⓒ Ⓓ Ⓔ	46 Ⓐ Ⓑ Ⓒ Ⓓ Ⓔ	71 Ⓐ Ⓑ Ⓒ Ⓓ Ⓔ	96 Ⓐ Ⓑ Ⓒ Ⓓ Ⓔ
22 Ⓐ Ⓑ Ⓒ Ⓓ Ⓔ	47 Ⓐ Ⓑ Ⓒ Ⓓ Ⓔ	72 Ⓐ Ⓑ Ⓒ Ⓓ Ⓔ	97 Ⓐ Ⓑ Ⓒ Ⓓ Ⓔ
23 Ⓐ Ⓑ Ⓒ Ⓓ Ⓔ	48 Ⓐ Ⓑ Ⓒ Ⓓ Ⓔ	73 Ⓐ Ⓑ Ⓒ Ⓓ Ⓔ	98 Ⓐ Ⓑ Ⓒ Ⓓ Ⓔ
24 Ⓐ Ⓑ Ⓒ Ⓓ Ⓔ	49 Ⓐ Ⓑ Ⓒ Ⓓ Ⓔ	74 Ⓐ Ⓑ Ⓒ Ⓓ Ⓔ	99 Ⓐ Ⓑ Ⓒ Ⓓ Ⓔ
25 Ⓐ Ⓑ Ⓒ Ⓓ Ⓔ	50 Ⓐ Ⓑ Ⓒ Ⓓ Ⓔ	75 Ⓐ Ⓑ Ⓒ Ⓓ Ⓔ	100 Ⓐ Ⓑ Ⓒ Ⓓ Ⓔ

Important: Fill in items 8 and 9 exactly as shown on the back of test book.

8 BOOK CODE (Copy and grid as on back of test book.)

0 1 2 3 4 5 6 7 8 9	A B C D E F G H I J K L M N O P Q R S T U V W X Y Z	0 1 2 3 4 5 6 7 8 9

9 BOOK ID (Copy from back of test book.)

10 TEST BOOK SERIAL NUMBER (Copy from front of test book.)

0 1 2 3 4 5 6 7 8 9	0 1 2 3 4 5 6 7 8 9	0 1 2 3 4 5 6 7 8 9	0 1 2 3 4 5 6 7 8 9	0 1 2 3 4 5 6 7 8 9	0 1 2 3 4 5 6 7 8 9

Quality ● Assurance Mark

Chemistry *Fill in circle CE only if II is correct explanation of I.

	I	II	CE*		I	II	CE*
101	Ⓣ Ⓕ	Ⓣ Ⓕ	○	109	Ⓣ Ⓕ	Ⓣ Ⓕ	○
102	Ⓣ Ⓕ	Ⓣ Ⓕ	○	110	Ⓣ Ⓕ	Ⓣ Ⓕ	○
103	Ⓣ Ⓕ	Ⓣ Ⓕ	○	111	Ⓣ Ⓕ	Ⓣ Ⓕ	○
104	Ⓣ Ⓕ	Ⓣ Ⓕ	○	112	Ⓣ Ⓕ	Ⓣ Ⓕ	○
105	Ⓣ Ⓕ	Ⓣ Ⓕ	○	113	Ⓣ Ⓕ	Ⓣ Ⓕ	○
106	Ⓣ Ⓕ	Ⓣ Ⓕ	○	114	Ⓣ Ⓕ	Ⓣ Ⓕ	○
107	Ⓣ Ⓕ	Ⓣ Ⓕ	○	115	Ⓣ Ⓕ	Ⓣ Ⓕ	○
108	Ⓣ Ⓕ	Ⓣ Ⓕ	○				

FOR OFFICIAL USE ONLY

R/C	W/S1	FS/S2	CS/S3	WS

CERTIFICATION STATEMENT

Copy the statement below (do not print) and sign your name as you would an official document.

I hereby agree to the conditions set forth online at sat.collegeboard.com and in any paper registration materials given to me and certify that I am the person whose name and address appear on this answer sheet.

Signature ______________________ Date ______________

By registering, you agreed not to share any specific test question with anyone by any form of communication, including, but not limited to: email, text messages, or use of the Internet. Doing so can result in score cancellation and other possible sanctions.

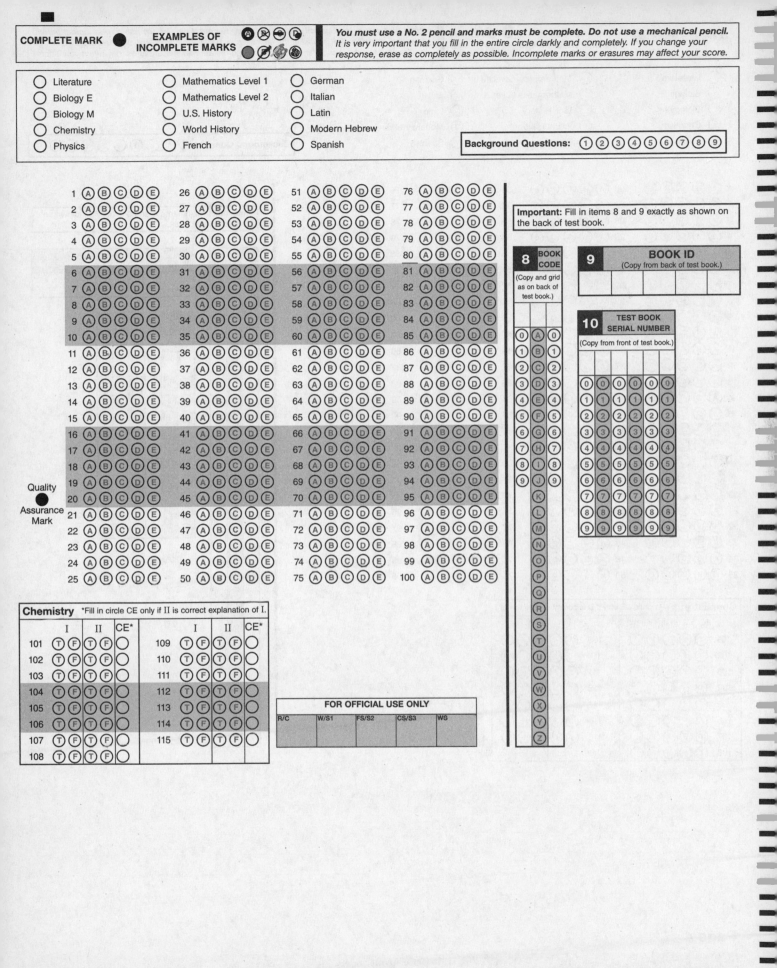

COMPLETE MARK ● EXAMPLES OF INCOMPLETE MARKS

You must use a No. 2 pencil and marks must be complete. Do not use a mechanical pencil. *It is very important that you fill in the entire circle darkly and completely. If you change your response, erase as completely as possible. Incomplete marks or erasures may affect your score.*

○ Literature ○ Biology E ○ Biology M ○ Chemistry ○ Physics
○ Mathematics Level 1 ○ Mathematics Level 2 ○ U.S. History ○ World History ○ French
○ German ○ Italian ○ Latin ○ Modern Hebrew ○ Spanish

Background Questions: ① ② ③ ④ ⑤ ⑥ ⑦ ⑧ ⑨

1 Ⓐ Ⓑ Ⓒ Ⓓ Ⓔ	26 Ⓐ Ⓑ Ⓒ Ⓓ Ⓔ	51 Ⓐ Ⓑ Ⓒ Ⓓ Ⓔ	76 Ⓐ Ⓑ Ⓒ Ⓓ Ⓔ
2 Ⓐ Ⓑ Ⓒ Ⓓ Ⓔ	27 Ⓐ Ⓑ Ⓒ Ⓓ Ⓔ	52 Ⓐ Ⓑ Ⓒ Ⓓ Ⓔ	77 Ⓐ Ⓑ Ⓒ Ⓓ Ⓔ
3 Ⓐ Ⓑ Ⓒ Ⓓ Ⓔ	28 Ⓐ Ⓑ Ⓒ Ⓓ Ⓔ	53 Ⓐ Ⓑ Ⓒ Ⓓ Ⓔ	78 Ⓐ Ⓑ Ⓒ Ⓓ Ⓔ
4 Ⓐ Ⓑ Ⓒ Ⓓ Ⓔ	29 Ⓐ Ⓑ Ⓒ Ⓓ Ⓔ	54 Ⓐ Ⓑ Ⓒ Ⓓ Ⓔ	79 Ⓐ Ⓑ Ⓒ Ⓓ Ⓔ
5 Ⓐ Ⓑ Ⓒ Ⓓ Ⓔ	30 Ⓐ Ⓑ Ⓒ Ⓓ Ⓔ	55 Ⓐ Ⓑ Ⓒ Ⓓ Ⓔ	80 Ⓐ Ⓑ Ⓒ Ⓓ Ⓔ
6 Ⓐ Ⓑ Ⓒ Ⓓ Ⓔ	31 Ⓐ Ⓑ Ⓒ Ⓓ Ⓔ	56 Ⓐ Ⓑ Ⓒ Ⓓ Ⓔ	81 Ⓐ Ⓑ Ⓒ Ⓓ Ⓔ
7 Ⓐ Ⓑ Ⓒ Ⓓ Ⓔ	32 Ⓐ Ⓑ Ⓒ Ⓓ Ⓔ	57 Ⓐ Ⓑ Ⓒ Ⓓ Ⓔ	82 Ⓐ Ⓑ Ⓒ Ⓓ Ⓔ
8 Ⓐ Ⓑ Ⓒ Ⓓ Ⓔ	33 Ⓐ Ⓑ Ⓒ Ⓓ Ⓔ	58 Ⓐ Ⓑ Ⓒ Ⓓ Ⓔ	83 Ⓐ Ⓑ Ⓒ Ⓓ Ⓔ
9 Ⓐ Ⓑ Ⓒ Ⓓ Ⓔ	34 Ⓐ Ⓑ Ⓒ Ⓓ Ⓔ	59 Ⓐ Ⓑ Ⓒ Ⓓ Ⓔ	84 Ⓐ Ⓑ Ⓒ Ⓓ Ⓔ
10 Ⓐ Ⓑ Ⓒ Ⓓ Ⓔ	35 Ⓐ Ⓑ Ⓒ Ⓓ Ⓔ	60 Ⓐ Ⓑ Ⓒ Ⓓ Ⓔ	85 Ⓐ Ⓑ Ⓒ Ⓓ Ⓔ
11 Ⓐ Ⓑ Ⓒ Ⓓ Ⓔ	36 Ⓐ Ⓑ Ⓒ Ⓓ Ⓔ	61 Ⓐ Ⓑ Ⓒ Ⓓ Ⓔ	86 Ⓐ Ⓑ Ⓒ Ⓓ Ⓔ
12 Ⓐ Ⓑ Ⓒ Ⓓ Ⓔ	37 Ⓐ Ⓑ Ⓒ Ⓓ Ⓔ	62 Ⓐ Ⓑ Ⓒ Ⓓ Ⓔ	87 Ⓐ Ⓑ Ⓒ Ⓓ Ⓔ
13 Ⓐ Ⓑ Ⓒ Ⓓ Ⓔ	38 Ⓐ Ⓑ Ⓒ Ⓓ Ⓔ	63 Ⓐ Ⓑ Ⓒ Ⓓ Ⓔ	88 Ⓐ Ⓑ Ⓒ Ⓓ Ⓔ
14 Ⓐ Ⓑ Ⓒ Ⓓ Ⓔ	39 Ⓐ Ⓑ Ⓒ Ⓓ Ⓔ	64 Ⓐ Ⓑ Ⓒ Ⓓ Ⓔ	89 Ⓐ Ⓑ Ⓒ Ⓓ Ⓔ
15 Ⓐ Ⓑ Ⓒ Ⓓ Ⓔ	40 Ⓐ Ⓑ Ⓒ Ⓓ Ⓔ	65 Ⓐ Ⓑ Ⓒ Ⓓ Ⓔ	90 Ⓐ Ⓑ Ⓒ Ⓓ Ⓔ
16 Ⓐ Ⓑ Ⓒ Ⓓ Ⓔ	41 Ⓐ Ⓑ Ⓒ Ⓓ Ⓔ	66 Ⓐ Ⓑ Ⓒ Ⓓ Ⓔ	91 Ⓐ Ⓑ Ⓒ Ⓓ Ⓔ
17 Ⓐ Ⓑ Ⓒ Ⓓ Ⓔ	42 Ⓐ Ⓑ Ⓒ Ⓓ Ⓔ	67 Ⓐ Ⓑ Ⓒ Ⓓ Ⓔ	92 Ⓐ Ⓑ Ⓒ Ⓓ Ⓔ
18 Ⓐ Ⓑ Ⓒ Ⓓ Ⓔ	43 Ⓐ Ⓑ Ⓒ Ⓓ Ⓔ	68 Ⓐ Ⓑ Ⓒ Ⓓ Ⓔ	93 Ⓐ Ⓑ Ⓒ Ⓓ Ⓔ
19 Ⓐ Ⓑ Ⓒ Ⓓ Ⓔ	44 Ⓐ Ⓑ Ⓒ Ⓓ Ⓔ	69 Ⓐ Ⓑ Ⓒ Ⓓ Ⓔ	94 Ⓐ Ⓑ Ⓒ Ⓓ Ⓔ
20 Ⓐ Ⓑ Ⓒ Ⓓ Ⓔ	45 Ⓐ Ⓑ Ⓒ Ⓓ Ⓔ	70 Ⓐ Ⓑ Ⓒ Ⓓ Ⓔ	95 Ⓐ Ⓑ Ⓒ Ⓓ Ⓔ
21 Ⓐ Ⓑ Ⓒ Ⓓ Ⓔ	46 Ⓐ Ⓑ Ⓒ Ⓓ Ⓔ	71 Ⓐ Ⓑ Ⓒ Ⓓ Ⓔ	96 Ⓐ Ⓑ Ⓒ Ⓓ Ⓔ
22 Ⓐ Ⓑ Ⓒ Ⓓ Ⓔ	47 Ⓐ Ⓑ Ⓒ Ⓓ Ⓔ	72 Ⓐ Ⓑ Ⓒ Ⓓ Ⓔ	97 Ⓐ Ⓑ Ⓒ Ⓓ Ⓔ
23 Ⓐ Ⓑ Ⓒ Ⓓ Ⓔ	48 Ⓐ Ⓑ Ⓒ Ⓓ Ⓔ	73 Ⓐ Ⓑ Ⓒ Ⓓ Ⓔ	98 Ⓐ Ⓑ Ⓒ Ⓓ Ⓔ
24 Ⓐ Ⓑ Ⓒ Ⓓ Ⓔ	49 Ⓐ Ⓑ Ⓒ Ⓓ Ⓔ	74 Ⓐ Ⓑ Ⓒ Ⓓ Ⓔ	99 Ⓐ Ⓑ Ⓒ Ⓓ Ⓔ
25 Ⓐ Ⓑ Ⓒ Ⓓ Ⓔ	50 Ⓐ Ⓑ Ⓒ Ⓓ Ⓔ	75 Ⓐ Ⓑ Ⓒ Ⓓ Ⓔ	100 Ⓐ Ⓑ Ⓒ Ⓓ Ⓔ

Quality Assurance Mark

Chemistry *Fill in circle CE only if II is correct explanation of I.

	I	II	CE*		I	II	CE*
101	Ⓣ Ⓕ	Ⓣ Ⓕ	○	109	Ⓣ Ⓕ	Ⓣ Ⓕ	○
102	Ⓣ Ⓕ	Ⓣ Ⓕ	○	110	Ⓣ Ⓕ	Ⓣ Ⓕ	○
103	Ⓣ Ⓕ	Ⓣ Ⓕ	○	111	Ⓣ Ⓕ	Ⓣ Ⓕ	○
104	Ⓣ Ⓕ	Ⓣ Ⓕ	○	112	Ⓣ Ⓕ	Ⓣ Ⓕ	○
105	Ⓣ Ⓕ	Ⓣ Ⓕ	○	113	Ⓣ Ⓕ	Ⓣ Ⓕ	○
106	Ⓣ Ⓕ	Ⓣ Ⓕ	○	114	Ⓣ Ⓕ	Ⓣ Ⓕ	○
107	Ⓣ Ⓕ	Ⓣ Ⓕ	○	115	Ⓣ Ⓕ	Ⓣ Ⓕ	○
108	Ⓣ Ⓕ	Ⓣ Ⓕ	○				

FOR OFFICIAL USE ONLY

R/C	W/S1	FS/S2	CS/S3	WS

Important: Fill in items 8 and 9 exactly as shown on the back of test book.

8 BOOK CODE (Copy and grid as on back of test book.)

0	A	0
1	B	1
2	C	2
3	D	3
4	E	4
5	F	5
6	G	6
7	H	7
8	I	8
9	J	9
	K	
	L	
	M	
	N	
	O	
	P	
	Q	
	R	
	S	
	T	
	U	
	V	
	W	
	X	
	Y	
	Z	

9 BOOK ID (Copy from back of test book.)

10 TEST BOOK SERIAL NUMBER (Copy from front of test book.)

0	0	0	0	0	0
1	1	1	1	1	1
2	2	2	2	2	2
3	3	3	3	3	3
4	4	4	4	4	4
5	5	5	5	5	5
6	6	6	6	6	6
7	7	7	7	7	7
8	8	8	8	8	8
9	9	9	9	9	9

COMPLETE MARK ● EXAMPLES OF INCOMPLETE MARKS

You must use a No. 2 pencil and marks must be complete. Do not use a mechanical pencil. *It is very important that you fill in the entire circle darkly and completely. If you change your response, erase as completely as possible. Incomplete marks or erasures may affect your score.*

○ Literature
○ Biology E
○ Biology M
○ Chemistry
○ Physics
○ Mathematics Level 1
○ Mathematics Level 2
○ U.S. History
○ World History
○ French
○ German
○ Italian
○ Latin
○ Modern Hebrew
○ Spanish

Background Questions: ① ② ③ ④ ⑤ ⑥ ⑦ ⑧ ⑨

1 Ⓐ Ⓑ Ⓒ Ⓓ Ⓔ	26 Ⓐ Ⓑ Ⓒ Ⓓ Ⓔ	51 Ⓐ Ⓑ Ⓒ Ⓓ Ⓔ	76 Ⓐ Ⓑ Ⓒ Ⓓ Ⓔ
2 Ⓐ Ⓑ Ⓒ Ⓓ Ⓔ	27 Ⓐ Ⓑ Ⓒ Ⓓ Ⓔ	52 Ⓐ Ⓑ Ⓒ Ⓓ Ⓔ	77 Ⓐ Ⓑ Ⓒ Ⓓ Ⓔ
3 Ⓐ Ⓑ Ⓒ Ⓓ Ⓔ	28 Ⓐ Ⓑ Ⓒ Ⓓ Ⓔ	53 Ⓐ Ⓑ Ⓒ Ⓓ Ⓔ	78 Ⓐ Ⓑ Ⓒ Ⓓ Ⓔ
4 Ⓐ Ⓑ Ⓒ Ⓓ Ⓔ	29 Ⓐ Ⓑ Ⓒ Ⓓ Ⓔ	54 Ⓐ Ⓑ Ⓒ Ⓓ Ⓔ	79 Ⓐ Ⓑ Ⓒ Ⓓ Ⓔ
5 Ⓐ Ⓑ Ⓒ Ⓓ Ⓔ	30 Ⓐ Ⓑ Ⓒ Ⓓ Ⓔ	55 Ⓐ Ⓑ Ⓒ Ⓓ Ⓔ	80 Ⓐ Ⓑ Ⓒ Ⓓ Ⓔ
6 Ⓐ Ⓑ Ⓒ Ⓓ Ⓔ	31 Ⓐ Ⓑ Ⓒ Ⓓ Ⓔ	56 Ⓐ Ⓑ Ⓒ Ⓓ Ⓔ	81 Ⓐ Ⓑ Ⓒ Ⓓ Ⓔ
7 Ⓐ Ⓑ Ⓒ Ⓓ Ⓔ	32 Ⓐ Ⓑ Ⓒ Ⓓ Ⓔ	57 Ⓐ Ⓑ Ⓒ Ⓓ Ⓔ	82 Ⓐ Ⓑ Ⓒ Ⓓ Ⓔ
8 Ⓐ Ⓑ Ⓒ Ⓓ Ⓔ	33 Ⓐ Ⓑ Ⓒ Ⓓ Ⓔ	58 Ⓐ Ⓑ Ⓒ Ⓓ Ⓔ	83 Ⓐ Ⓑ Ⓒ Ⓓ Ⓔ
9 Ⓐ Ⓑ Ⓒ Ⓓ Ⓔ	34 Ⓐ Ⓑ Ⓒ Ⓓ Ⓔ	59 Ⓐ Ⓑ Ⓒ Ⓓ Ⓔ	84 Ⓐ Ⓑ Ⓒ Ⓓ Ⓔ
10 Ⓐ Ⓑ Ⓒ Ⓓ Ⓔ	35 Ⓐ Ⓑ Ⓒ Ⓓ Ⓔ	60 Ⓐ Ⓑ Ⓒ Ⓓ Ⓔ	85 Ⓐ Ⓑ Ⓒ Ⓓ Ⓔ
11 Ⓐ Ⓑ Ⓒ Ⓓ Ⓔ	36 Ⓐ Ⓑ Ⓒ Ⓓ Ⓔ	61 Ⓐ Ⓑ Ⓒ Ⓓ Ⓔ	86 Ⓐ Ⓑ Ⓒ Ⓓ Ⓔ
12 Ⓐ Ⓑ Ⓒ Ⓓ Ⓔ	37 Ⓐ Ⓑ Ⓒ Ⓓ Ⓔ	62 Ⓐ Ⓑ Ⓒ Ⓓ Ⓔ	87 Ⓐ Ⓑ Ⓒ Ⓓ Ⓔ
13 Ⓐ Ⓑ Ⓒ Ⓓ Ⓔ	38 Ⓐ Ⓑ Ⓒ Ⓓ Ⓔ	63 Ⓐ Ⓑ Ⓒ Ⓓ Ⓔ	88 Ⓐ Ⓑ Ⓒ Ⓓ Ⓔ
14 Ⓐ Ⓑ Ⓒ Ⓓ Ⓔ	39 Ⓐ Ⓑ Ⓒ Ⓓ Ⓔ	64 Ⓐ Ⓑ Ⓒ Ⓓ Ⓔ	89 Ⓐ Ⓑ Ⓒ Ⓓ Ⓔ
15 Ⓐ Ⓑ Ⓒ Ⓓ Ⓔ	40 Ⓐ Ⓑ Ⓒ Ⓓ Ⓔ	65 Ⓐ Ⓑ Ⓒ Ⓓ Ⓔ	90 Ⓐ Ⓑ Ⓒ Ⓓ Ⓔ
16 Ⓐ Ⓑ Ⓒ Ⓓ Ⓔ	41 Ⓐ Ⓑ Ⓒ Ⓓ Ⓔ	66 Ⓐ Ⓑ Ⓒ Ⓓ Ⓔ	91 Ⓐ Ⓑ Ⓒ Ⓓ Ⓔ
17 Ⓐ Ⓑ Ⓒ Ⓓ Ⓔ	42 Ⓐ Ⓑ Ⓒ Ⓓ Ⓔ	67 Ⓐ Ⓑ Ⓒ Ⓓ Ⓔ	92 Ⓐ Ⓑ Ⓒ Ⓓ Ⓔ
18 Ⓐ Ⓑ Ⓒ Ⓓ Ⓔ	43 Ⓐ Ⓑ Ⓒ Ⓓ Ⓔ	68 Ⓐ Ⓑ Ⓒ Ⓓ Ⓔ	93 Ⓐ Ⓑ Ⓒ Ⓓ Ⓔ
19 Ⓐ Ⓑ Ⓒ Ⓓ Ⓔ	44 Ⓐ Ⓑ Ⓒ Ⓓ Ⓔ	69 Ⓐ Ⓑ Ⓒ Ⓓ Ⓔ	94 Ⓐ Ⓑ Ⓒ Ⓓ Ⓔ
20 Ⓐ Ⓑ Ⓒ Ⓓ Ⓔ	45 Ⓐ Ⓑ Ⓒ Ⓓ Ⓔ	70 Ⓐ Ⓑ Ⓒ Ⓓ Ⓔ	95 Ⓐ Ⓑ Ⓒ Ⓓ Ⓔ
21 Ⓐ Ⓑ Ⓒ Ⓓ Ⓔ	46 Ⓐ Ⓑ Ⓒ Ⓓ Ⓔ	71 Ⓐ Ⓑ Ⓒ Ⓓ Ⓔ	96 Ⓐ Ⓑ Ⓒ Ⓓ Ⓔ
22 Ⓐ Ⓑ Ⓒ Ⓓ Ⓔ	47 Ⓐ Ⓑ Ⓒ Ⓓ Ⓔ	72 Ⓐ Ⓑ Ⓒ Ⓓ Ⓔ	97 Ⓐ Ⓑ Ⓒ Ⓓ Ⓔ
23 Ⓐ Ⓑ Ⓒ Ⓓ Ⓔ	48 Ⓐ Ⓑ Ⓒ Ⓓ Ⓔ	73 Ⓐ Ⓑ Ⓒ Ⓓ Ⓔ	98 Ⓐ Ⓑ Ⓒ Ⓓ Ⓔ
24 Ⓐ Ⓑ Ⓒ Ⓓ Ⓔ	49 Ⓐ Ⓑ Ⓒ Ⓓ Ⓔ	74 Ⓐ Ⓑ Ⓒ Ⓓ Ⓔ	99 Ⓐ Ⓑ Ⓒ Ⓓ Ⓔ
25 Ⓐ Ⓑ Ⓒ Ⓓ Ⓔ	50 Ⓐ Ⓑ Ⓒ Ⓓ Ⓔ	75 Ⓐ Ⓑ Ⓒ Ⓓ Ⓔ	100 Ⓐ Ⓑ Ⓒ Ⓓ Ⓔ

Chemistry *Fill in circle CE only if II is correct explanation of I.

	I	II	CE*		I	II	CE*
101	Ⓣ Ⓕ	Ⓣ Ⓕ	○	109	Ⓣ Ⓕ	Ⓣ Ⓕ	○
102	Ⓣ Ⓕ	Ⓣ Ⓕ	○	110	Ⓣ Ⓕ	Ⓣ Ⓕ	○
103	Ⓣ Ⓕ	Ⓣ Ⓕ	○	111	Ⓣ Ⓕ	Ⓣ Ⓕ	○
104	Ⓣ Ⓕ	Ⓣ Ⓕ	○	112	Ⓣ Ⓕ	Ⓣ Ⓕ	○
105	Ⓣ Ⓕ	Ⓣ Ⓕ	○	113	Ⓣ Ⓕ	Ⓣ Ⓕ	○
106	Ⓣ Ⓕ	Ⓣ Ⓕ	○	114	Ⓣ Ⓕ	Ⓣ Ⓕ	○
107	Ⓣ Ⓕ	Ⓣ Ⓕ	○	115	Ⓣ Ⓕ	Ⓣ Ⓕ	○
108	Ⓣ Ⓕ	Ⓣ Ⓕ	○				

Important: Fill in items 8 and 9 exactly as shown on the back of test book.

8 BOOK CODE (Copy and grid as on back of test book.)

0–9 | A–Z | 0–9

9 BOOK ID (Copy from back of test book.)

10 TEST BOOK SERIAL NUMBER (Copy from front of test book.)

0–9 (six columns)

Quality Assurance Mark

FOR OFFICIAL USE ONLY

R/C	W/S1	FS/S2	CS/S3	WS

PLEASE DO NOT WRITE IN THIS AREA

SERIAL #